AN ISLAND IN THE AUTUMN

Dorothy

with love

John

16 October 2013

AN
ISLAND
IN THE
AUTUMN

JOHN SMITH

Librario

Published by
Librario Publishing Ltd.

ISBN : 978-1906775261

Copies can be ordered from retail
or via the internet at :

www.librario.com

or from :

Brough House
Milton Brodie
Kinloss
Morayshire
IV36 2UA

Tel / Fax : 01343 850178

Cover design and layout by Steven James
www.chimeracreations.co.uk

Printed and bound in Great Britain

CONTENTS

Appendices

INTRODUCTION

On 6th March 1957, on leave from West Africa, I joined a small crowd outside the new High Commission in London to applaud the raising of the flag on the morning of Ghana's independence. On 14th July 1979 I was in Westminster Abbey to celebrate the independence of Kiribati. For nearly thirty years dismantling of empire was my trade: in Nigeria, in the Solomon Islands, and in the Gilbert and Ellice Islands. In 1967, while enjoying a semester as a 'distinguished visitor in residence' at Duke University in North Carolina, I had both the time and the environment in which to think and write about my first few years in the Colonial Service. Duke University Press was kind enough to publish *Colonial Cadet in Nigeria* in 1968.[1]

I stayed on in Nigeria for ten years after independence, part of the conspiracy of optimism that believed that peoples, who had lived within arbitrary colonial boundaries for a mere sixty years, could readily be welded into a nation, despite diversities as great as those between Finn and Greek or German and Portuguese. Duke University again provided me with the tranquillity to sort out my perception of why and how things had gone wrong. *Nigeria: crisis and beyond*, not a memoir, was published in 1971 under a pseudonym, John Oyinbo.[2]

Now, long into retirement from overseas service and after full-time second and part-time third careers, I have written about my last eight years working once again in empire. *Colonial Cadet* viewed that task from the bottom of the ladder from where I could try to put my gloss on the policies and timetables of others with little effect on either. *An Island in the Autumn* views it from the topmost rungs. I was responsible for some of the policies and I had influence over the timetables. It is a personal but selective memoir of the happy and interesting, if sometimes frustrating, years I, and my family, spent in the Western Pacific.

I have followed the pattern I used in *Colonial Cadet*, writing about those issues that at the time seemed and, in the dimmed recollection of the present, still seem most significant, spiced with anecdote to provide

---

1. J H Smith, Colonial Cadet in Nigeria, Durham, Duke University Press 1968.
2. John Oyinbo, Nigeria: crisis and beyond, London, Charles Knight 1972.

a flavour of the life we lived. This time I have had the advantage of being able to read accounts by others of events in which I took part and of being able to browse in the British National Archives. It has been salutary to read again, in the hushed calm of Kew, letters and reports I wrote more than thirty years ago, sometimes, I fear, upon matters that had long since escaped my memory, and even more salutary to read the comments upon them made by officials in the Foreign and Commonwealth Office! In *Colonial Cadet* I appended some touring and other reports I had written as an example of what the job was about. Here, with the same intention, I have chosen some documents that will, I trust, give some indication of what I was about, first as Financial Secretary in the Solomon Islands and then as Governor of the Gilbert and Ellice Islands. Finally, in an epilogue, I reflect upon my career as an administrator in the twilight of the British Empire.

I have been fortunate to be able to draw upon the scholarship of both Professor Harry Maude and Professor Barrie Macdonald. The former was a distinguished predecessor in the Gilbert and Ellice Islands with whom I was able to correspond from time to time and the latter a welcome visitor during my time as governor there. Both have made significant contributions to Pacific history and I am indebted to them. My sincere thanks are owed to Rose and Chris Cochran, friends from my time in Honiara, both for their encouragement and for reading the Solomon Islands chapters in draft on which they made many valuable comments as well as correcting errors. I am grateful, too, to Mike Walsh, Consul General for the Gilbert Islands, who was the government economist in Tarawa when I was there, both for his friendship and for reading and commenting upon the chapter on Ellice separation. Mike accompanied Sir Leslie Monson on his visit to the Ellice Islands and was responsible for the statistics in the Monson report. Mike described to me how Sir Leslie wore his usual Whitehall garb of pinstriped suit to go ashore, bearing his papers in an HMG labelled leather briefcase. His many years in the Colonial Office and knighthood did not, alas, rank him of sufficient status to have his canoe carried aloft in Vaitupu when the shallows were reached, impressive figure though he must have been. That honour was reserved for the monarch or her personal representative. I like to think that as Sir Leslie paddled the last few yards, ruining his trousers, he at last appreciated why shorts were popular with the colonial administrators he had ruled from a distance for so long.

Tom Layng, friend and colleague, has kindly given me access to his splendid collection of Pacific photographs. I am most grateful to him for the opportunity to share once again those days when we worked closely together on the separation of the Gilbert and Ellice Islands.

I am especially indebted to Professor David Murray. Both he and Dr Ruth Finnegan, his wife, were immensely helpful to me while they were at the University of the South Pacific, frequent visitors to the University Extension Centre in Tarawa and welcome guests in Government House. David, who advised both me, personally, and the government of the Gilbert Islands, on constitutional matters, kindly read the chapters on Gilbert's independence and those dealing with the Banaban issue. His knowledge of both the people and the events were of great help in drafting what was, for me, the most difficult part of the book. All opinions and any errors are, of course, mine.

Prologue
How it Began . . .

When a telephone call interrupted discussion of my future, the Assistant Under Secretary acknowledged his caller with an endearment I had not heard since my childhood. While he dealt with an apparent domestic crisis, I looked around the room. 'Dearie' was in tune with the bowler hat and tightly rolled umbrella on the stand, his black jacket, pinstripe trousers and stiff collared white shirt. Appearance and manner suggested a home civil servant rather than a diplomat, belonging to the 'C' rather than the 'F' of the Foreign and Commonwealth Office. (FCO) Perhaps he had originally belonged to the old Colonial Office, but later, when he sent for an underling to remind him of the dependencies where a vacancy might soon occur, the Dominions Office seemed to have a better claim. He advised me to do nothing rash or in a hurry. He was confident of finding me 'an island in the autumn'.

It was January 1970. I had spent nearly twenty years in Northern Nigeria, half of it before and half of it after independence. Nigeria's civil war had just ended. I had stayed on but had made up my mind that, much as I loved the people and the country where I had spent the best years of my life, and however acceptable I appeared to be, it was time to make a break. My wife, Sylvester, who had only known Nigeria in the troubled last five years, and the family which had started to arrive deserved a less harrowing environment and I had no doubt that peace would aggravate rather than appease the xenophobia which is an understandable trait of new nations. I had, moreover, never expected to continue in the Overseas Civil Service for as long as I had. Appointed in 1950, already three years after the independence of India, I had then given myself a certain five years, a possible ten and a lucky fifteen.[1] At the age of twenty-two, fifteen years is still the greater part of a lifetime.

Training successors had been an important part of the preparation for independence undertaken in Nigeria and I had been directly involved, first supervising an administrative service course and, later, setting up and directing a staff development centre. As a result I was known on the

---

1. JH Smith *Colonial Cadet in Nigeria* p6. Durham, Duke University Press 1968.

training circuit and job offers had come my way from time to time. That January I had been offered an academic post in public administration at the newly established University of the South Pacific but I also had an immediate commitment to teach a semester at Duke University. The Vice Chancellor in Suva wanted me at once despite my having always said that I would not be free until the middle of the year. His expectation of what I could do in a part of the world and for a civil service about both of which I knew nothing was worrying. I did not relish running programmes for permanent secretaries within a week or two of arrival. I certainly did not want to forgo my semester in North Carolina. I knew the people at Duke. They had been good to me and I was obligated to them, especially to the Provost, Professor Taylor Cole and to Professor Bill Hamilton, both keen observers of and shrewd commentators on the transition of power in Africa. The William Perkins Library was a treasure house for anyone with Commonwealth interests. At Duke I would be able to research and write at leisure, unwinding gently from close involvement in the trauma of coup, counter coup, civil war, the creation of states and, more personally, the tragedy of embitterment between friends.

On that cold and grey January day, an island in the autumn seemed highly desirable. I said 'yes' to the Assistant Under Secretary, 'no' to the Vice Chancellor and set off to Durham, North Carolina. On my return to England in July I was offered the post of Financial Secretary to the Western Pacific. A half hour in my public library taught me a number of things I had not previously taken in: notably that Guadalcanal, famous as a Second World War battlefield, was not an American administered island, which the Japanese had invaded, but one of the British Solomon Islands. Its main town, Honiara, was the seat of the Western Pacific High Commission. The High Commissioner had responsibilities for the Anglo-French Condominium of the New Hebrides and for the Gilbert and Ellice Islands Colony as well as for the British Solomon Islands Protectorate. My one powerful memory of relevance was the delight with which I had read Arthur Grimble's radio talks that later were to be published in book form as *Pattern of Islands*.[2] In the early months of my first tour in Nigeria, alone in the bush, I had eagerly awaited the weekly copies of the *Listener*, in which the radio talks were

---

2. Arthur Grimble, *Pattern of Islands*, London, John Murray 1952.

published. It had never occurred to me then that my career might one day take me to the Pacific and now that I knew it would, but to the Solomon Islands, it did not occur to me that not only the people about whom he had written so delightfully but the legacy of Arthur Grimble himself would dominate the final years of my service.

THE BRITISH SOLOMON ISLANDS

CHAPTER ONE
PACIFIC CONTRASTS

We had only a couple of weeks in which to plan and pack. There was little time for reading or coming to terms with the reality of what lay ahead. We assumed that we were a travelled family and could manage. Longitudinal flights to and from West Africa were, however, no preparation for a latitudinal flight to the opposite longitude and then on again. I had crossed the Atlantic several times but only as far as the eastern seaboard. Fortunately we decided to stop over in Los Angeles, where we had good friends who had worked with us in Nigeria, and then in Fiji, at the time the hub of Pacific air communications. Because Sylvester had two sisters who had emigrated to New Zealand and whom she had not seen in many years, she and the children would visit New Zealand for a couple of weeks from Fiji while I went on to Honiara, settled in and got things ready for their arrival. The High Commissioner, a bachelor, had, moreover, kindly invited me to stay on arrival and, as a former *aide de camp*, I was anxious to avoid landing Government House with the potential embarrassment of a very young family.

The Crown Agents wrote to confirm travel arrangements. We were travelling first class to Nadi. I was then continuing to Honiara with the luggage. The family were going to do the New Zealand leg and return economy class, taking only a suitcase between them. This appeared to have caused consternation. I was booked into one hotel, Sylvester into another, and the three children, all aged less than four, into a third. I enquired why we could not stay in the one hotel. I was assured that because I was travelling first all the way I must stay in a hotel appropriate to my status! Nobody could explain how the management of a hotel might react when three infants turned up unaccompanied. I gave up the struggle. I was paying for the accommodation and decided to make my own arrangements on arrival.

We landed at 3.00 am and opted for the hotel into which the children had been booked. It turned out to be much the best choice as we discovered the next day when we took a taxi ride around Nadi. The children were seized by Fijian stewards, gentle giants of the kindest disposition, sorted out and put to bed. It was wonderful to be back in the tropics again, to feel the warmth, enjoy the sharp dawn and dusk, pick up the sounds, scents and colours of familiar birds, insects and plants, above all to squeeze a lime over my breakfast pawpaw.

I saw the family off to New Zealand a couple of afternoons later and had an evening to myself before an early departure on the HS 748, which then flew to Honiara via Port Vila in the New Hebrides. The flight from Los Angeles, via Honolulu, had already impressed upon me the immensity of the Pacific Ocean. Crossing the dateline for the first time had also given me an understanding flash of identity with the discomfort that must have been felt in 1752 when eleven days in September were 'lost' even if the supposed riots were a myth. Now flying both more slowly and at a lower altitude, the reality of the scale of my new surroundings sunk in. The Sahara, across which I had once driven, seemed a modest barrier compared with these endless seas. I had never had any difficulty relating to Nigerians. However great the apparent differences in culture, we shared the northern hemisphere, a seasonal basis for agriculture, a long history of trading contact, similar patterns of urban growth, and similar paths of political development. Now in the Pacific even the night sky was unfamiliar. I wondered how I would cope and how I would relate to Solomon Islanders. Despite the immensity of their oceanic environment there were few of them, a mere 161,000 scattered between six larger and countless smaller islands. The population of Honiara, the capital, numbered only some 12,000 of all races. In West African terms it was a very small town.

At Nadi I had selected a couple of cases to take with me and consigned the rest of the luggage airfreight, and, with first class baggage allowance for five of us, there was a lot of it. I assumed it would travel on the next flight some three days later. To my anguish when the ADC who met me at Honiara went to collect my two bags he found the lot! There was no way it would fit into the Government House Jaguar. Luckily he was able to find somebody with a truck. There was still the embarrassment of what to do with it on arrival. I could guess what the staff thought about the overnight guest arriving with over a dozen trunks and suitcases!

Sir Michael Gass, the High Commissioner, had come to the Pacific from the then Gold Coast where he had been commissioner in Ashanti. It gave us a West African bond. We had been used, from our cadet days, to Africans playing a major role in administration, at first chiefs and their senior advisers and, later, politicians and civil service colleagues. Commerce had been as much, if not more, an African than an expatriate concern. We had no experience of white settlers and not much sympathy for them. I was soon to be irritated by the tag of 'African exile', applied to the likes of me by expatriates whose service had been confined to the Pacific and by educated Pacific Islanders, starting to take an interest in politics. It made no concession to the difference between those of us who had served in West Africa and those who had served in East and Central Africa. I defined that difference neither as a matter of ability nor of administrative experience but as an understanding of our expatriate role. West African service, service in the 'white man's grave' and service under the principle of indirect rule, inculcated an understanding of the transitory part we played in the history of great kingdoms and dynamic peoples. And indeed, often not appreciated, formal colonial rule in much of West Africa had lasted for a mere sixty or so years. In my new environment I began to understand how most of us in the colonial service were as much affected by the peoples with whom we worked and by their culture as they were by us and by our culture. Sir Michael had also been Chief Secretary in Hong Kong and had acted as Governor there. In many ways a shy man, he was easy to get on with and that first encounter was to grow into a warm friendship, disrupted, sadly, by his death all too early in his retirement.

After a few days I was passed on to Tom Russell, now the Chief Secretary and until my arrival my predecessor as Financial Secretary. A kind and considerate host with a wealth of knowledge about the islands, he was an anthropologist by training and had a real understanding of, as well as a deep affection for, Solomon Islanders.[1] He was a knowledgeable historian of the Pacific generally and, a former paratrooper, particularly aware of the Second World War and the fighting whose traces were still evident all over Guadalcanal. I could not have had a better tutor.

Newcomers arriving at the top, displacing those climbing up the local promotion ladder, are bound to be treated warily. I knew, too, that having spent the last ten years working for an independent African government I would have very little, if any, feel for dependent territory

---

1. Tom Russell, *I Have The Honour To Be*, Spennymoor, The Memoir Club 2003 is especially interesting on Marching Rule in the Solomons.

status and the hand of the FCO, into which the Colonial Office had been absorbed. Nigeria was a large territory and prior to independence I had had no job senior enough to involve me in direct links with Whitehall, although both as an ADC and private secretary to governors I had gained some experience about how relations were handled at higher levels. Since independence, as a permanent secretary, I had dealt with the British High Commission in Nigeria and occasional visiting dignitaries but much in the same way as I had dealt with the United States and other embassies and I was used to dealing directly with international agencies. I needed to tread cautiously and to learn fast.

Getting to know Honiara in those first few days, I was startled to find expatriate women, some of them the wives of civil servants, at cash tills in the stores, and the Guadalcanal Club and the Yacht Club still the exclusive preserve of expatriates. I learned that the Mendana Hotel, the principal of the two hotels, had but recently been forced to admit Solomon Islanders after sit-in protests led, to their credit, by young expatriate administrative officers, inspired by Martin Luther King's civil rights protests in the United States. Although it was pleasing for everyday office wear to be able to use shorts, which had never been popular in Muslim Northern Nigeria and after independence had become an unacceptable symbol of colonialism, I was both amused and irritated to observe expatriate staff, among whom there were a good many Australians and New Zealanders, insistent upon long sleeved white shirts, white long trousers, socks, shoes and a panama hat for playing bowls in the evening at the club, but content with shorts, an unbuttoned shirt or T-shirt and flip-flops for work.

It was also strange to find that every one of my senior staff, including secretaries, was an expatriate. At first the only Solomon Islanders I met in the working day were the handful of elected members of the Governing Council, messengers and drivers. The most senior local civil servants were doctors, trained at the excellent Fiji medical school, and teachers in the government secondary school and teacher training college. The one Solomon Islander administrative officer so far appointed was on secondment in the Gilbert and Ellice Islands Colony. Outside the office I was equally conscious of the many differences in scale to what I had been used. Honiara, an artificial settlement developed as the centre of government and the port of entry, understandably had the largest concentration of expatriate population, some 1,300, of whom 500 were Chinese. At something like one in seven of the total population, expatriates were very noticeable. They were not obviously arrogant or patronising and many enjoyed excellent relations with Solomon Islanders but they didn't behave like strangers or guests in somebody else's country. It was their workplace and home and they considered it was the business of government to look after their interests. Post World War II, the provision of primary education for expatriate children was standard in larger centres throughout the colonial world and entirely justified but I was surprised to find the children of expatriates, entitled to educational grants and passages, using places in the island secondary schools. One of my senior expatriate staff even thought it right that on completing secondary education his children should be provided with employment. This expatriate confidence and self-regard was demonstrated on New Year's Eve when the Chief Secretary read out the New Year's Honours list at mid-night in the exclusively expatriate Guadalcanal Club.

One reason for expatriate dominance was the lack of any obvious significant Solomon Islander. There was neither paramount chief nor a well-established local businessman. The Town Council was the only, and somewhat token, recognition of local participation in government. Most Solomon Islanders living in the capital were government clerks, policemen, hospital staff, labourers and their families, more often than not extended by young school leavers seeking work and known as 'lieus'. They struck me as being shy, overwhelmed by the expatriate presence, and somewhat dour in consequence. There was little of the cheerful waving and smiling which greeted the expatriate passer-by universal to West Africa. Only in the fruit and vegetable market and at the post office counter did I need to deal directly with Solomon Islanders. The Christian Churches, too, of which there were many denominations, had large numbers of expatriate missionaries and teachers working in their schools.

The capital was, of course, not typical of the country as a whole but politically, it seemed to me that the majority of the expatriates naively assumed that because most of the Solomon Island population appeared disinterested in national affairs there was no need for urgency. There was, in fact, a lively, if sometimes unnoticed, interest in the local issues that affected everyday lives. I was aware that such issues that may not be matters of much concern to the British administration could easily become the major issues after independence. It struck me, too, that the mildest of Solomon Islander comments about localisation, for example, often produced almost a 'backs to the wall' response. We needed to wake up and achieve a more adult relationship with the people to whom we were going to hand over power much sooner than many expected. There were only seventeen elected members of the legislature but Special Branch, with two full time expatriates in charge, seemed to me to be on their tails as though they were busy planning revolution!

Living conditions also contrasted sharply with those to which I had been used. Honiara had a more humid climate than I could recall, except for some months spent at Lokoja at the confluence of the Niger and Benue rivers, although there were sparkling and breezy days when the view over the sea to the volcanic island of Savo was spectacular. Our airy bungalow, built on stilts to survive earth tremors, was on a ridge high above the main town on the coastal plain. It was surprisingly mosquito free. Like all buildings throughout Guadalcanal it was subjected to systematic spraying, part of a World Health Organization programme aimed at the eradication of malaria. In theory the malarial cycle could be broken given a relatively small island population. Alas, despite great efforts over the years and the use of huge resources, the programme failed. But the risk of malaria was much less than it had been in Nigeria and none of the family fell prey to it. All the children did, however, succumb to an extremely common but unpleasant eye infection. They would wake up literally unable to open their eyelids until we had bathed away the sticky mucus that had accumulated overnight. Unused to being ill they found it very frustrating and Sylvester's patience was sorely tried. The other minor health hazard was head lice. Solomon Islanders tended to have very full heads of hair. Our daughter, who was less than a year old when we arrived and got carried around quite often, soon had lice. I caught them from her and was acutely embarrassed until I had got rid of them.

Earth tremors, of which I had no previous experience, were frequent and earthquakes registering on the Richter scale not uncommon. My first quake occurred soon after lunch. I had in my office Peter Salaka, Chairman of the Honiara Town Council. He suddenly seemed to be swaying and I hardly had time to suspect that this was the result of lunching too well before he leaped up, grabbed me and rushed me along the corridor, down the stairs and into the open, shouting that it was a quake as we ran. The next occurred the weekend after our sea baggage had arrived and been delivered. I had just hung up a picture and stood back to admire it, when it fell promptly to the ground. The rattling of crockery and glassware was evidence that it was not the result of my incompetence. I never got used to earthquakes. There was something especially sinister about the way in which water in a swimming pool would go on sloshing to and fro for a long, long time after the initial movement. Ruth, our little daughter, just learning to walk would get very angry when events over which she had no control threw her to the ground.

I was of a generation for whom both school and work on a Saturday morning had been the norm. Now, for the first time in my life, week-ends began on Friday evening rather than midday Saturday and although the 9 - 5 working hours were less suited to the tropics than those I had been accustomed to in West Africa, where we worked from 7 - 9 and 10 - 2, I was able to lunch every day with the family. Salary was more than adequate and for the first time ever in my career I was able to save for more than the next leave.

The stores were surprisingly well stocked and although the market was disappointingly small, in no way a central meeting place and lacking any hustle or appreciation of bargaining, even at the end of the day, good quality fruit and vegetables could usually be found. The market reflected the family orientation of the subsistence economy. Unlike in Africa trading was rare and markets all but unknown. In one or two islands with population pressure, the saltwater people traded with those inland, exchanging fish for yams, usually on a family-to-family basis. Even in Honiara with the main population living in the cash economy – civil servants, police, school and college students, the market had never developed. To my amazement the fish market was an expatriate enterprise, run in conjunction with soft ice cream, by an American whom I had last met through the University of Southern Illinois when, as Managing Director of English Language Services Inc, he was involved in compiling and marketing a course for teaching English as a foreign language! He and his partner now had their sights set on exporting crayfish to the United States and the fish market was their way of establishing themselves locally. It was culturally and economically rather shaming to buy a top grade pineapple and see the vendor go off to spend the 10 cents you had paid for it on a synthetic ice cream.

As I was to discover, one factor limiting the liveliness of the market was excessive legislation. The Protectorate had a dynamic public health department without the counter balance of any effective local commercial and trading interests. Neither agricultural extension staff, whose concern was food and cash crop production, nor Co-operative staff, whose interest was the export of copra and the distribution of imported goods, seemed to play any part in the development of local markets. Used to the vibrant markets of West Africa that first visit to Honiara's was to influence much that I tried to achieve by way of development.

I had looked forward to living by the sea after twenty years spent hundreds of miles inland but the perils of the Solomons were perils of the sea: stonefish, sharks, and seawater crocodiles. Even the locally accessible beaches, usually with grey rather than golden sand, were home to tiresome and persistent sand flies. The best way to relax was to walk up a river and cool off in a mountain pool, although there were one or two pleasant enough beaches protected by the reef where we used to bathe. Eventually we were to build a small swimming pool in which the children all quickly learned to swim and in which we, and our friends, spent many a happy hour. It compensated for any of the inconveniences of life in Honiara.

My job tied me to the Secretariat and I was aware how untypical of the rest of the country Honiara must be. I determined to take whatever opportunities might arise to get out and to visit other islands. On one of my first Sundays and before the family arrived, I jumped at the chance to join a launch party planning to picnic on Savo, the prominent volcanic island a few miles away. Others were providing the food so I promised to produce the drink. I went to the main store and bought a case of beer. It was New Zealand beer but that did not surprise me. Two of the party were Australian Marist brothers from a Catholic secondary school. Once out of harbour, I offered them a beer which they accepted delightedly, but one sip and the bottles went overboard to the un-brotherly comment, 'we don't drink piss, haven't you got any real beer?' I quickly learned that not only Australians but most islanders were as loyal to their Melbourne or Sydney lager as any Englishman to his local real ale.

Fortunately Solair's light aircraft provided an inter island air service and this way I was able to take day trips to Auki, Gizo and Kirakira, respectively the headquarters of Malaita, Western and Eastern districts, which gave me a feel not only for the scale and variety of the country but also for my colleagues in the administration. Later on two district officers were kind enough to invite me go on tour with them. Jim Tedder, in charge of Central District, took me on a splendid few days trek along the Weather Coast of Guadalcanal, across from Honiara.[2] Tom Layng, District Officer of Western District, invited me to join him on a launch tour, which enabled me to visit Kolambangara, Munda and Rendova. All the districts covered many islands, often with small and scattered populations and some islands, such as Tikopia, were huge distances away. The logistical challenges to administration were substantial. Good use was made of radio links and there were periods set aside morning and evening when anyone could ask for a message to be sent, an unusual and impressive public service. What little I saw of the districts reinforced my initial impression that while the Protectorate was well governed its administration was ill balanced. The head was bigger than the body warranted.

In October I put some of these first impressions in a letter to Denis Glason, responsible for the Solomon Islands in the Overseas Development Administration and a former colleague of mine in Nigeria:

> *There is a general frustration which, I think, stems from the fact that the territory is grossly over-administered, both locally and by London. We have a full run of departments, often staffed by first-rate men who are unable to achieve half of what they would like to do. Neither could a community of 161,000 fairly unsophisticated people possibly absorb and sustain all that heads of departments would like to do. This has led to a curious concentration on procedural details and a proliferation of petty rules and regulations, as well as a surprising amount of printed information and reporting. All this occupies people's time and provides some job satisfaction but it really achieves very little indeed for the overall*

---

2. James Tedder, *Solomon Island Years: a district administrator in the islands* 1952 – 1974, Stuarts Point NSW, Tautu Studies 2007 gives an excellent account of a district officer's job.

economy. It might surprise you to know, for example, that the excellently run Government Press handles an average of 14 jobs a day throughout the year, and I think I have seen more circulars in two months than we used to see in two years in Northern Nigeria.

If localisation is to be achieved within a sound economy I foresee, if not a cutback, at least a stabilisation of many government services at their present level. We must also be extremely cautious about the flow of expertise from your end which, I fear, will steadily increase as British commitments elsewhere decline. An able and powerful personality in a particular specialised field can distort things very seriously however well intentioned and professionally expert the advice.

I was going to have to get to grips with administering the finances and economy of the equivalent of a small town, spread over hundreds of islands set in a vast area of ocean. And somehow or other I had to find ways to balance taking full advantage of the huge resource of expatriate talent and experience with getting Solomon Islanders more closely involved in what was their country and in building their confidence so that their opinions and aspirations became the dominant force. It could not have been more different from West Africa.

CHAPTER TWO
MAKING THE
CONSTITUTION WORK

My arrival coincided with the introduction of a new constitution moving the country on from Crown Colony status. It drew on the experience gained when Ceylon first began its constitutional route to independence and on English local government with its extensive use of committees. It had been drafted with the sound intention of helping the process of the transfer of power and the understanding of representative government. The Constitutional Order provided for the Governing Council with an elected majority, sitting in public as the Legislature and in private as the Executive. All elected members were also appointed to committees dealing with specific portfolios, and were, therefore, involved in the discussion of ideas, the preparation of plans and the formulation of policies from start to finish.

The High Commissioner presided. The Chief Secretary, the Attorney General, and the Financial Secretary, all British overseas service officers, were ex-officio members. There were seventeen elected members, of whom two were expatriates: a planter of a paternalistic disposition balanced by a radical priest of the Melanesian Mission. All were elected as individuals; there were no political parties. Initially the Secretary for Protectorate Affairs, the Director of Medical Services, the Director of Public Works, the Director of Agriculture, the Director of Education, the Commissioner of Land and Surveys and the Commissioner of Labour, all expatriates, were public service members. English was the language of the house and there was no interpretation. The committees, to which elected members were appointed, were at first five in number: Communication and Works, Finance, Internal Affairs, Natural Resources and Social Services. Later, a sixth was added: Commerce and Industry. The committees dealt with all matters within their portfolio *ab initio* before discussion within Governing Council, meeting in private. External Affairs, Security and the Public Service remained the direct responsibility of the High Commissioner and were dealt with by the Chief Secretary. I chaired the Finance Committee. Solomon Island elected members chaired the other committees.

The Constitutional Order provided for some flexibility, giving the High Commissioner power to reduce the number of public service members, to increase the number of committees and to appoint a chairman to preside over public meetings of the Governing Council. The latter he did in August 1971, appointing Mr Silas Sitai MBE, BEM, a respected elder with a distinguished war record. In December of the same year the last public service members left the Council. These careful moves by the High Commissioner sustained the reality of constitutional progress and development, as well as ensuring that he retained the initiative, important to successful de-colonisation because once lost so, too, is the goodwill necessary to oil the tricky processes of transition. As members grew in experience the Governing Council began to work well as the legislature. Debates were lively and good use was made of question time and private members' motions. As the public service members were phased out so elected chairmen were obliged to accept greater accountability for the actions of the departments within their portfolios. Their awareness of what was politically acceptable, in turn, forced civil servants to view their proposals and actions with greater sensitivity to public needs, perceptions and prejudices.

There were, however, problems. Government departments remained many and small. Responsibility to a particular committee of Governing Council did not itself bring them together or provide the cohesion which might have been found in a smaller number of larger, more comprehensive ministries. In my own sphere of influence, the Treasury, Inland Revenue, Customs and Excise, and Statistics were separate departments, jealous of their identities. There was little sense of common purpose and interest. The lack of cohesion was even greater between departments such as Agriculture, Forestry, Geological Survey and Lands in the Natural Resources group. It was far from easy, indeed virtually impossible, for the elected chairmen to exercise leadership over professional departments with strong and experienced heads. As the chairmen grew in confidence and gained in experience they began to question their status. It was also difficult for them to establish this when they travelled elsewhere in the region, representing their country. As committee chairmen they did not automatically receive the courtesies extended to ministers and this could be hurtful, especially when they were denied direct access to their political equivalents, as sometimes happened.

The distinction between Governing Council, meeting as Executive and then as Legislature could also be confusing and, for those who had already exhaustively expressed their views in one of the committees, somewhat tedious. It also became increasingly difficult to guarantee support of an individual through all three stages, often to the embarrassment of the chairman concerned. Finding ways to counteract these constitutional deficiencies would be the main thrust of the next Select Committee's recommendations.

In the meantime there was also a leadership vacuum nationally. Governing Council as an executive met too infrequently to act as a cabinet. The day to day affairs of a country cannot await decisions from a body that meets only three or four times a year. Inevitably, the elected members tended to presume that the government was still the trinity of High Commissioner, Chief Secretary and Financial Secretary. In fact the High Commissioner was retreating from the strong executive position he had once held. He was required constitutionally to consult and to act upon advice. Of the three ex-officio members of the Governing Council, the Attorney General, as law officer to the government and responsible for legal drafting and public prosecution, had to act as a public servant rather than play a political role. The Chief Secretary's portfolio was limited to external affairs, defence and the public service and was not the concern of a committee. I, on the other hand, as Financial Secretary, was responsible for economic development as well as fiscal and financial policies, all of which had a bearing on the activities of every department. With nearly every issue before Governing Council having financial or economic implications I was on my feet far more frequently than my ex-officio colleagues in both private and public meetings. Because the Finance Committee had the other committee chairmen among its membership it inevitably became the most influential of the committees. The scenario was set for me to provide leadership. My post independence experience in Nigeria and the fact that, as a newcomer, I was free of local connections or memories gave me an advantage.

Not that I thought much about it at the time. I was daunted by the knowledge that within ten weeks of arrival I not only had to face my first public meeting of Governing Council but, after some introductory formal business, to be the very first speaker moving the Appropriation Bill and making the annual budget speech. I had experience enough of drafting speeches, but nearly always for somebody else to make. I rather prided myself on being able to suit the words both to the style of delivery of the individual and to the likely mood of their audience. It was rewarding when few if any changes were made to the draft and the speech was delivered as I hoped it might be. In Northern Nigeria an assistant secretary would have penned the first draft of the budget speech and it would have moved up the hierarchical ladder, importing sections from other ministries, to the permanent secretary and minister who would have discussed sections of it with the premier and other colleagues. My enquiry as to who in my office started the ball rolling received the curt response, 'you do'. In a territory dependent upon United Kingdom grant-in-aid to meet annual deficits in the recurrent budget, the Appropriation Bill had become something of a technical chore and under the former constitution there had been little in the way of effective local political response. Unofficial members' eyes no doubt glazed over as the Financial Secretary ploughed through his figures in much the way as do those of the faithful few attending the AGM of a local club when the treasurer presents his accounts.

I decided that this speech mattered hugely to the successful establishment of the new constitutional order and to my being able to participate in it effectively. I began by saying so:

Mr Chairman, this is the first Appropriation Bill to be debated since the establishment of the Governing Council in accordance with the constitutional advances introduced by the British Solomon Islands Order 1970. More significantly, it is the first time that a Protectorate Budget has been presented to a legislature which has an elected majority. It is also, Mr Chairman, the first time that I have had the honour of presenting a budget and, indeed, the first occasion on which I have had the privilege to speak in this House. I am, therefore, Sir, most conscious of the special circumstances which surround the 1971 Budget. With a new Constitution, a new Legislature, and a new Financial Secretary I would like to be able to offer, if not a new look in budgets, at least something rather special.[1]

---

1. Governing Council Debates, Official Report, 16 November 1970.

The only thing special I could offer was the manner of my presentation. I was determined that members should understand not only what I was saying but also realise that there was nothing particularly esoteric about budgets, despite the mouthful of the seldom used word 'appropriation' in the bills presenting them. A development plan was in formulation and I tried to set the budget within the context of development, explaining that future budgets would be the annual expression of the development plan and emphasising the role of the committee chairmen in the whole process. I broke with the tradition that the Financial Secretary drew attention to all major events over the past year. I confined myself to matters that fell within the finance portfolio and left everything else of importance for colleagues to deal with in their speeches. Surveying the economy I called attention to the lead that Japan had acquired as the principal importer of Solomon Islands' produce, notably timber, taking 43% of exports in value compared with the 16% that went to the United Kingdom and Australia. I had quickly realised on arrival that the United Kingdom could never have a long-term economic interest in her Pacific dependencies. They were both far too distant from Europe and that much closer to the fast growing major economies on the Pacific rim to be viable trading partners for the UK. Introducing the directions of government expenditure I endeavoured to lay the foundations for changes that I felt to be essential. A third of local revenue was absorbed by expenditure in the administrative sector and almost as much by social services. Far too little was devoted to the productive sector. I drew attention to specific anomalies:

> *For example, expenditure on agriculture, the basis of wealth of the Protectorate, will in 1971 be only 5.5% of total expenditure. There is a staff of 132 in the Department. The Police Force, in what I believe we regard as an unusually happy and law-abiding community, numbers 341. The average Solomon Islander is, therefore, more likely to meet a policeman than an agricultural extension worker.*[2]

As one does on these occasions, I sensed that what I saying was going down well with elected members. It may have seemed rather too

---

2. Ibid.

'political' for official members who were not used to one of the team exposing weaknesses. I was disappointed to see only two or three in the public gallery and somewhat annoyed that none of my staff were in the officials' box. 'We'll be there, when you need answers in the Committee of Supply', I was later told. I made it clear that in future I would expect support on the occasion of any major speech. I was also a firm believer in the training value of participation, however minor and routine, in the great occasions of the annual cycle of state events. How could one convincingly persuade people of the value of the democratic and representational processes we were introducing if one had never seen them in action? I also knew that elected chairmen would need their officials close by them when they had to face public scrutiny of their proposals. If they were to trust me it was important that I, and my staff, should set an example.

There was one person, however, upon whom the budget speech had exactly the effect I had hoped. Francis Bugotu was the most senior Solomon Islander in the education department. He was also closely involved with *The Kakamora Reporter*, a monthly magazine, edited by Henry Raraka and backed by a group of young, well educated and radical Solomon Islanders with the *sub-rosa* support of Tony Hughes, an exceptionally able and far-seeing but relatively junior British administrative officer. These were the people who had led the assault on the 'expatriates only' policy of the Mendana Hotel. Francis very kindly wrote to me:

> I have just been reading your speech on the 1971 Appropriation Bill and wish to say how very happy I am to read it. I hope you don't mind me saying this and sending you this little note, but this is the first financial secretary's speech I could follow and understand with a lot of agreement.

That note gave me much satisfaction. I felt that I had begun to establish myself with the people upon whom the future of the country lay and hoped that I could escape the 'African exile' categorisation and gain the trust and confidence without which I could achieve nothing. The Finance Committee gave me the opportunity to get closer to my Solomon Island colleagues and, alongside the formal business, assess their expectations, their strengths and their weaknesses through informal discussion. A newcomer and totally ignorant about the country, I was able to pose many questions and arouse their curiosity and interest. The Finance Committee became as close to a Cabinet as the country had.

CHAPTER THREE
DEVELOPING THE ECONOMY

The opportunity to play a part in economic development was the main attraction of my job. I was a generalist administrator, neither an economist nor an accountant. Economic history had been part of my undergraduate studies but the only directly relevant formal training I had ever had was one year of intermediate economics (equivalent to 'A' level) in my first year at university. I had learned about finance and development on the job: holding accounts, preparing and managing budgets, inspecting local government treasuries, drafting grant applications, helping local councils with projects, building the occasional road and rest house, learning to understand company accounts as a government appointed director and finally, as Permanent Secretary to a state ministry of finance in Nigeria bringing previous experience together and learning how to cope with a deficit budget. My generation held Maynard Keynes in awe and, even if few of us had read him in the original, his was the dominant influence. I had read and absorbed the easily accessible J.K. Galbraith. Most of us, who were colonial administrators, saw our duty extending well beyond law and order. Our predecessors had seen to the provision of the economic infrastructure basic to the needs of governance. Our task was actively to seek the means that would encourage economic take-off in order to sustain political and social development.

We took economic planning seriously and, although there were enormous problems associated with statistics in subsistence economies, it was probably easier to plan effectively in a small, undeveloped economy than in the huge and complex economies of the developed world. In later years economic planning, especially in the three or five year plan mould, was to be derided in the Western world, primarily for party political reasons. Other fashions took its place. The mission statements, business plans, annual operational plans and research assessments, which became all important during the 1980s in the universities where I spent my subsequent career, in practice performed, with far more (and pointless) bureaucracy, much the same function as the intelligently addressed, three or five year plans of my colonial days. The aim, and certainly the aim I had in 1970 in the Solomon Islands, was to gather sound information about the economy, think ahead in terms of objectives, assess executive capacity and try to determine priorities and the means of achieving them. Once agreed, implementation of a plan had to be flexible and effectively monitored; in essence it was no more than good housekeeping, but none the worse for that.

I considered that realistic planning could only be undertaken in the context of what was actually achievable financially and, therefore, believed in a close alliance between economic development and financial and fiscal policies. This was also the system of which I had had direct experience in Nigeria as Permanent Secretary to a state ministry of finance. I had observed that separate ministries of economic planning had not always facilitated development. Inter-ministry rivalry encouraged the planners to bypass the Ministry of Finance by appealing directly to the prime minister who would, then, quite soon need his own economic advisers to help arbitrate between planning and finance.

I also had personal motivation. Treasuries have many technical responsibilities related to banking, currency, excise, taxation and the keeping of public accounts, all somewhat dry and some, by definition, unpopular duties. Responsibility for development and economic planning gave opportunities for getting closer to peoples' aspirations, for excitement and, of course, for popularity. A government statistician had recently been established and Gerald Finkle was bravely beginning to put some kind of order into figures already collected and starting to try to compile the kind of statistical summaries that were essential to understanding what was happening. Peter Hill, an economist working in my office, was available to all departments for cost benefit analysis of projects but there was not, at the time of my arrival, a planning unit as such. In the Western Pacific High Commission, however, a Regional Development Planning Unit (RDPU) had been established by the Overseas Development Administration (ODA) to advise all three governments.

It was based in Honiara and was engaged in formulating a three year plan, 1971 to 1973, for the Protectorate, the sixth plan it had had and the first to have had the advantage of substantial economic expertise. There were three members of the unit, two economists and an experienced finance man with a colonial service background. John Pell, the senior economist, was critical of the Protectorate administration and anticipated a battle with me, just as I had been warned in London to expect one with him because it was known that the RDPU was proving unpopular with heads of departments. I was delighted to have economists able to conduct the studies and analysis necessary to underpin an effective plan. My prime concern was to ensure that the plan would be well balanced. Lessons I had learned as a de-coloniser were: that people adapt with remarkable ability to both the advantages and the constraints of their environment; that you should never assume that you know what is in their interests better than they do; that governments have a major role in ensuring that infrastructure is in place but are not good at managing businesses; that marketing is a crucial component of any scheme to improve or introduce natural resources production; and, above all, that it is easy to implement the administrative sector of a development plan – a new legislature, public service housing and the like, relatively easy to implement the social sector – education and health, and extremely difficult to implement the productive, natural resources sector, on which, of course, every other sector depends.

I was anxious, too, that the plan be designed so that it could be easily understood and would automatically become the structure for future annual budgets. Annual appropriation, the tradition of the Westminster parliamentary model, was originally established to ensure that the monarch had to summon parliament at least once a year and would always be time limited in unnecessary and costly adventures abroad. Still a sound principle in many ways, annual appropriation has the obvious disadvantage that most projects in the modern world require a substantial lead time for research and design and then may take several years to implement. In the colonies we made a clear distinction between the recurrent and capital budgets. Logically a three-year plan would be the capital budget for those three years and would also indicate priorities in each year's recurrent budget. John Pell had no difficulty in accepting my position and we worked well together. Often deliberately provocative, he was always stimulating, his contribution full-blooded and extremely valuable. I presented the

Sixth Development Plan to Governing Council in 1971.[1] The RDPU had done an excellent job.

The economy was heavily dependent on external aid, which financed about 41% of expenditure on monetary GDP (valued at market prices). Expatriates accounted for 80% of post-secondary human resources. Public sector recurrent expenditure had trebled over the previous decade but locally raised revenue met only 80% of the total so the Protectorate was the recipient of grant-in-aid, a budget deficiency grant. Deficiency grants inevitably create a substantial bureaucracy. Energies get directed at process rather than objective. As was the position in many dependencies, the government dominated the economy both because it was responsible for a range of services in which the private sector had not yet obtained a foothold, and because it was the single largest employer. So, for example, the churches played a major role in education, particularly at the primary level, but were in receipt of substantial government grants, and it was the Government Stores that imported the educational materials used by these schools, such as exercise books, pens and pencils, which could not be produced locally. One of my early objectives was to run down dependence on the Government Stores in order to provide an incentive for the private sector.

The cash economy was dependent on copra and timber. Some 25,000 tons of copra, half of it from expatriate owned plantations, was exported each year, a tiny percentage of the world market. Local producers, usually in a Co-operative, were at a great disadvantage because of the high costs of collection and transport to the few anchorages that could be used by even relatively small tramp steamers, then, fortunately, still sailing the oceans. Our position in the world copra market was so small that there was little possibility of being able to add value locally in the manner in which, for example, Jamaica with its much larger production and superior communications was able to do. Some seven million cubic feet of hardwood was exported each year, all from expatriate owned forest. The timber trade offered no opportunity for local participation except as employees. There were no individual pit sawyers as were found in West Africa. The Colonial Development Corporation (CDC) was in the process of establishing an oil palm plantation with facilities for

---

1. Governing Council Debates, Official Report, 10th May 1971.

outlier participation. The Agricultural Department was encouraging coffee and cocoa production but both crops have a long lead-time and as yet the effect on the economy was negligible. Their day would come, I used to say, when the people of China acquired a taste for both. There was some prospect of mineral exploitation and in 1970 there was active engagement with the Mitsui Mining and Smelting Company of Japan about bauxite mining on Rennell, an outlying Polynesian island to the south of Guadalcanal.

The Solomons are an archipelago of many islands with the population mainly living along the shore, fish the main protein in the diet and nearly everyone a fisherman. My office looked out on to the Coral Sea. At any time of day I could see great shoals of fish. Outside territorial waters Japanese, Taiwanese and American tuna fleets operated with absolutely no benefit whatsoever to the local economy. They did not even need to come ashore to bunker. I became convinced that there had to be an economic future for the country in the Pacific Ocean's abundant supply of fish. Even the scheme to export crayfish to New York restaurants, albeit they were thousands of miles away, looked plausible on paper although I had my doubts about the reality. Solomon Island fishermen would catch the crayfish, store them in locally made sea cages and sell them weekly to a visiting boat with freezer facilities. Once back at Honiara the frozen crayfish would be flown to the USA in containers. Freight costs would be high but could be borne by a luxury item. The major problem was the journey from Honiara to Fiji, where a jumbo could complete the journey to New York. It took some eight hours to Fiji in a DH Heron. There were two flights a week but opportunities for delay and cancellation were many with a small airline covering the entire range of Pacific islands, especially in the hurricane season.

The UK government was providing project funding for fisheries surveys elsewhere. All, however, were aimed at upgrading local subsistence fishermen into commercial fishermen without attention being paid to the huge problems of marketing. The projects tended to be run by enthusiasts with little if any experience of either tuna fishing or large scale commercial fishing. In the Gilbert Islands between 1970 and 1980, £1.64m of aid was allocated to fourteen fishing projects. At the end there was still no effective commercial industry. One of the projects was directed at an engine powered fishing dory to replace the sailing canoes, which the Gilbertese built themselves . The dories could not be beached and repaired in the way canoes were. The Gilbertese are excellent sailors and fishermen but not mechanics. In Papua New Guinea and in Fiji, where efforts were being made to create joint ventures with foreign long-lining fleets, the main benefit was some limited employment. I wanted something better and I was soon to be immersed in the development of both bauxite mining and commercial fishing. Such was their importance that they deserve a chapter to themselves.

Initially there were many other aspects of development to consider. Long since persuaded by Professor Arthur Lewis, the West Indian economist, that the imposition of export duties kills the goose that lays the golden egg, I was concerned that Protectorate revenue relied so heavily on export duties. The export duty on copra had been around 15% on f.o.b. values in the last ten years and a much larger proportion of the 'beach' price paid to local farmers, nearer 20% to 25%. My objective was to transfer taxes on production to taxes on consumption. My instincts were in favour of immediate abolition of the export duty on copra but it was to take time. As the recipient of grant-in-aid the annual budget of the Protectorate had to be scrutinised and approved by the FCO and I knew that I would have to have some alternative sources of revenue to quote. Few things gave me greater pleasure than being able to announce in my 1971 budget the abolition of a specific duty of $7 a ton even if, alas, at that stage I still had to maintain the *ad valorem* duty. I did, however, pledge that there would no change in its rate nor would there be any re-imposition of a specific duty before 1975.

One of the main strengths of any nation is its human resources, still referred to as manpower in the less politically correct 1970s. There had been a manpower survey in 1970 as well as a census. 8.5% of the population was in wage employment and this accounted for 33% of the available male workforce, a high proportion by the standards of most developing economies at the time, but there was one expatriate in employment to every eleven Solomon Islanders. Localisation was a key issue. Tom Russell called a heads of department meeting to discuss it soon after my arrival. Because I had spent several years running so-called 'crash' courses in order to hasten localisation in Northern

Nigeria, which had lagged massively behind Southern Nigeria in terms of education, I was asked to share some of my experience. I listened to several heads of departments unconcernedly talking in terms of a decade or two before most senior expatriates could be replaced, justifying their views on the known secondary school population, the percentage likely to qualify for university, the time needed for professional training and gaining experience on the job. A number of colleagues were of the view that it would be wrong to countenance any lowering of standards 'while we are in charge'. There was neither a sense of urgency nor appreciation of the fact that the elite to whom power would inevitably be handed over much sooner than many expected was already identified.

Several heads of department were non-graduates and not all possessed the professional qualifications they were now demanding of local staff. They had had military and other experience, worked their way up from the bottom and learned on the job. It would have been invidious to make any direct comparisons, so I simply commented that whether we thought it a good idea or not, independence – and this was probably the first time the word had ever been voiced at a meeting – would happen sooner than anyone expected. I explained that in Northern Nigeria ten years prior to independence there had been a mere handful with a school certificate, let alone a degree, in a population of many millions. We had to be pragmatic about standards, paying more attention to character and proven ability than formal education. Our task was to make the best possible use of the human resources we had and train Solomon Islanders as quickly as possible to the minimum level of skills required for any particular job. Nearly all present were ex-servicemen and I reminded them of the speed with which men had been prepared for combat in World War II.

These were pioneering days and it was important to expect people to move on quickly and to recognize that in terms of localization some posts were far more sensitive that others. The administration and the police would need to be localized first. At the time there was only one Solomon Islander Administrative Officer and he, sensibly, had been sent on secondment to the Gilbert and Ellice Islands where he could learn on the job without the pressures of family and local connections. Recognising that there was both insufficient a pool of potential administrators to try and establish a local course and that the educational programme was beginning to produce a steady flow of graduates, I proposed that the Administration should rob other departments of suitable staff. In Northern Nigeria I had recruited an archivist, an archaeologist and a biologist into the administration and as time had gone on such people were, in turn, courted by the private sector, often finishing their careers as chairmen of local divisions of multinational companies. The same, I was sure, would happen in the Solomons. The first Solomon Islanders we had entertained at home were both graduate teachers. They had impressed me and I suggested to Tom Russell that they should be approached, without any pressure, to join the Administration. They both agreed to do so. Eight years later these two, Baddeley Devisi and Peter Kenilorea,[2] were to become the first Governor-General and the first Prime Minister of an independent Solomon Islands.

Localisation was not just an issue for the public service. It was significant for the private sector. Experience suggested that the nationalist pressures there would follow, rather than coincide with, those in the public sector because the transition to independence is invariably accompanied by a substantial growth in economic activity and trade, providing increased employment opportunities. That expansion, however, would often call for the import of new expatriate skills at the very moment when the call for the withdrawal of those already there is beginning to heat up. I was not worried about the handful of large expatriate commercial enterprises. The CDC and Levers, for example, had plenty of corporate experience of de-colonisation elsewhere and not only understood the political issues but had commercial incentives to localise. Levers' Pacific Timbers, the major logging operation, already set a good example by employing Ghanaians and Nigerians at the middle management level on secondment from their timber activities in West Africa. It was good for the Africans, earning hard currency without a swarm of relations close by to help spend it, cheaper for Levers than employing expatriates from Europe and, important for the local economy, providing a role model for Solomon Islanders to emulate. One of the hardest tasks of localisation everywhere was to persuade appropriately qualified job seekers to opt for a tough, outdoor life in remote places when there were always soft and well remunerated office jobs available in the capital.

---

2. Peter Kenilorea, *Tell It As It Is*, Taipei, Center for Pacific-Asia Studies 2008 is a rare autobiography from the hand of a prime minister of a newly independent state.

Of more concern were the small expatriate family businesses, some of which probably survived on underpaid family labour, content with a known lifestyle rather than being career ambitious.[3] Localisation could spell disaster for them. One option was for them to seek Solomon Island partners and with their help expand to absorb the additional costs. The Churches, too, faced difficulties. Collectively they were a powerful force in a country where all but a very small percentage of the indigenous population were active churchgoers. On Good Friday there was an ecumenical way of the cross service in Honiara, when a huge congregation moved from station to station set up at the various churches. The only people wondering what it was all about would be newly arrived expatriates on their way to the club or beach. The Churches were, in the main, alert to the need for localisation but concerned that returning graduates and others with specialist training in whom they had invested would be persuaded to join government service.

With a view to becoming less dependent on overseas grants, some of the churches had become involved in commercial activities. The Melanesian Mission, for example, had a well-managed boatyard and some plantations. The objectives were legitimate but in encouraging the development of Solomon Islander owned business ventures it was important to ensure that mission owned enterprises did not use the tax advantages granted to charities to compete unfairly. Dominicans from the United States province had a mission station in the Western District. Among their number was Fr Meese, the least likely monk I ever met. He came to complain to me about some legislative measure that I was presenting to Governing Council. Dressed in an expensive suit and sporting a large pearl tiepin, he argued the merits of free and unrestricted enterprise strongly. As he spoke it became evident that he was not arguing theoretically on behalf of members of his flock, who had been hard done by, but championing his own entrepreneurial activities. I discovered that among other money making businesses he was the Solair agent in Gizo and an insurance broker. There were many who supported him; he provided an efficient service, had access to the latest in radio communications and was clearly a good entrepreneur. Personally I found

---

3. Lucy Irvine, *Faraway*, Doubleday, London 2000 gives an excellent background to how small family firms managed.

it distasteful that a missionary was engaged in tasks that with effort and training a Solomon Islander might well be found to undertake.

A large part of my job was to raise awareness about the need for development, the advantages of balanced planning and the dangers of heavy reliance on external aid. I spoke to an educational conference on the *Financing of Primary Education*. As in most developing countries there was an instinctive and understandable conviction that universal primary education was the highest priority. It was a basic human right that nobody should be denied. My job was to explain that moral commitment to that aim must not cloud my investment judgement. Investment in primary education takes at least seven years before there is any return and in terms of professional level human resources many more years, over twenty years, for example, to produce a doctor. Investment in secondary and higher education had, therefore, to be the immediate localisation priority and the production of teachers had to be well established before there could be wide expansion of primary education. The highest immediate return would be from a three-year investment in higher education so that on completion of their courses Solomon Islanders could replace expensive expatriate labour.

I also needed to emphasise that it was not so much the capital costs of school buildings that mattered but the recurrent expenditure needed to put them to proper use, year after year. Younger expatriates than myself, who had grown up in the post-war welfare state of the United Kingdom, were apt to argue that the amount of aid required was minimal by UK standards and would put to me that I would best be employed extracting as much aid as possible. After citing the facts and figures about how far we were dependent on aid and how substantial was the deficit in local resources, I went on to say:

> *Perhaps you see no harm in living this way. While I agree that the rich nations should help the poor, I cannot subscribe to the view that total dependence on aid is acceptable. A people which has to beg to survive, or a government which has to beg to survive, are just as degraded as human beings as the individual beggar who, as yet, has no place in the Solomons. But as the man who has to go out and about with the begging bowl I can assure you that as a people we are beggars, that as*

a government we do beg; and I find it degrading. We need an adult relationship with the rich nations of the world that will mean a fair return for the export of our produce and skills and not the undignified tied relationship of budgetary aid.

Constantly harping on the same themes, throwing out challenges in an endeavour to stimulate the economy and always willing to accept an invitation to speak, I began to sense that the reality of change, the coming of independence and the need for development was getting into the bloodstream at least of the major participants in the process of transition. My views seldom went unchallenged, not least by expatriate colleagues, as occurred when I imposed a duty on imported meat. The Solomons was not short of protein. The seas were abundant with fish, many families kept pigs and poultry, and cattle, used to graze in coconut plantations in order to keep the grass down, provided beef for the better-off. Large quantities of corned beef were, however, imported because Solomon Islanders who had worked on the Queensland plantations, in the early days as indentured labour little short of slavery, had returned with a taste for the rice and corned beef that had been their staple diet. Rice was now being grown locally and a tariff had already been imposed on imported rice. In 1971 I proposed a duty of 5% *ad valorem* on imported meat. Introducing this in my budget speech I said:

This is a deliberately low initial duty to indicate to the private sector the seriousness of our intention to expand the beef industry and our desire to see the establishment of a local cannery as soon as the quantity of meat production permits. I hope that in the meantime more initiative will be shown in providing retail outlets for fresh meat at a price that the average Solomon Islander can afford. Government itself must not frustrate this objective by inflexible application of public health standards of a level unsuited to the local environment.[4]

That final sentence caused the Director of Medical Services, no longer a public service member of Governing Council, understandably and

---

4. Governing Council Debates, Official Record 11th November 1971.

fairly, to express his concern. He feared my comment was an open invitation to slaughter in any old manner and would enhance the danger of meat unfit for consumption getting into the food chain. He also pointed out that inspection was free and did not add to the costs of slaughter. In fact, however, there was only one licensed abattoir, owned by an expatriate company. I knew that two Solomon Island parties seriously interested in establishing abattoirs had been snubbed by the public health authorities. I had used the meat import duty as an opportunity to warn generally about the danger of setting standards that automatically excluded local participation and ensured the retention of expatriate monopolies. We had an excellent medical department under the leadership of Dr MacGregor, and there was a strong and effective public health team. It was an example of the concern I had expressed on arrival about the Protectorate being over-administered. Well-qualified and hard working expatriates were finding things that needed doing and applying the latest international standards. Public health by-laws, for example, required bread to be wrapped. This put the establishment of a modest bakery business beyond the capabilities of most Solomon Islanders. Again it was an expatriate monopoly. In West Africa there were dozens of bakers in every town, some of them the cooks of expatriates moonlighting! In every French village people collected unwrapped baguettes from their *boulangerie* two or three times a day. In West Africa women would cook food and sell it by the plate to workers outside large departments, such as the public works, construction sites, factories and the like. Even in wealthy and advanced Hong Kong there were numerous simple eating places on the side of the street that would not have been permitted in Honiara. These basic development incentives and opportunities that get an economy moving were missing in the Solomons partly, at least, because the relevant regulations were those appropriate to a sophisticated, well off Western urban community. I wanted to get the government machine away from the notion that whenever somebody came up with a good idea it was the job of the civil service to put obstacles in its path.

I was in general hard on medical services because I considered that health had had too generous an allocation of revenue at the expense of education. In the development plan and in each budget I was trying to adjust that balance within an overall limit necessary to avoid the inevitable pressures for both health and schools to run away with the plan at the expense of the much less glamorous but productive natural resources sector. Standards were high and it would have been politically inept to attack them. The localisation record was also the best of all departments because the excellent medical school at Fiji was able to provide most of our doctors and had not yet aspired to the award of metropolitan qualifications which would enable Fiji trained doctors to work elsewhere than in the Pacific. My main concern, therefore, was to avoid any substantial expansion and endeavour to avoid legislation that might hinder development.

The Headmaster of King George VI Secondary School also took me to task when, invited to speak to senior students about development, I argued that so long as staff and pupils all dressed in white shirts and shorts there was little incentive to anyone thinking of setting up a tailoring business. Like everything else in the country, uniforms were supplied through a contract with the Government Stores. I light-heartedly suggested that they rebel against school uniform and demand the option to wear clothes of their choice on suitable occasions. The fairly recently arrived and excellent Head, Alistair Macbeth, was privately anxious to brighten uniforms but such was the heavy hand of government that he assumed it would all have to be publicly funded. My aim was to allow fashion to create demand. I wanted students to work in their holidays to save enough to invest in brighter shirt or fashion cut pants (it was the age of narrow trousers), not to stand in a queue to have them handed out free!

If the Government Store's monopoly was one obstacle inhibiting business entrepreneurship, the banks were another. There were two banks, the Commonwealth Bank of Australia and the Australia New Zealand Bank (ANZ). They were expatriate banks with expatriate staff. Their prime interest was in securing the custom of expatriate business. They played no part in the extension of credit to Solomon Islanders and, to be fair, the development of banking facilities to people only just beginning to break out of a subsistence economy is a difficult and highly skilled task in which the return on investment will not be seen for many years. The record of trading banks in introducing those at the bottom end of society to credit has nowhere been good because it has not been their function. Where there has been success in extending credit to people operating below the usual banking threshold, Credit Unions and Co-operative Societies have been the vehicles. The Co-operative movement was relatively well developed in the Solomons, with 8,000 members in 153 primary societies, directed towards trading and marketing. There was also an Agricultural and Industrial Loans Board, which had been making loans of a type that an effective trading bank should have welcomed. The development plan proposed reconstituting the Loans Board as a small business credit scheme introducing Solomon Islanders to handling credit and, in due course, handing them on to the trading banks.

The banking services on offer locally were, however, primitive compared with those of an international bank, such as Standard or Barclays International. The Commonwealth and ANZ still operated pretty much as the savings banks they had originally been. The local managers were pleasant enough and anxious to help but not only did they have little authority they didn't really understand what I was talking about. They employed no local staff in positions where they might learn about banking and took it for granted that Honiara would remain a posting for young Australian and New Zealand staff. Work, unfortunately, never took me to either Australia or New Zealand so I had no opportunity to raise the issue informally at a higher level but I determined to encourage a bank with strong international connections and experience to establish in Honiara. I had promising talks with Barclays DC&O in London while on leave but eventually it was the lively Hong Kong and Shanghai Bank that took the plunge.

The Protectorate used Australian currency. A substantial sum was paid to the banks to cover the cost of imported specie, significant in an economy where coin was preferred to paper money by the majority of the population on grounds of its durability. Thatched buildings are a ready prey to fire and in houses with only mats for walls and virtually no furniture, the thatch is where you store belongings of importance. Using Australian currency had its advantages but there were downsides in addition to the cost of specie import. Long term the issue of currency would inevitably be raised within the context of coming independence and when I found that the United Nations Development Programme (UNDP) regional team had a development economist with the right experience to advise us, I commissioned a report. Ed Dommen reported in April 1972 setting out very clearly the advantages and disadvantages of establishing a Solomon Islands currency, the financial implications, the administrative issues, a suggested timetable for the establishment of a local currency and a draft currency ordinance. The report, succinct, well written and without a single word of jargon, was a model of what is needed for presentation to and discussion by non-experts with the authority to take a decision. Dommen was clearly in favour of the establishment of a local currency board in order to provide effective investment of foreign reserves, currently held in pockets and hidden in the thatches of Solomon Islanders, to yield valuable statistical information on currency circulating, to offer the denominations of coin and note best suited to local needs and to give the Solomon Islands Government control of exchange rates. He saw it as a step along the way to nation building. The advantages were primarily political. A nation's own currency can be a useful symbol of national unity and there would be the opportunity for the designs to reflect traditional forms of money, such as there were. There would, however, also be a modest revenue gain to replace what amounted to an interest free loan to Australia. There would be greater knowledge of the economy and as experience grew there would be the opportunity to travel further along the road towards control by establishing a central bank. It all came to pass but long after I had left the country.

CHAPTER FOUR
MINING AND FISHING

A United Nations aerial geophysical survey of mineral resources had indicated possible reserves of 36 million tons of bauxite on Rennell, a small outlying atoll, 110 miles to the south of Guadalcanal, some 40 miles long and less than five miles in breadth. The Government had invited tenders internationally to explore with a view to develop and in 1969 had issued a prospecting licence to the Mitsui Mining and Smelting Company of Japan. After initial investigations had proved promising, Mitsui and the government had signed a Memorandum of Understanding in January 1970 that required Mitsui to produce a feasibility study. The next set of negotiations were scheduled to follow my first session of Governing Council in November 1970, when Mitsui planned to present the feasibility study and hoped to be able to reach agreement on exploitation in line with the Memorandum of Understanding.

Alumina, the essential ingredient of aluminium, can be extracted from bauxite. How the bauxite had occurred on Rennell was something of a mystery. One school of thought suggested that it was of the *terra rossa* type, formed by solution of silica from clay left after the calcium and magnesium carbonates of the limestone of the coral atoll had been dissolved. This view was disputed because of the huge quantity of limestone that would have needed to be dissolved. Moreover, bauxite was not common to other Pacific atolls so that its occurrence on Rennell suggested that it depended on a factor not common to all atolls. For example, Bellona, a small atoll close to Rennell, had phosphate deposits but no bauxite. Another theory concluded that the bauxite had been formed from volcanic ash. There was, however, no known recent volcanic activity in the vicinity and the direction of prevailing ocean currents and winds did not identify a more distant source. The geology was fascinating but as an administrator I could not afford to dwell on it. My job was, if possible, to encourage exploitation of a significant asset to the best possible advantage of the Solomon Islands.

I had little time in which to get myself up to speed. Fortunately, my last job in Nigeria had been in the Benue-Plateau State where tin was mined and smelted so I had learned something about the economics of mining. Mining requires massive investment at the start of a project and a guaranteed return over some twenty years, by the end of which the only asset remaining is usually a hole in the ground. Almost all mining devastates the environment. Smelting close to the mineral source lowers costs and adds value locally, usually a political as well as an economic advantage. I read the papers and was briefed by Tom Russell and John Pepys-Cockerell, responsible for the natural resources schedule, but I began negotiations without having had a chance to visit Rennell, one of three Polynesian islands in the Solomons group, and home to some 1,200. An airstrip had been one of the immediate benefits of prospecting so that the island and its people were no longer quite as isolated as they had previously been, but the impact of a major extractive industry was clearly something not to be lightly wished upon on a small and remote island.

The Ministry of Overseas Development, as it then was, had supported the original discussions with a mining consultant and had now appointed Mackay and Schnellman, leading mining consultants, and Allan, Charlesworth & Co, Chartered Accountants, to provide assistance with the assessment of the feasibility study and with subsequent discussions with Mitsui. I was fortunate in the quality of the team thus assembled. The immensely experienced Dr Fred Fitch oozed the technicalities of mining engineering from his finger tips and picked up on innumerable technical issues which no layman could ever have spotted, although I was later to realise how painful it was for him to negotiate with Japanese whose prisoner of war he had been. The immediately likeable John Laurence of Allan, Charlesworth was able to talk about share holding, company formation and management, royalties and all forms of taxation in language we could easily understand. He was to become an extremely good friend and ally over the years. His expertise and the manner of its presentation was the most valuable UK aid that I experienced anywhere, a model for technical assistance, sadly, not always emulated. Later in the negotiations I obtained through the UNDP the services of Charles (Chuck) Lipton, an extremely able and experienced United States lawyer specialising in mineral rights and negotiations. Chuck's expertise was unique. For a couple of decades he was involved in nearly every major minerals development in the Third World.

The consultants shared my own unhappiness with the Memorandum of Understanding and disagreed completely with the advice that had previously been given. Briefly, the government had been advised not to seek any royalties, the usual tax on the extraction of an irreplaceable mineral, but to rely on a dividend producing shareholding in the industry through a locally registered company. The government was to have an initial 'free ride' of 25% of the shares and would have the right to purchase a further 20%. There was to be a tax holiday of sixteen years, while the government undertook not to impose royalty or export duty and to waive all the usual rents and fees required under lands and mining legislation. Allan, Charlesworth were to report that the Memorandum of Understanding had 'frankly been an embarrassment to all concerned'. In fairness to those in the Protectorate it had been their first significant venture into the hard world of commercial negotiation as well as mining and, understandably, they had accepted the professional advice given to them in areas about which they knew little. Fortunately, caution had prevailed to prevent formal ratification of the agreement until more information was available and it is possible that tougher negotiations earlier on might have put Mitsui off altogether. As it was, prospecting had confirmed the potential for mining and Rennell now had an airstrip and had benefited from some casual employment.

Mackay and Schnellman were as unhappy about some of the technical aspects of the Mitsui feasibility study as Allan, Charlesworth were about the revenue implications of the Memorandum of Understanding. There were many matters related to the composition, quality and size of the deposit, to the proposed methods of extraction and so forth but there were two especially significant issues. At that time there was no open market for bauxite because aluminium producers obtained bauxite from their own captive sources. Unlike other minerals, where chemical analysis is the prime factor in valuation, with bauxite the costs of freight and extraction were paramount. Neither was there a satisfactory formula for relating the value of any particular bauxite to known bauxite, alumina and aluminium prices, significant because bauxite represents only 1½% of the value of fabricated aluminium. In the feasibility study Mitsui had used for valuation the price of bauxite mined at Gove in Northern Territory, Australia for the supply of which they had a twenty year contract with Nabalco. Our consultants argued that the Gove price was known to be low and contested the adjustments made for *premia* and penalties in connection with mineral and moisture content. We wanted the highest possible valuation and Mitsui the lowest. We were aware that Mitsui need not be concerned whether the Solomon Islands mining company was profitable because it could take its profits anywhere down the line from the alumina operation. The other factor Mackay and Schnellman wanted further investigated was the possibility of adding value by locating alumina extraction on Rennell. This would greatly reduce the freight costs and open up the possibilities of producing phosphate in part of the same plant and of utilising the 'red mud' waste product of extraction usefully, providing additional products to compensate for the environmental disorder mining was bound to create.

None of this made for easy negotiations around the table. It was my first encounter with the Japanese and I found the Mitsui team somewhat stiff and formal. David Kausimae, the excellent Chairman of the Natural Resources Committee, was my main support but like me he was coming to it for the first time. We let the consultants discuss many of the technical issues with their opposite numbers in the Mitsui team without our participation and tried to keep things moving along at plenary sessions. We established that since their last visit the Constitution had changed, that there was now a government with an elected majority and that our present circumstances demanded guaranteed and sustained revenue from the beginning of the venture. It soon became clear that Mr Kaneko and his colleagues had arrived expecting their feasibility study to be accepted with little modification, followed by the negotiation of a joint venture agreement. When we realised that no further progress could easily be made we discussed with our consultants how serious they considered Mitsui's intentions were. Their view was that potentially there could be a deal much more favourable to the interests of the Protectorate than that envisaged in the Memorandum of Understanding, but to achieve it more investigation was needed. I decided that it would be best to bring the shutters down on the current negotiations but make it clear that we remained extremely interested and wanted to continue talking with Mitsui. Mitsui had now twice come to Honiara for quite lengthy negotiations. It seemed that if we suggested meeting next in Tokyo it might both sweeten the failure of the current round of talks and indicate the seriousness of our interest. I foresaw a problem, however. In Honiara, as host, I had chaired the negotiations. If Mitsui were the host in Tokyo Mr Kaneko would rightly expect to chair the discussions, but on no account did I want to lose the advantages that chairing confers in difficult negotiations. A solution occurred to me at our final meeting. I proposed talks the following April in Tokyo under the auspices of the British Embassy. I did not press Mitsui but suggested that both sides write and exchange notes of our understanding of where we had got to and then make arrangements.

I had done all this without consultation and now faced negotiations with the FCO and the Embassy in Japan. I had no idea how helpful or difficult London or Tokyo would prove to be. My being a new boy of whom they had as yet little knowledge helped. I explained that all I wanted was space in which to hold meetings and luckily I was not turned down. In the event there was an empty house in the Embassy compound that was put at our disposable and embassy staff in the Commercial Department, headed by John Whitehead, some years later to return to Tokyo as Ambassador, were extremely helpful in many other ways.

My record of the major points discussed at the Honiara meeting became the agenda for the Tokyo negotiations that took place in April 1971. It was my first visit to Japan. I travelled via Hong Kong where I was able to catch up with one or two old friends and get accustomed again to all the sophistication of a big city. Mitsui were extremely hospitable, almost overwhelmingly so. None of their team ever seemed to go home and I had quickly to establish that we needed time to ourselves for discussions, as surely they did, and on some days made it clear that we were not available until the following day. I was very glad to be in the chair and be able to control the agenda and timetable.

At the week-end Mitsui took us to Kamioka, a copper mine. An old and long established mine, its operation was as modern as could be found anywhere in the world. The technology was the most impressive I had ever seen anywhere. Suitably dressed in dungarees, boots and helmets we were taken underground. We could have gone in city suits and hardly have had a speck or two of dust to brush off. In the entire hour we spent underground we only encountered two human beings. They were playing table tennis in a rest area. Untended machines were undertaking the drilling and extraction. Unmanned trolley trains glided along the galleries. When we reached a shaft our approach was spotted by camera, an unmanned cage arrived, doors opened and closed again, once we were all in, as if by magic. On our return to the surface we were taken to the control room. Removing our boots and donning slippers we entered an air-conditioned room with a central control panel where the operator had in view a battery of closed circuit TV monitors which had recorded our progress enabling him to summon trolleys and cages on our behalf. There was an impressive row of computers, substantial in those days, with several engineers in charge of the operation, but on each of their desks, in this space age control room, sat an abacus! Any doubts I might have had about Mitsui's ability to undertake the building of an alumina plant on Rennell, if that were to prove feasible, were dispelled.

From the space age mine we were transported back to the middle ages. We were staying in the company guesthouse overnight. In the stone covered hallway traditionally dressed women, one to each of us, came forward on their knees to persuade us to sit down on a wooden bench so that they could remove our boots. They put slippers on our feet and then led us along wooden corridors to our rooms. I was privileged with a room in which the Crown Prince had recently stayed. It was easy to appreciate the protocol: outside footwear on stone, indoor slippers on wood and bare feet on the rice matting of the bedroom, except that there was no bed, but a futon. You exchanged footwear before using the toilet or the baths where you learned to wash from a bucket before lounging and chatting in a splendid communal hot tub. In the evening we all donned company kimonos and sat cross-legged to enjoy an extremely good meal. In that atmosphere our hosts relaxed and completely changed character. A rather severe accountant, who had never once opened his mouth during discussions either in Honiara or Tokyo but had sat assiduously clicking his abacus and making copious notes, became the life and soul of the party, telling innumerable jokes. Mr Kaneko no longer seemed to be conscious of his Managing Director status. He laughingly explained to me how Japan managed labour relations by setting aside a week in April every year, the week we were there, for demonstrations and strikes on the understanding that everyone was back to work as normal the following week.

After the week-end visit, which included a visit to Kyoto and entertainment in a Geisha house, negotiations became much easier. Both parties gave way sufficiently for us to be able to agree the principles to be embodied in a future Joint Venture Agreement between the Protectorate and Mitsui Mining and Smelting. David Kausimae and I signed a preliminary agreement to this effect on 28 April before leaving Tokyo. Chuck Lipton played a major role in the drafting and, on his advice, the final clause stated that the agreement would be 'null and void and of no further force and effect in the event that the Joint Venture Agreement is not executed on or before December 31, 1972'. That gave Mitsui just over eighteen months in which to conduct trial mining and for both parties to resolve some outstanding issues. Sadly, we never did reach the point of drafting a joint venture agreement. Events elsewhere in the world and their affect on the aluminium market and the costs of mining on a remote Pacific island intervened. Perhaps for the people of Rennell it was just as well and should there ever again be a demand for their bauxite, the deposit remains intact.

At the time I was confident that we had done as well as we could and David Kausimae and I returned to Honiara especially well satisfied because we had used our time there to reach another agreement with a Japanese company in an entirely different field but one which we both thought had much greater potential than mining for the future well-being of the Solomons. In that we were to be proved right.

There had long been a small export trade from Honiara of *beche-de-mer*, managed by the Chinese community, but the received wisdom was that the obstacles to commercial fishing could not easily be overcome. The investment required was huge and access to markets required insider knowledge. What little fish was available for sale in Honiara market was a sideline of the trade to the USA in crayfish that the two Americans were trying to establish. Their intended business was at the mercy of a long and complex airfreight haul. I was not surprised that they found selling ice cream to Solomon Islanders more reliable. But I had only to look out of my office window at any time of day to see the sea teeming with fish.

Then one day in February 1971, John Pepys-Cockerell told me that he thought he was on to something. He had with him Captain Honda of Taiyo Fisheries of Japan. Pleasant and unassuming, Captain Honda explained that he had been in the Solomons as a fighter pilot during the Second World War. Coming from a family of fishermen he had been excited by the quantity and quality of the fish he had seen while flying over Solomon Island waters. Now a master fishermen himself, he had, after years of effort, persuaded Taiyo to let him come and investigate. John Pepys-Cockerell,who was immensely knowledgeable about the natural sciences, also knew all about Taiyo, the largest fisheries company in the world, the huge demand for skipjack tuna and the pole and line fishing techniques then in use. His knowledge and enthusiasm were enough to persuade both David Kausimae, Chairman of the Natural Resources Committee, and me that here was a golden opportunity to be seized. Captain Honda was given every facility to learn as much as he could.

David and I decided to take advantage of our planned April visit to Tokyo for the bauxite mining negotiations with Mitsui to explore the fisheries option further. The Natural Resources Committee authorised us to negotiate with Taiyo while there. Conscious that not only had I never caught a fish in my life but that I had never even tried to do so, I had to learn fast, expertly tutored by John Pepys-Cockerell, who understood the international fisheries scene, and David Kausimae, who knew about Solomon Islands' fishing. Our discussions with Taiyo and the Memorandum of Understanding, which David and I signed on 28 April 1971, were to result in a major industry for the Solomons, very quickly employing hundreds and earning thousands.

Acting on the spot and without the opportunity to consult either colleagues or consultants we took a risk but that was what we were paid to do. There were other Pacific countries courting Japanese investment. We could not afford to delay and the agreement did no more than give Taiyo priority rights for eighteen months to conduct a survey of fishery resources and to examine the potential for the development of a shore based fishing industry. On one page of foolscap, the memorandum had eight clauses. The Government gave Taiyo priority but not exclusive rights for eighteen months, beginning on 1 June 1971, to conduct a survey of fishery resources and the development of a fishing industry within our territorial waters. We agreed on four catcher boats and two refrigeration ships to undertake the survey. All six were named to ensure that they and they alone were used in the survey. Taiyo contracted to provide a full report at two monthly intervals throughout the survey, to provide training facilities and to employ Solomon Islanders to the maximum extent feasible, and to produce a proposal for the establishment of a locally based fishing industry within three months of the completion of the survey.

Skipjack tuna fishing at that time was done with pole and line from a catcher boat. Skipjack is migratory and shoals are huge, numbering thousands of fish. No other species are involved or caught by mistake. Hooks are not baited. When a shoal is sighted and near to hand, live bait fish are thrown into the sea, the tuna rise and are caught on lures. Some fifteen or so fishermen cast their lures, bring the fish up and as they toss the line over their shoulder with a skilful twist of the wrist dislodge the skipjack which are collected by a couple of other crew and stored in brine until transfer to the mother ship at the end of each day. Although a huge tonnage of fish can be caught very quickly, the migratory habits and rapid movement of the skipjack tuna, the skill required both in locating the shoals and in using pole and line, and, crucially, the size and number of catcher boats permitted are effective conservation measures. Long-lining and purse seining methods of fishing are an entirely different matter.

With some apprehension I joined the large crowd that, in anticipation, had gathered at Point Cruz wharf on the evening of the last day of May. Just before dusk the Japanese fleet arrived, the biggest concentration of Japanese vessels to have been seen off Guadalcanal since the battle of the Coral Sea. They were the named ships and boats in the agreement and on time. Throughout all the negotiations with Taiyo I found that, however difficult it was to reach agreement, once obtained the Japanese were punctilious in keeping to every detail exactly. My problems were more with my own colleagues. Our Comptroller of Customs undertook a minute and lengthy examination of every ship demanding duty on whatever he could stretch the legislation to cover. The Commissioner of Police discovered that the Japanese had blue movies on the mother ships. He proposed confiscation lest the Solomon Islanders be corrupted, who, under terms of the Memorandum, were to be aboard the mother ships to confirm survey figures independently. Both had the letter of the law on their side but made it difficult for David Kausimae and me who were endeavouring to made Taiyo as welcome as possible.

There was also a political battle to be won in Governing Council. Although foreign involvement in copra and timber had long been the norm, there was strong opposition to it in fishing. As the Rev Kiva, Member for Nggela, Savo and the Russells eloquently put it, 'these seas, they are as our gardens'.[1] The revered Canon Fox, the grand old man of the Melanesian Mission and still a powerful influence, expressed his opposition vigorously. I suspected that his lazy cook had failed to give him his favourite fish for lunch one day on the excuse that Taiyo had caught them all! Others demanded penal taxation, hardly the best way to get a survey done at no cost to the country. Underlying the opposition, however expressed, was considerable anti-Japanese feeling, mainly among expatriates, including government staff, who went out of their way to make life difficult for Taiyo. It was an uphill task persuading those concerned on this and other issues that our job was to achieve a viable economy, not to put obstacles in its way.

By the August meeting of the Governing Council a considerable head of steam had built up. There was some resentment that we had negotiated with Taiyo without Governing Council's authorisation. Probably the most anti-colonial of members, Solomon Mamoloni, even complained that we had negotiated without the knowledge of the British Government! A motion to restrict Japanese fishing to waters outside the three mile limit demonstrated the limited understanding of maritime law. That was indeed the law, the named Taiyo boats being the only exception to it. There was complete freedom for anyone from anywhere in the world to fish waters outside the limit. They did so without any benefit to the Solomons and, especially at night, often fished within the limits about which, without a navy, nothing could be done. The length of the survey was seen to be excessive, but because skipjack are migratory it was essential to check movement and the effect of weather upon the migration over a full year. Accused of rousing emotions akin to those of Marching Rule, of depriving Solomon Islanders of their everyday sustenance, even of encouraging sharks to eat people because Taiyo had caught all the fish, it was not easy to win Governing Council over to understand and to accept that the survey did no more than open the way for future negotiation of a

---

1. Governing Council Debates, Official Record 29th August 1971.

commercial agreement. David and I emphasised that the investment required, even for the survey, was well beyond our means; that, while members constantly called for services for which the government had to find the revenue, our seas were rich in potential, but a potential which we could only exploit with a partner with both capital and access to the market. To protect local fishermen Taiyo had undertaken not to fish within 500 yards of the shore and the fish so far caught were mainly over two years old and, as I enjoyed pointing out, would otherwise have lived to die of old age.

It was a rough ride but we pulled through. A fishing industry was, at heart, everyone's aspiration. We had succeeded in getting the biggest fisheries in the world interested. There was no commitment beyond the eighteen months. It would cost us nothing. Solomon Islanders would be employed and the Japanese would be spending freely. Within days of their arrival Captain Honda had recruited a substantial number of Solomon Islanders and the political pressure eased as soon as the community began to benefit directly. The Solomons was a small country with a population of only 161,000. Even one job made a noticeable difference. Fortunately, the public expression of opposition, which highlighted the matters of most concern to Solomon Islanders, coincided with bumper catches and so it suited both Taiyo as well as the government to re-negotiate the agreement. Taiyo wanted to enlarge the survey. The government, convinced that Taiyo was serious, wanted to establish principles with respect to a future joint venture agreement and to reach that point as soon as possible. A further Memorandum of Understanding, signed on 17 September 1971, reduced the period of the survey from eighteen to fifteen months and increased the number of mother ships to five and catcher boats to fifteen. To compensate for the fish caught and subsequently sold, each catcher boat would pay a premium of $A500 per month. In the interests of conservation, it was also agreed that no more than five catcher boats would ever operate from a single anchorage or fish together.

The major conservation problem with which the survey was faced was in the procurement of bait fish. Bait fish are caught inshore. Finding a supply for skipjack fishing was, therefore, in direct competition with local fishing for food. Taiyo had agreed not to fish within 500 yards of the low water mark and the bait fish problem was ameliorated by Taiyo training Solomon Islanders in catching and conserving bait fish, which Taiyo then bought from them. Taiyo also undertook not to export any bait fish. Looking to the future, Taiyo agreed to establish a shore-based experimental plant for the processing of skipjack. It was agreed that the fishing operation would be managed by a locally registered company, in which the government would have an equity option, and that the industry would be shore-based, with as much processing done locally and as many Solomon Islanders employed as possible, Taiyo providing managerial, financial, technical, administrative and marketing services. It was agreed that the company would make a direct contribution to revenue in addition to the usual statutory tax obligations, and vessels used would bunker and be slipped locally where possible. Finally it was agreed that the government would impose limitations on the annual catch as required and extend its jurisdiction from three to twelve miles within which it would give the company exclusive commercial fishing and export rights.

In that first year 9,587 tons of skipjack were exported and government revenues gained directly by $A69,754 and indirectly from duties paid on goods purchased by Taiyo employees. It all looked extremely promising but I was conscious how ill equipped we were to continue any further without professional support. The government had neither fisheries legislation nor a single fisheries officer. I sought the assistance of UNDP and obtained the services of a British lawyer at the Food and Agricultural Organization of the United Nations (FAO) with experience of fisheries legislation to draft a fisheries ordinance, those of an Icelandic fisherman, Mr Kristjonsson, with extensive experience of Pacific tuna fishing to assist in technical assessment of the survey results and a fisheries economist from Poland. From the UK, through the Overseas Development Administration, we secured the services from the accountancy and taxation advisers Allan, Charlesworth, and of our friends from the mining negotiations, John Laurence and Alistair Macdonald. They would be able to advise on the complexities of how and where a vertically based industry such as Taiyo could pick up its profits. Our biggest problem was the extension of fisheries jurisdiction from a three mile to a twelve mile limit. The UK, anxious to protect its own fishing fleets, had interests contrary to countries, such as the Solomons, arguing for archipelago rights. It was not usual for a minor colony to contest the policy of the metropolitan power but we did and secured agreement for an economic zone beyond the standard territorial waters, for which, of course, the UK was responsible under international law. The trump card was the business plan with exciting figures that actually gave promise to the possibility of an end of grant-in-aid but my relations with London were not helped by the concurrent 'cod war' with Iceland, with whose approach the Solomons could sympathise, and by the fact that our principal fisheries advice came from an Icelander!

Alongside all that had to be done to have the necessary legislation enacted it became apparent that there was a question to be resolved that, as the reality of a major fishing industry got closer and closer, concerned Taiyo ever more seriously. Captain Honda and I had established excellent relations and he had arranged for local shore management to be the responsibility of a delightful young Japanese man, Morio Mito, educated in the States, whose wife was Canadian. When I sensed that Taiyo was getting cold feet and seemed reluctant to proceed I was told that it was the express wish of the President of Taiyo that peace be made with the Japanese war dead on Guadalcanal and in the Coral Sea, of whom his brother was one. The Japanese had been reluctant to raise the issue because they expected a rebuff. There had long been a procedure for American war dead found after the battle and I knew that nothing had ever been done about the Japanese. There was indeed little that could be done about the many battleships sunk in the Coral Sea but I felt that we could and should help with the dead from the land battle. Taiyo introduced me to associations of the bereaved from the battles and to the government ministry concerned with veteran affairs.

This was the first formal contact between the governments, twenty six years after the end of the war. With the assistance of the Japanese Government and at their expense, a planeload of veterans arrived. I offered every assistance, stipulating only that they employ as many Guadalcanal Islanders as possible to assist. Over several weeks the veterans systematically searched for their dead. It was extraordinary to watch them at work, not difficult because many of us lived closer to the battlefield than we had ever imagined. A group came to our own compound. One of them obviously remembered the location well, although thirty years earlier there would have been neither house nor garden, and knew exactly where to look. They dug near an old bunker and very quickly came across bodies, which had once been hurriedly buried there. After about a month the remains of several hundred dead had been collected. The Japanese wanted to arrange a Shintu cremation. Finding a suitable site was not easy. My own liberal instincts inclined towards using the war memorial in Honiara where there was ample space but, understandably, such a suggestion was unmentionable to the strong group of expatriate ANZAC veterans, and the High Commissioner and I agreed that there was no point in creating any additional opposition to the fishing proposals. In any case, the public health authorities were unhappy about using anywhere in the capital, as were the police. I was getting desperate when Olly Torling, a Dane who was trying to establish a small beach resort some fifteen miles up the coast at Tambea, in order to support his copra plantation at a time of falling prices, came to see me and offered to host the cremation. He knew about the problem because some of the Japanese veterans were staying there. Knowingly or not he was taking a shrewd commercial decision. For several years afterwards he benefited from a steady flow of well-behaved Japanese visitors, mainly the widows, girlfriends and children of the fallen.

The cremation ceremony took place in the presence not only of those who had been involved in the project but of other veterans and bereaved relatives who flew in especially. Among them was an elderly and very small admiral who spoke impeccable English. He kept himself apart from some of the senior army veterans and confided to me that he had as little time for them now as he had had for their behaviour during the war. When I somewhat impertinently congratulated him on his command of the language, he curtly replied, 'but of course my English is good. I was trained at Dartmouth.' That had been before the First World War. The ceremony was impressive if difficult to follow and, rather curiously, after it was over those of us who had honoured the invitation to attend were all presented with alarm clocks! My children, who had ghoulishly relished the whole business, were made a great fuss of and I was pleased that it had added a sober dimension to living on a former battlefield and the constant finding of wartime debris. (On his sixth birthday my eldest son received among presents from his friends a Japanese helmet, an American helmet, a bayonet and two defused hand grenades.) The older Taiyo representatives assured me that they now felt able to operate in the Solomons and soon after, it was possible to arrange for a simple permanent Japanese war memorial on a ridge high above Honiara.[2]

The survey period ended on 31 August 1972 and Taiyo did not delay in submitting a proposal. It was time to negotiate a Joint Venture Agreement. Conscious of the suspicions which still abounded and of the importance to the country of obtaining the best possible Joint Venture Agreement, I decided to hold the final negotiations in public in the High Court, which doubled as the Governing Council Chamber and had ample but segregated public seating. I wanted to avoid any accusations of secret deals and I wanted to guarantee ratification by the legislature. The three days of negotiations were not exactly prime time television entertainment and those who did turn up seldom stayed for long, but the pressure was taken off and the fact that David Kausimae and I were prepared to do everything in public earned respect and inspired confidence. My admiration for Taiyo grew even more when they bravely accepted the challenge of negotiation not only on our ground but also in public. It confirmed my conviction of the seriousness of their intent.

The Agreement was signed on 4 November 1972 and ratified by Governing Council on 9 November. The objective was to secure the maximum value added to the economy in the shortest time, utilising to the full all available local resources, and ensuring a sound revenue stream while leaving the management of the operation firmly in the hands of the undoubted experts. Solomon Taiyo was formed, Taiyo having 51% of the equity and the Government an option up to 49%, the first 25% of which was a 'free-ride'. Solomon Taiyo was permitted to catch up to 30,000 metric tons of skipjack tuna a year with provision for the imposition of smaller quotas should the situation require. The types of fishing vessels and the techniques of fishing to be used were all subject to the new Fisheries Ordinance, which incorporated the latest FAO wisdom with respect to conservation. The Agreement was restricted to pole and line fishing. Progressive quotas were set for the localisation of the company, starting at 30% for the sea operation and 86% for

---

2. I wrote more fully about this in *The Round Table* No 393, December 2007.

the shore-based operations, moving to 60% and 90% respectively over five years. Local fishing rights were protected. Bait fish supply was dealt with and the important prohibition on its export maintained. A fisheries training course for Solomon Islanders was established at the Marine Training School. Some concessions were made with respect to import duties, specifically on fuel, and an export duty was imposed on fresh and frozen skipjack starting at 7% f.o.b. and rising in the third year to 9%. To encourage maximum added value there was no export duty on canned tuna. The agreement was to last for ten years.

The first of two canneries was opened in 1973 at Tulagi, the former capital of the Solomons, bringing much needed activity back to what had become a depressed backwater. The first exports of canned tuna were made in 1974. They were of excellent quality. Taiyo was able to bring catcher boats direct to the wharf alongside the cannery and so the tuna canned had, unusually, never spent any time frozen on a refrigeration ship. Taiyo maintained that it was the best canned tuna in the world. They were probably right and, until the troubles this century in the Solomons put an end to the cannery, I always looked with pride and pleasurable anticipation for the Solomon Taiyo label in the supermarket. It certainly tasted better to me than any other canned tuna.

Few things in my career gave me as much satisfaction as the Solomons Taiyo Joint Venture Agreement. Although such agreements are now often disparaged almost as a matter of principle, at the time it was regarded as a model of fairness and practicability. The entire deal had been achieved without a dollar of government investment. There had been a benefit to the economy from the first day of the survey. A shore-based local company had been established with the emphasis on maximum value added. The Solomons had achieved up to date and technically effective fisheries legislation. Conservation of fish stock was a paramount concern of both legislation and the joint venture. Domestic fishing was protected and with the largest fisheries company in the world as partner there was reason to suppose that Taiyo would to some extent take the place of a navy, to which the country could never aspire, in discouraging illegal fishing. The Solomons also now had the experience of having negotiated and established a major joint venture that involved both traditional fishing and seamanship skills and the entirely new ones of food processing. It was a valuable experience that could serve the new nation well in future economic endeavors.

Many, many years later when all things imperial were assumed to have been exploitative and bad I spoke about Solomon Taiyo at a conference seeking answers to the question '*How Green was the Empire?*'[3] One could argue that the motive for the industry was to achieve revenue streams that would reduce dependency on the mother country and grant-in-aid but this was crucial if political independence was to be in any way meaningful, and that was what concerned me. No doubt, forty years on, there is now knowledge available about fishing generally and tuna in particular that would have enabled us to improve on the conservation measures in the Joint Venture Agreement, but at the time it was as green as we could get. Certainly, it is also since then that forms of tuna fishing far less green than pole and line have been introduced. There are those who argue that it was wrong in an essentially subsistence economy both to introduce commercial fishing on a large scale and to invite a major foreign company to be partner. If that advice had been followed Solomon Islands waters would have been fished by others without any constraint and without any benefit to the Solomon Islanders. Would that really have been better?

My sorties into Japan to seek partners in developing the economy caused the occasional raised eyebrow in Whitehall. While I always sought, and obtained such help as I thought the UK could best provide, such as the first class services of Allan, Charlesworth, there were those inclined to ask, 'What's in it for us?' and at one stage I was warned of mild ministerial irritation that the Solomons and their Financial Secretary in particular seemed disinterested in helping the UK economy in any way. I knew and had collaborated with Bridget Bloom at the *Financial Times* (FT) and through her good offices was able to arrange for a Solomon Islands supplement. Michael Southern, FT's man in Sydney, did an excellent job in editing it with the limited material available. My role was to point him in the right directions and, in order to cover costs, encourage local businesses to advertise. There was an immediate and excellent response from Taiyo and local businesses including even the small Chinese stores. There were two exceptions: the two major British commercial interests, the Commonwealth Development Corporation

---

3. *How Green was our Empire?* Ed. Terry Barringer, Occasional Paper No 2 of the OSPA Research Project at the Institute of Commonwealth Studies, London.

(CDC), setting up the palm oil industry, and Levers, which had both copra and timber companies, declined the invitation to advertise. I was disappointed. Perhaps they already knew what I was soon to discover. The supplement was published on 9 August 1972, admittedly not a good time of year to attract attention in the UK, but I received a mere six letters in response to a large advert proclaiming investment opportunities and seeking commercial enquiries. Of these only one was a genuine trade enquiry! Thereafter, I could at least offer hard evidence to anyone from the FCO complaining that I seemed more interested in helping the Japanese economy than the British. Of course, my job was to help the Solomons' economy. It was obvious to me that, given the huge distances involved and the relatively minute size of the Solomons' economy that future trading partnerships had to lie with the developed countries on the Pacific rim. It was pointless to ask me, 'What's in it for us?' That was never, whatever may be said to the contrary, the primary motivation of those who worked in the imperial services in the field post World War II. The interests of the people we served were paramount. More often than not, that approach was usually the one that would best serve the long-term interests of Britain.

CHAPTER FIVE
AMONG OTHER THINGS . . .

Exciting and absorbing as the mining and fisheries negotiations might have been, they were only a part of the job. Routine tasks took up much of the time. Annually there was the budget to prepare and once the Development Plan was approved, an annual review of its progress. Grant applications for plan projects had to be drafted and cases carefully argued. At each of the three Governing Council sessions a year there were questions to be answered and decisions to be taken on how to respond to the many motions put forward by private members. There were also staffing and other matters related to the departments under my direct control and occasionally I would be required to attend regional meetings connected with development or transport. I was fortunate to be supported by an excellent staff. Two colleagues who served me exceptionally well and became good friends were John Yaxley and Tony Davies, the latter on secondment from the ODA.

When Peter Hill, our economist and a helpful colleague, left I was lucky enough to be in England when a successor was being recruited and I was invited to the interviews. I was looking for somebody who was not only a good economist, as were all the candidates, but who would be able to give advice in terms laymen could understand, pointing in the direction of somebody whose general education and cultural interests were broad. I had then been in Honiara for a couple of years so I was also concerned to find someone with the personal resources to cope with the restrictions of the intellectual and social environment in which he or she would be working.

The candidate who most impressed me in every way happened to play the violin and said he would take it with him. The rest of the interviewing panel was uncomfortable when I declared that I much preferred the candidate who played the violin, but I got my way! Patrick Spread was a great success, made his reputation and ever since has been involved in development plans and other economic matters all over the world. In his spare time he has earned a doctorate and has written several books, challenging classical economic theory and arguing very convincingly that what makes the world tick is support bargaining.[1]

My deputy when I arrived was John Hunter who had served for a number of years in the Solomons and knew the Finance branch inside out. He had every reason to expect that the job of Financial Secretary would be his but served me loyally and well until his abilities were recognized by promotion to be Chief Secretary in the Gilbert and Ellice Islands. John was the Solomon Islands Director of Pacific Airways and had taken a great interest in the development of tourism with the aim of riding on the back of what was beginning to be a substantial industry in Fiji. A project dear to his heart, which we never managed to get off the ground, was to attract Travelodge to Honiara, although eventually his efforts led to the up-grading and better management of the Mendana Hotel.

The prospect of a better air service with the rest of the world, which tourism might bring, was superficially attractive but I was less convinced than most about the potential added value of tourism to the local economy. A survey to discover the profile of a typical airline tourist visiting the Pacific identified an older West Coast American woman, recently widowed and spending some of her late husband's life insurance on the holiday of a lifetime! Such tourists were unlikely to be adventurous. They expected the creature comforts of the USA, including air-conditioning, and the type of food to which they were accustomed. So it suited the hotels to serve canned Hawaiian pineapple rather than fresh and that pattern was repeated from top to bottom. Tourists might purchase a few local handicrafts and watch some local dancing but for the most part everything they needed had to be imported. The Solomons also lacked easily accessible good beaches and the water sports that go with them in popular tropical resorts.

A few times a year a cruise ship would call and once even the huge *Canberra* came alongside the wharf. Cruise passengers were mainly Australians and New Zealanders. Honiara did not have the infrastructure to support several hundred tourists on a day visit. There were no public toilets and after a visit there would be a letter from the shipping company asking that they be provided before the next time they called! There were

---

1. Patrick Spread, *Support-Bargaining*, Brighton, Guild Publishing 2008.

no buses and no taxis. Expatriates used to offer their services to take passengers on a drive round in return for a donation for the Red Cross. Not every tourist got the message and some could be rude and tiresome as well as mean. There was, indeed, little for them to do except look at the handicrafts for sale on the wharf or stroll to the Yacht Club or Mendana Hotel for a beer. The hotel usually arranged exhibitions of island dancing. The dancers were immigrant Gilbertese who had been resettled in the Solomons when drought had severely affected the Phoenix Islands, where they once had lived. Like all their countrymen and women they took their dancing seriously and were always ready to oblige. The Gilbertese are Micronesians and their culture is strikingly different to that of Melanesians. They are a people with a strong sense of community. Solomon Islanders did dance but their island groups were disparate and did not seem to care much about sustaining their particular culture away from their home islands. I doubt whether many tourists realised that they were watching Micronesian dancing on a Melanesian island. They were after all visiting Pacific islands and these were Pacific Islanders.

A cruise ship, some of whose passengers did get to see a bit more of the country, was that taking the New Zealand contingent to the world scout jamboree in Japan. To finance the trip parents, siblings and friends, in some cases grandparents too, had been invited to come along. Having all their family on board with them was not what most of the scouts regarded as much of an adventure. We arranged for the ship to overnight in Honiara and all the scouts were taken off to camp with Solomon Island scouts leaving their parents to make the most of the town. Many of us took them around and offered them hospitality. If nothing else our gesture made for a happier voyage on to Japan. I had enjoyed being a scout as a boy and took an interest in scouting locally. The Solomons had a full time organiser and trainer appointed by the UK Scout Association and he suggested that I lend a hand with the Venture Scouts, all of whom were in secondary schools. I enjoyed the opportunity to get to know some younger Solomon Islanders better than my formal duties ever gave me opportunity to do. I was made aware of the potential talent available once another generation or two had made their way through the education system.

The Air Pacific board met in Suva, the capital of Fiji, and provided an interesting insight into airline politics. The nationalized airlines of those days were very much in the hands of professional aviators and British Overseas Airways (BOAC) had a major share holding in Air Pacific and chaired the board. BOAC's interest was in having a feeder airline to attract passengers to its long haul international flights, which in the 1970s still had to land in Fiji to refuel. BOAC was represented by pilots of great experience but with little understanding of or interest in island politics and economies. Their concerns were technical and commercial. They took a keen professional interest in the type of aircraft to be purchased and were subject to massive lobbying by the British and other governments to persuade them that the products of their aviation industry could best serve Air Pacific's interests. The company, originally known as Fiji Airways, had moved from eight seat De Havilland Doves to sixteen seat DH Herons and about the time I became a Director it was time to move on again and before long the purchase of a jet became an issue. Those of us on the board representing island interests were primarily concerned with a regular and adequate service. The problem with the advancing technology was that planes not only became faster and could fly farther, which everyone welcomed, but needed longer runways, more sophisticated ground navigational aids and offered capacity way beyond the means of most island communities to take up. A weekly flight offering forty seats would have been ideal but when Air Pacific moved to an eighty plus seat BAC 1-11 it was not long before the airline had to look around for longer distance hauls between places with substantial populations to provide an effective payload. Inter island services were reduced in favour of flights to New Zealand and Australia, a move that, for the company, fortunately coincided with the arrival of the jumbo jet able to cross the Pacific without refuelling in Fiji.

The phosphate rich island of Nauru, which had become an independent member of the Commonwealth in 1968, enjoyed the highest per capita income in the world in the 1970s. Every member of its small population was in receipt of mining royalties. Living on a remote, isolated and very small island, only a few square miles in all, Nauruans had the income to indulge their interest in travel. Before the arrival of the jets, extending the regular flight from Fiji through Funafuti, in the Ellice Islands, and Tarawa, in the Gilbert Islands, to Nauru added another hour plus to an already long journey that was touching the limits both for a single pilot and the available hours of daylight, significant where navigational aids were limited and runways were without lighting. In Nauru a stretch of the only road, which had to be closed when an aircraft was due, served as the runway. There was seldom any traffic to be picked up in Funafuti or Tarawa en route to compensate for the passengers disembarking in those places because, although both the Gilberts and the Ellice provided the bulk of the phosphate miners on Nauru, they travelled there by ship. Recruitment was spread around all the islands and contracts provided for families to accompany the men. So Air Pacific never provided Nauru with the adequacy of service it wanted and to which it felt it was entitled. The President, Hammer DeRoburt, was a non-executive board member. I understood his frustration and considered the ready and patronising dismissal of his pleas by the executive board members politically inept. Here was the one board member really worth courting. Nauru could easily have financed the airline's move into the jet age.

Unable to obtain co-operation, despite the support of myself and one or two other island directors, the President walked out. I recall being accused by the BOAC chairman of being the kind of director who had recently ensured the failure of Rolls Royce! The President went off and bought his own jet, a Fokker 48, cheaper and more economical to run than Air Pacific's BAC 1-11. Air Nauru began to offer an extremely effective and frequent inter island service, as well as flights to Melbourne needed for maintenance of its lone aircraft. Economically there was not, of course, room for two airlines but for a few years the islands were better served than they had ever been or would ever be again. Air Nauru was usually a delight to fly with but did have its problems, devastating for passengers, when the President, who understandably tended to think of it as his personal airline, was on board and ordered deviations to the scheduled flight!

President Hammer DeRoburt's vision of the central Pacific being brought together encouraged him to invest in sea as well as air communications. The merchant vessel *Cenpac Rounder* unfortunately failed to break into the established shipping and trade patterns but for a while was extremely useful. When, for example, John Hunter and his family were transferred from Honiara to Tarawa they were able to move lock, stock and barrel on a four or five day direct voyage.

Without the *Cenpac Rounder* they could have been months without their loads, which would almost certainly have had to be shipped to Australia and then out again.

As well as tourists the air services brought a good many official visitors of one sort or another and some came by sea. In March 1971 HRH the Duke of Edinburgh came on a visit in HMS *Britannia*. Anchored offshore and splendidly lit at night, her elegant lines sent a tingle of pride down one's spine. While in the army I had served in a joint services force based at Aqaba in Jordan, the naval part of which was a frigate whose first lieutenant Prince Phillip then was, and I had met him a number of times in mess and wardroom when everyone was in uniform. On the Honiara visit I noticed his sharp eye for ties when he quickly picked out John Green of Customs as a former submariner. Meeting HRH once or twice since I have always contrived to wear a tie that would attract his eye and it always has. The strain of meeting hundreds of people day in, day out, many of whom are over-awed by the grandeur of the occasion, must be huge. *Britannia* provided a much needed haven on longer royal tours which would have been unbearable if every night had to be spent as guest of governor or ambassador.

There were, of course, a good many visitors from the FCO. The more senior were usually guests at Government House. We often put up the less senior. Dependencies were now subject to FCO inspection, something unheard of in Colonial Office days and the cause of much speculation when first encountered. I was delighted to be able to reciprocate hospitality to one of the team, an old colleague from Nigeria, Douglas Brown, with whom I had often stayed in Lagos when he was Private Secretary to Sir James Robertson, the Governor General. Douglas had joined the FCO after leaving the Overseas Service and was able to fill me in about inspections. In addition to assessing security, communications and procedures (for which there was a substantial guide to be kept up to date), they looked at all manner of local conditions such as cost of living, accommodation and recreational facilities. Dependencies were as novel to Foreign Service Inspectors as inspections were to dependencies and it was immensely valuable to have Douglas around who had experience of both services. A lot of what the inspectors did was to sort out pretty esoteric issues concerned with the sanctity of staff gradings. At that time there was some discussion about absorbing the tail of the Overseas Administrative Service into the Foreign Service. It came to nothing and never had much chance in the first place, but it was amusing to listen to Douglas explaining how the quality of a particular government house would never do for the top diplomatic service grades, all of which would have the knock-on effect of demoting everyone in the dependency! In later life Douglas and I were to meet again when we both made second careers in university administration and found ourselves college secretaries within the University of London, he at St Bartholomew's Medical School and I at the suitably named Imperial College.

The two services had, of course, entirely different purposes although there were those who made the transition between the two with great success. In retirement, when mistakenly introduced as a former diplomat, I have explained the difference between the two services by explaining that if in some remote part of the world the drains were offensively smelly, the diplomat would put his hand to drafting a witty dispatch on the adversity with an apt classical quotation indicating the superiority of Roman sanitation, reminding the office of his erudition, deserving of appointment somewhere more significant! The colonial servant, on the other hand, would roll up his sleeves, do something about it and waste no time making a record.

We also had a ministerial visit from the FCO Minister with responsibility for the Pacific Dependent Territories, Mr Anthony Kershaw MP. He was a gentlemanly, shires Tory of the old school, well briefed, full of common sense, charming and easy to get along with. His private secretary was a young married woman and pregnant. His concern for her welfare was such that suggested that he might have been her PS! His visit was just after Christmas and it was arranged that I would escort him to Yandina, on Ngela, where Levers had their largest plantations. The two of us flew over early one morning with Solair, the local airline flying light aircraft between islands. First called Megapode Airlines after the megapodes which nested on the shores of Savo, our local volcano, the name was abandoned when somebody read a biological description of the megapode as having difficulty in getting airborne and being ungainly in flight! We were met by Levers manager, Joe Walton, who loved not only his job, at which he excelled, but every palm in his plantations. To the layman one coconut palm looks very much another but Joe would wax lyrical on variations we could not discern and when the minister was unwise enough to enquire about the effect of hurricanes I began to think that we would still be there at nightfall. Even the unexpected information that ailing palms were treated with tetracycline, the cure-all of the seventies, did not revive us. The temperature was high; it was extremely humid and uncomfortable. Eventually Joe noticed our straying attention and suggested that we stop and have a drink. For a moment we relaxed, savouring the very thought of a cold beer. Not for long: we were treated to hot coffee and Christmas cake!

There were a number of specialist advisors to the Secretary of State and I have always remembered going to the High Commissioner's office to discuss health projects with him and the visiting health advisor, a distinguished medical consultant. The room was heavy with smoke, the pair of them chain smoking throughout the hour or two I was there, hardly the atmosphere in which to discuss health, especially as Richard Doll's research into the relationship between smoking and cancer was beginning to take effect. So much so, in fact, that we had decided on health grounds not to try and obtain local added value by import substitution of tobacco products. To be fair, however, I had given up the idea of importing the raw materials and manufacturing cigarettes as soon as my enquiries revealed that the smallest machine available would spew out the annual consumption in less than a week. I did not pursue the helpful suggestion from an American friend that I try museums in Virginia to see if they wanted to dispose of an early nineteenth century machine!

The two visitors whose memory I most relish came in private capacities. Raymond Firth, the revered anthropologist, whose work with the Tikopians, who lived on an extremely remote Polynesian island hundreds of miles away from Honiara, was world famous, dined with us one evening while staying at Government House (GH). Tall, lean and sprightly as well as a splendid conversationalist it was difficult, at my age then, to believe that he was over 70. He told us that he was on his way to New Zealand to celebrate his father's hundredth birthday! Another GH guest whom we were privileged to host was Lady Alexandra Metcalf, one of Lord Curzon's daughters, whose late husband 'Fruity' had been Private Secretary to the Duke of Windsor. I did not then know what I do now about her own colourful and exciting life but I was overwhelmed by thoughts of her father, the most regal of all India's Viceroys, who had subsequently been waiting in vain for the call from the Palace to form a government when I was barely one year old. From that moment it was clear that the aristocracy would never again be in a position to exercise the enormous influence in public affairs that had been their expectation certainly until the Great War. And here was his daughter, dripping with pearls and every inch the natural aristocrat at our table. President of Save the Children, she had flown in from Papua New Guinea where 'posh nobs' were unlikely to make their mark on the frontier style Australian administration. The airport was also very much a do it yourself affair. I asked how she had managed her baggage. "There was no problem," she replied. "I saw a man in a uniform and told him to carry my bags. He did." It was the captain of her aircraft! I hope that he was as enthralled as I to be of assistance to this grand old lady.

CHAPTER SIX
HIGH OFFICE :
RITUALS AND SURPRISES

Towards the end of 1972 the High Commissioner invited me to join him on a tour to the Gilbert Islands. It would be his last because the Colony was soon to be detached from the Western Pacific High Commission and the Resident Commissioner there was about to be appointed Governor. It was an enjoyable few days in which I had no duties to perform and a pleasure to meet up with those, such as the Hunters, whom I had known in the Solomons. On my return to Honiara I told Sylvester that I thought we had been very lucky in our posting. The Gilbert and Ellice Islands would have been a difficult place with three small children. Not long after that and while the High Commissioner was on tour elsewhere, a secret telegram arrived from the Foreign Office that he was required to decipher personally. The cipher officer cabled back to say that he would not be available for several days and was told in reply that I should decipher it. I had never much enjoyed the tedious business of deciphering the double Playfair codes that were standard throughout my service. I went over to Government House. After instruction to ensure that I remembered how to tackle it, I sat down to begin the laborious task, wondering what could be so urgent and why I was involved, rather than the Chief Secretary, who was the officer administering the government in the absence of the High Commissioner. Fortunately it was not a long telegram; its purport that the Secretary of State was of a mind to recommend my appointment as Governor of the Gilbert and Ellice Islands in succession to Sir John Field who would be retiring in 1973. Before the recommendation went to the Palace, my agreement was required.

I was enjoying my job, which was broad in its scope, fulfilling and always interesting. I was beginning to see the fruits of my endeavours and starting to plan the next steps. I felt that I had gained the acceptance of Solomon Islanders and many, if not all, of my expatriate colleagues. There was confidence in me. I was seen as somebody who could make things happen. My friend and colleague in Nigeria, Trevor Clark, who had been persuaded by me to forsake the fleshpots of Hong Kong, where he was never entirely happy, to take up the post of Deputy Chief Secretary, had but recently arrived and I knew that together we could achieve much.[1] The family was happily settled in Honiara. My brief visit to Tarawa had shown me the limitations of atoll life. While obviously pleased that I had been considered for promotion the timing was wrong. I had been in Honiara for just over two years. I dearly wanted to say that I was not interested but common sense warned me that it is nearly always a mistake to turn down an opportunity. I had a young family and another twenty years of working life ahead of me. The one person I could have shared my doubts with was Sir Michael Gass and he was not available. I sent off the telegram committing my future. When Sir Michael returned from tour he made it plain that my answer had been the correct one. He had, I suspect, in his generous and unselfish way promoted my cause but, like me, was not altogether happy about the timing. So I confided in Sylvester and we prepared ourselves for the difficult task of saying nothing to anyone over the next few weeks, which included Christmas and the New Year, and doing nothing which might arouse suspicions while we quietly organised a short leave and transfer in the summer of 1973.

When the news finally broke, such was the unfair reputation of the Gilbert and Ellice Islands that those primarily concerned with the comforts of civilisation commiserated with us rather than offered congratulations. The more politically orientated expressed regret that I was being forced out of a job where I could be active and effective into one where my role would be more that of representative and referee. Some were even convinced that I was being removed before I did 'more damage'! The *Kakamora Reporter* had this to say:

> *We are rather dismayed at Mr Smith leaving us at this time. We are probably being selfish because we realise he is going to become a big man as Governor of the Gilbert and Ellice. We can't look that far, and it does not make sense from what little we know of Mr Smith. All we know is that*

1. Trevor Clark, *Good Second Class*, Spennymoor, The Memoir Club 2004 contains an amusing comment on the differences between diplomatic and colonial services.

as Financial Secretary of the Solomons he is a 'namba wan'
man. Nevertheless we can only say that we are sorry to see
him go and hope that he will happy in his new post'.[2]

My disappointment at being moved on so soon was, however, somewhat
alleviated by what else was written in the *Kakamora Reporter* editorial. It
suggested that I had managed to achieve one of my objectives:

> *John Smith has been a breath of fresh air in administration*
> *to the present generation of Solomon Islanders. In the short*
> *two and a half years he has been here he has shown Solomon*
> *Islanders that government need not be something that*
> *mysteriously must be hidden from the people being governed.*
> *That government and its work can be explained simply to the*
> *people so that they know where they are heading and what*
> *the government is actually trying to do for the country. He*
> *has done a lot to dispel the typical Solomon Islander's view*
> *of the 'gavman' who comes ashore with the big stick – to be*
> *carried with awe and trembling by the 'natives' above the*
> *breaking surf so that his white stockinged delicate feet hurt*
> *not against the stones and wet.*

Of course I had been very fortunate to arrive in the job at the time
that the new constitution came into force and I had simply made sure
that that context became a breath of fresh air. I had never had the
chance of being carried ashore in the Solomons but was about to enjoy
such rituals in full measure in the Gilbert and Ellice as *Te Unimane*, the
old man, and that required a uniform.

I had not worn uniform as Financial Secretary. For many years I had
been a customer of the Army and Navy Stores in Victoria Street, which
had equipped me with all I needed when I first set sail for West Africa
more than twenty years before. Later, after I had been confirmed in my
appointment, they had made my colonial service uniform. Had I still
had it, it could have been readily adapted to suit the requirements of a
governor. But Northern Nigeria had modified the uniform, lengthening

2. *Kakamora Reporter* 36, March 1973.

the patrol jacket to below the knees in order to meet Islamic standards of propriety and replacing the solar topee with a Sukarno style lamb's wool cap. My topee had long since been given to a peripatetic Nigerian barber who, specialist in cutting expatriate hair, had no compunctions about so colonial a symbol, and the jacket to my steward. Only the boots and the sword remained. I wrote saying that I would be requiring a governor's uniform and trusted that the Stores would be able to provide it. A charming reply informed me that the Stores had not realized such dinosaurs as colonial governors still existed and regretted that they no longer had a tailoring department up to the job. They recommended a military tailor in Tooley Street. Dickensian in atmosphere the premises were situated under the arches of London Bridge station, now host to the London Dungeon. A small rotund gnome like gentleman in a waistcoat entered my details into an immense ledger in fine copper plate handwriting, dipping nib into inkwell as my generation had all done at school. When I pointed out the urgency of my requirement – one of the few occasions on which a governor wears uniform is on arrival for his swearing in, there was much pursing of lips and wagging of fingers. 'Can't be done, Sir. There's a royal wedding next year and we are flat out fulfilling all the orders for that.'

Eventually I persuaded him to take me seriously and was given a date for a fitting. The day arrived and the uniform was fitted. I enquired about the hat. I had always thought that 'swan feathers, twelve inches long, pointing outwards' on top of a topee looked particularly ridiculous and had opted for the more elegant blue fore and aft alternative, devised to wear with the temperate climate gubernatorial uniform. "Can't be done, Sir. Velour is hard to get these days and swan feathers are near by impossible." My protest that I had seen swans happily swimming in the lake at St James's Park that morning helped not at all. We searched through the uniform bible issued with the authority of the Lord Chamberlain and I invented my own headgear – an army staff officer's cap with suitable braid and badge. It arrived just in time and I was able to wear uniform at my swearing in. It provided opportunity for some light relief in my induction speech. I said that some would have noticed that I had arrived without the customary gubernatorial plumage, an early indication of changes on the way now that the country was approaching independence.

Some weeks later this part of my speech caught the eye of one of the staff on the Pacific desk in the Foreign Office. Concerned lest imperial dignity be offended, he kindly rang around the specialist tailors. He was told by Moss Bros that they had sold the last governor's hat to Ted Leather who had not long before been appointed Governor of Bermuda but when pressed said that they thought they might be able to convert an admiral's hat. Some weeks later it arrived, together with an invoice, for governors paid for their own uniforms, and I was able to wear it at my first Queen's Birthday parade. In 1997, when Hong Kong was returned to China, a Dutch TV channel made a programme about the end of empire and came to my home in Dulverton to interview me. I showed them the hat and demonstrated how it was put together. This was to inspire the title of the programme *Swan Song* which began with me putting together and explaining the gubernatorial plumes. My uniform now resides in the British Empire and Commonwealth Museum.

Our children were still very young and we had said very little about it all to them other than that we were going to live on another island after our leave, but not much escapes the attention of a six year old. I was walking into town with him one day when a truck pulled up and the driver, leaning out of his cab to seek directions, called out, "S'cuse me, Guv'nor . . . " After he had gone on his way Gerard looked up at me enquiringly and asked, "Dad, how did he know?"

Governors, like ambassadors, are appointed by the monarch and are invited to 'kiss hands'. The FCO arranged my audience with the Palace. We lived in Windsor and it was immediately prior to Ascot week when the Queen is in residence at the Castle. It would have been very easy to stroll from our house twenty minutes up the Long Walk, but the protocol surrounding the monarch is inevitably strict and rightly so. It is sound practice to combine the honour of a private audience with a reminder of the humble place to which one belongs and to London we had to go. The half hour audience, which ended with Her Majesty dismissing us with, "How good of you to have called before leaving", required me to hire a morning suit, which I did not possess, a lengthy and expensive excursion by Sylvester to the better dress shops in Windsor to seek her outfit, arrangements for somebody to look after our children for the day and then a journey to London where the FCO sent a car to collect us from my club. Our appointment was for 12.30. Perhaps, I thought, we would conclude with a pre-lunch gin and tonic. As the car stopped at the gates, summer visitors still remaining from the changing of the guard, lent forward hoping for a glimpse of, if not royals, at least celebrities. The policeman on duty asked my name. Those within earshot fell back disappointed at the reply 'John Smith'.

The top hat and gloves that I had been instructed to wear were removed by a flunkey. An equerry welcomed us and drilled us in the form as he escorted us to Her Majesty's study. It felt rather like entering a film set, so familiar was the room from many formal photographs. The Queen was charming, knowledgeable and easy to talk to but one was left in no doubt that it was an audience for one of her governors and not a social call. Throughout, she neither addressed a remark directly to Sylvester nor made any comment about our family circumstances. I had met Her Majesty in Nigeria in 1956 when I was one of the Marshals for the durbar in Kaduna, probably the last great imperial occasion with its thousands of gaily caparisoned horsemen, and a state visit by General Gowan, the Nigerian head of State, whom I had known since he was a schoolboy, was imminent, so conversation was easy. We talked for some fifteen minutes about Nigeria and some of the personalities she would soon be meeting. She then moved on to the problems the King of Spain was having and discussed the previous night's edition of the BBC current affairs programme *Panorama* which had focused on the crisis and which she had watched 'fortified by a couple of strong gins and tonic'. The half hour was up and that was as close to the real thing as we got. I don't recall the Gilbert and Ellice Islands getting a mention. And the royal hand was shaken not kissed. Sadly, unlike ambassadors, colonial governors were not invited to a second audience at the end of their term of office. When we left there was one solitary top hat on a table by the door. As we approached a Palace flunkey picked it up, searched for my initials, which he knew quite well wouldn't be there, and handed it to me with disdain.

A week or two later we were due to fly from Heathrow. The FCO telephoned to say that a car would be arranged to take us to the airport. I was delighted, gave details of our flight and suggested the time that the car might pick us up. 'Our car', I was told rather sternly, 'can only collect you from a London rail terminus.' It was a twenty minute drive to Heathrow from our house in Windsor and I saw no point in the hassle and expense of a taxi to the station, a train journey to London and then a thirty to forty minute drive back in the same direction with three young children. I declined the offer and said that we would make our own way to the airport. The snub was not appreciated but I was told that we should go to the Alcock and Brown suite where we would be met. On the day, I passed that information on to the cabbie. "Never heard of it, mate," was his response and neither, it seemed, when on arrival we asked several uniformed officials, had anyone else. After ten minutes of fruitless driving around I told the driver to make for terminal three and we checked in. We had settled down in the first class lounge, the children making free of the nuts and other nibbles generously provided, when an indignant and pompous official arrived and told me that I had no right to be there. We were to follow him immediately, which reluctantly we did. The Alcock and Brown suite, looking rather like a prefab village hall, was tucked away alongside terminal three. It was empty except for a junior official from the FCO department dealing with the Pacific. He had been there some time with nothing better to do than enjoy the bar but to our children's dismay there were neither nuts nor crisps.

They were simmering with rebellion when the airport official re-appeared. "Your flight is ready to depart. Instruct your driver to follow me and I will lead the way to the aircraft." "But we have no driver." "Then how did you get here?" "By taxi." "But all our VIPs have their own drivers. How are you going to get to the plane?" "That is your problem. We were content to be embarked with the other passengers. You brought us here." After more expostulation we bade our farewell to the FCO man, who sank back on his couch with relief, and we squeezed into the extremely small car of the airport official. He had recovered his equanimity by the time we drew up alongside a lone aircraft well away from the terminal. "You are the last to embark. The plane will take off as soon as you are on board." We shook hands to show that there was no ill feeling and, as he drove off, climbed up the gangway into an absolutely empty aircraft!

We found our seats, sat down and debated how long before somebody realised we were missing. It was a sobering thought that, if necessary, by setting off on foot with three small children, we would probably bring the entire operation of the world's busiest airport to a standstill. We were saved from putting that to the test by the arrival of the aircrew, rather startled to find us on board. They were soon followed by the cabin crew and then by the other passengers. Life returned to normal as our flight, direct to Los Angeles, took off. Some hours later we were passed the flight information bulletin. I avoided Sylvester's eyes as we read that we would shortly be arriving at Winnipeg!

The plane was the right one; a strong headwind was enforcing an additional refuelling stop. Our children were of an age when they liked to help and we saw little of them on the flight as they took over the cabin crew and overwhelmed the other passengers with BA goodies. At LA we thanked the crew profusely and guessed they heaved a great sigh of relief as we left. Alas for them! We were staying in the same hotel for the same length of time and, bless them, they spent a lot of time in the pool with the young Smiths, all the more noble because they knew they now had us on the next leg to Fiji. They even sent the children a card from Australia promising to see us on Concorde in a couple of years. How good flight crews could be in those far off days when they worked regularly together as a team and knew one another well.

After a night in Nandi we boarded a Pacific Islands Airways flight to Tarawa. A couple of hours after our arrival I had to dress up in my uniform and be sworn in. We were lucky to have people we knew around. John Hunter had been acting in the interregnum and his wife, Elizabeth, whom the children remembered from Honiara, was able to sweep them off. Renn Davies, Attorney General in Honiara, had made a special journey to do the honours. The ceremony lasted about half an hour and then there was a reception in Government House where we had our first meeting with the notables of the Gilbert and Ellice Islands Colony.

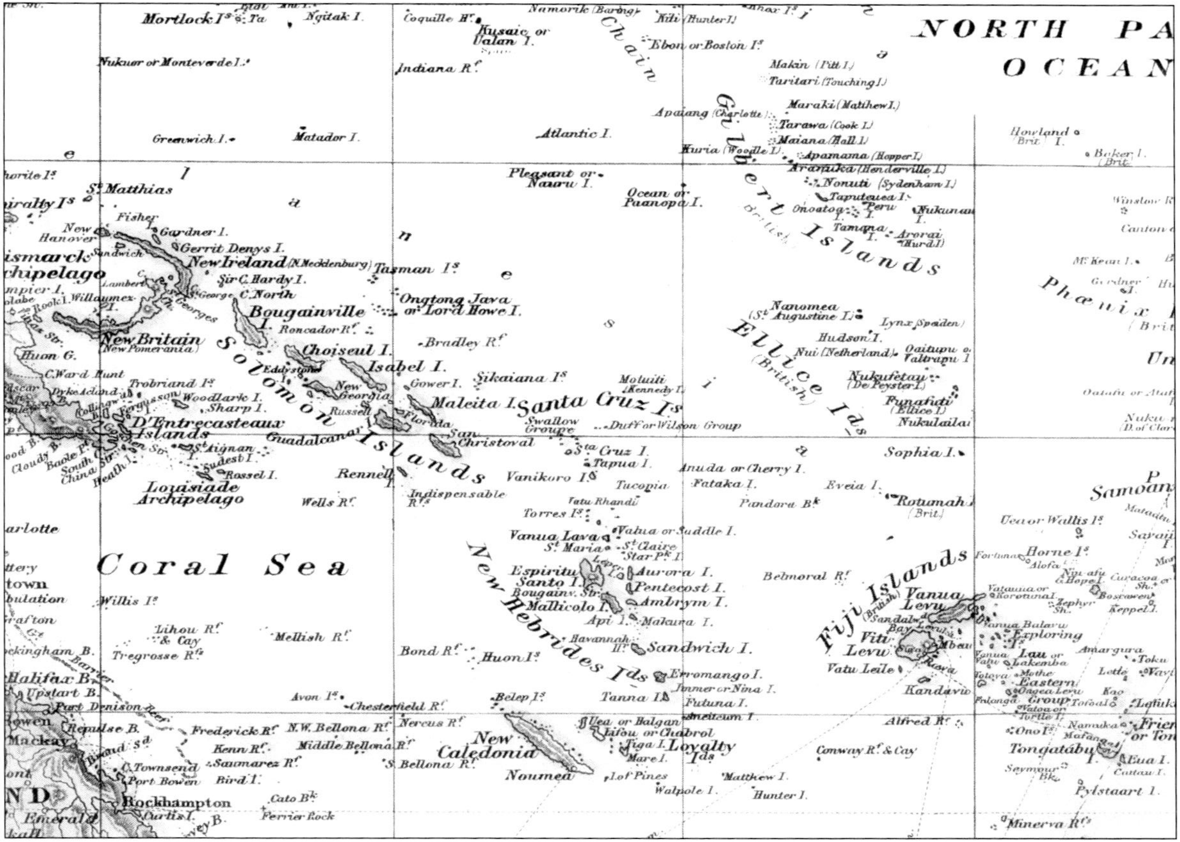

NORTH PACIFIC OCEAN

Gilbert Islands (Kingsmill Chain)

Phoenix Islands

Ellice Islands (British)

Samoa

Fiji Islands

New Hebrides

New Caledonia — Nouméa

Solomon Islands

Santa Cruz Is

Coral Sea

New Britain — New Ireland

Bismarck Archipelago

Louisiade Archipelago

D'Entrecasteaux Islands

In Tokyo with Peter Kenilorea and David Kausimae

Fishing on Point Cruz wharf

Son Peter swapping his cycle for a bird with a
Solomon Island friend - also called Pete

Guadalcanal - typical hinterland

Lagoon village on Malaita

Mendana Avenue - Honiara's main street

Honiara Secretariat - the centre of government

Welcome dance by Solomon Islands women

Solomon Islands traditional war canoe

Governing Council 1972 - Sir Michael Gass,
the High Commissioner in uniform

Ysabel village built over the lagoon

Solomon Taiyo cannery at Tulagi

At work in the Solomon Taiyo cannery - Tulagi

THE
GILBERT
AND
ELLICE
ISLANDS

CHAPTER SEVEN
TE UNIMANE

The adjustment from being an active Financial Secretary with an extensive schedule of duties to becoming a Governor supposedly remote from day to day administration was more difficult than moving from the relatively well provided Solomon Islands to the remote and environmentally limited Gilbert and Ellice Islands. Much of my role was now representational and ceremonial. While I chaired both executive and legislature, my formal portfolio of duties was confined to external affairs and security, neither issues likely to arise very often. Fortunately, there were several outstanding political matters that needed to be resolved and on which I was expected by the FCO to make early judgements so it was important to learn quickly as much as I could about my new command as well as to establish relationships with as wide a number of people as possible.

Within a civil service there is a hierarchy and that I had to respect. The Chief Secretary was in charge of the day-to-day transaction of government business and it was his duty to keep me informed of what, in his judgement, I needed to know. John Hunter I knew and respected and he was both able and effective. I could also deal directly with the Financial Secretary, Douglas Freegard, the Attorney General, John Hobbs, the Commissioner of Police, Collis Kenworthy and the elected leader of government business, Reuben Uatoia. Former government departments concerned with potentially commercial business, such as the marine and public works, had been made part of the Gilbert and Ellice Islands Development Authority (GEIDA) with a remit both to seek out opportunities for development and make government more aware of the cost of the services it provided. The Chief Executive, Suter Brown, had been recruited from industry. He and the General Manager of the wholesale Co-operative Society, David Harrison, were also people with whom I could have a direct relationship, as were the Catholic bishop and the head of the Gilbert Islands Protestant Church. But, with the exception of the Chief Secretary, none of these would have expected a summons to Government House or a visit to them as other than an infrequent occurrence.

I was, of course, able to visit government departments, schools, and other institutions as part of my familiarisation and to honour invitations to special functions but, understandably, nobody wanted the hassle of a gubernatorial visit more than occasionally. My main contacts came, therefore, through presiding at meetings of the Executive Council, which was attended by elected members with portfolios as well as by the heads of several departments. My job was to get the leader of government business and elected members to express their views effectively and to try and avoid domination of the proceedings by the expatriates. As the latter were in the majority and English was the language of both memoranda and discussion this was not always easy to achieve, the more so because Micronesians are not only by temperament diffident and taciturn but do not expect to have to defend an opinion by argument. In their own culture they achieve agreement slowly and, often it seems, largely in silence, one elder occasionally expressing an opinion but never criticising the views of another. My own opinions on any matter were really of no importance. What mattered was to use each constitutional step forward as preparation and training for the next. So I insisted on more matters being put to Executive Council in order to get the concept of cabinet government established, above all to cultivate a sense of collective responsibility, in the hope that it would become second nature to govern by consultation with colleagues, and to give members as wide an experience in problem solving as possible. Given the circumstances, this training role was the main source of my job satisfaction but not one that was understood by all of my expatriate colleagues who, understandably, were more concerned with getting a particular problem resolved. It was a relief when constitutional advance allowed me to phase out the expatriate heads of departments and appoint ministers to replace members with portfolios.

There was far less satisfaction in chairing the legislature where, as Speaker, my role was formal and largely dictated by set procedures. Having greatly enjoyed my membership of Governing Council in the Solomons and used it politically, it could be extremely frustrating to see a member of the government team lose an opportunity to make a valid point. I also very quickly learned the need for impartial body language. I once allowed myself a quiet smile when a member made an amusing remark, unaware that another member saw it both as directed at himself and insulting. He walked out in a huff and never really accepted my subsequent apology. He had been much more upset by my recognition of apparent humour than by the substance of the joke itself.

One other way I could get to know people was by entertaining them. Government House provided the venue, the equipment and the staff at no expense to myself. Governors do not pay Customs and Excise duties so that drink is relatively cheap. I did not have an entertainment allowance as such but a duty allowance of $A 1,500 a year. Sylvester and I decided that we would entertain as much as we could, in a modest fashion, that would enable us to get as many people inside the house as possible and also in a style that islanders would enjoy. Initially we had a few expatriate heads of department, usually on their own, to our normal supper, so that we could get to know them but we avoided formal dinner parties as much as possible. Our usual form of entertainment was an informal buffet supper party with between thirty to forty guests. Both Gilbertese and Ellice are musical and they love entertaining. We never had a problem in getting a local choir to come and sing, accompanied by guitar or mandolin, the kind of music to which it was extremely easy to dance. The twist was popular at the time. We had wonderful parties this way and whereas some of our younger island guests were embarrassed by having to hold a conversation with us – one young man once implored me to stop talking to him because more important people were present and I was making him ashamed – there were no inhibitions about dancing with us. Indeed, when on tour, I used to think I must have danced with every woman on the island before I was allowed to escape!

This way we made sure that every expatriate, who rightly expected an invitation, was entertained at least once but alongside islanders who we always tried to keep in the majority. Every year on the Queen's Birthday we held our largest party with several hundred guests, immediately after the formalities of the morning parade. It was always an enjoyable occasion at which the Butaritari brass band, which had provided music at the parade, reinforced with beer, played again with great verve in a more informal style. Their German instruments dated from the twenties and thirties and I enjoyed raising money to help re-equip them during my governorship. I got the bandmaster to teach his band *Sussex by the Sea*, the regimental march of the Royal Sussex with whom I had spent my national service, and was later honoured by a march he composed and dedicated to me. Inevitably on such occasions as the Queen's Birthday the guest list almost wrote itself, and we were always looking for ways to get more ordinary folk into the house. So, for example, we had all the enumerators at the conclusion of the census, the finalists playing in a soccer league and so on. Noticing that volley ball was popular and, where space was at a premium and cash short for equipment, a relatively undemanding and inexpensive sport, I suggested a volley ball competition and provided a prize. I had expected some dozen or so teams to compete. Volley ball suddenly took off. Every office and organisation produced teams, sometimes several of them. What we expected to last a couple of weeks took nearly two months, ending with a huge and enjoyable party in Government House.

Apart from our entertaining in Government House to get known and to get to know people, it had a role as a hotel. There was a small and well-run hotel on the island, the Otentai, but guests of importance expected to stay with us for at least part of their visit and there were those who spent all their time with us. As for much of our five years there was only one plane a week, we had houseguests more often than not. We often saw one guest off on the plane bringing in the next. On our sons' last summer on holiday from England we had houseguests every night of their five week stay. It could be trying. Luckily, there were two good guest rooms with their own bathroom and sitting room. Our house rule was that guests had breakfast in their own quarters so that we could breakfast as a family. When there were guests the children usually ate separately at lunch and they always ate before us in the evenings. After an afternoon cup of tea with guests I would excuse myself, before meeting them again at 7.30 pm for a drink before dinner, so that I could spend time with my family. The vast majority were understanding, some such good friends, for example Garth Pettitt of the ODA, John Laurence of Allan Charlesworth, Eddie Neilsen, our civil aviation adviser and Denis Stoneham, Government Printer, both of whom we had known in Honiara, that they happily joined in our family activities, which all guests were welcome to do at week-ends when we had the huge privilege of the Governor's launch to take us to Bikeman, a delightful sand bar in the lagoon where we could swim. But just occasionally there was a guest who found my behaviour unacceptable. One rather haughty lady enquired "why on earth don't you get a nanny?" and a man from the

FCO once interrupted our family breakfast to demand that a telegram be sent off immediately (an impossibility until the lines were opened) and seeing two apples on our table said "I'll have one of those" leaving us with one apple to share between the five of us. The two had been our ration from the Co-op when the last ship had come in. It would be six weeks before the next. We did not share apples with guests who would be able to buy all they wanted within a matter of days! He was also the guest who arrived on a Tuesday with a *Sunday Times* in his cabin bag which I had spotted at the airport when I met him. I told Sylvester that a treat was in store – a Sunday paper in the week of publication. Alas he did not offer it to us to read and did not even discard it in his wastepaper basket before he left!

Running what was in effect a hotel was undoubtedly the toughest part of life for Sylvester. Luckily we had an excellent cook, Tatake, and housekeeper, Nei Koi, both of whom took everything in their stride and never failed to ensure the highest standards. As a family we were very content with the island diet of fish and coconuts. The coconut is a wonderfully versatile fruit and the variety of fish available, all eaten within hours of being caught, was fabulous. I used to drink fresh toddy, sap from the coconut palm, at breakfast and for elevenses in preference to coffee. Not everyone cares for the smell but toddy provides all the vitamins and minerals you need. Much can also be achieved with breadfruit and pandanus, and rice was always available. There were, however, those who hankered after steak and chips and, understandably, local guests expected something different from everyone's everyday diet when they came to Government House. Imported food was available in small quantities every six weeks or so when a ship called, provided the container had not been left behind, which sometimes happened. Sylvester wisely made sure that she never asked for special treatment and we never took more than the ration that the Co-op store provided to all and sundry. We didn't broadcast this and many probably assumed that we flew in our own supplies, something some expatriates did but we were not among them.

Living conditions were relatively tough for expatriates and were the main reason why a two year contract was as much as many felt they wanted. Recently married young expatriates who thought that a couple of years on a tropical island would be an extended honeymoon were often disappointed. A wonderful honeymoon it could be for those with a sense of adventure and plenty of initiative, but for some it was their first time abroad and they had been unable to imagine a world without the facilities to which they were used at home. It was particularly difficult for wives without young children to look after and keep them busy. Their husbands were kept occupied and interested by their jobs but these did not involve wives much if at all. While the aim was to offer joint appointments where possible, usually easiest in education, there were no jobs for expatriate women without specific qualifications. There were limited opportunities for voluntary work and most families rightly employed local women to do the housework, laundry and cooking, a sort of economic *quid pro quo* for being there. Those who really enjoyed learning about the place, the people and their language or who were enthusiastic about fishing, bird watching or sailing got the most out of it. There was also the fun and excitement of planning their leave, making use of the huge opportunities for stop-overs in exotic places that a round the world ticket provided.

There was not only a substantial expatriate staff turnover but I soon realised how ill prepared for atoll life some new arrivals were. I sometimes wondered whether there were those in London who, understandably and perhaps fairly, believing that the Western Pacific was behind the times and needed shaking up, would be encouraged to use recruitment for some social engineering, appointing candidates who did not come from the usual background. It certainly seemed that way on occasions, with results that were not always as might have been expected. There was an unhappy incident at the secondary school in the first week of my arrival. Three boys raped an expatriate teacher. The blame was generally laid at the door of an expatriate teacher who had formed a pop group that the other staff believed had got out of hand. When all this was relayed to me I assumed that the staff who objected would be older expatriates with experience and the man who had initiated the pop group, allowed it to rehearse in his house and 'even allowed the boys to use his lavatory' would be a young and recent arrival. It was the other way round. The man blamed for the ill discipline was an older member of staff, from a conventional background and with experience elsewhere. Those who objected to his behaviour were young, recently arrived and from families with no tradition of serving empire.

When things had settled down I went to the school to speak to the staff. Nobody stood up when I went into the room. No doubt they thought that I represented a fuddy-duddy old style hierarchy but it seemed to me that their lack of good manners, casual approach to dress and time keeping would have encouraged poor discipline among pupils who had been brought up to respect elders. I doubt whether the pop group had much to do with poor discipline although it had certainly split the staff into two groups. Among the school staff at that time was somebody who in later life was to become a talented and renowned playwright, Alan Bleasdale.[1] I have been uncertain whether to be pleased or sorry that he never turned his hand to writing about the Gilbert Islands in the 1970s! A proud Liverpudlian, I remember him coming to Government House for a party, rather scruffy in dirty shorts and T-shirt (the usual dress being slacks and an island shirt) and making it clear that it was a pain to be there. We had been married in Liverpool, Sylvester had taught in a Scotland Road primary and could speak Scouse as well as anyone. I think she rather surprised him!

With an expatriate civil service that was predominantly contracted and often ill-prepared for atoll life, I decided to introduce an induction course that would cater for new arrivals three or four times a year. I opened each course with a general introduction during which I always emphasised that we were guests in somebody else's country. It was not for us to set standards or determine values. We were there to help the islanders on their way to statehood in the twentieth century, introducing them to some skills they might not have but also enjoying the opportunity to learn from them skills that our own society had either long since forgotten or never possessed. We should respect their customs, even if they seemed a little old world, just as we would at home when visiting elderly relatives. There was plenty of sun, sand and surf; beach attire was fine in its proper place but inappropriate for work and shopping. No doubt it sounded pompous, prudish and paternalistic but dress was an issue that did cause irritation locally. Others followed me, explaining how government worked, providing helpful information about health services and hazards, supplies, banking, mail services and so forth. The morning concluded with everyone who had participated

---

1. Best known for the TV drama *Boys from the Blackstuff*.

coming to lunch at Government House, providing an opportunity for more informal and personal contact. This occasioned some amusing incidents. Somebody, unhappy with his own housing, remarked "You do yourself alright here, don't you mate?" The Sunday after another induction course, a recently arrived VSO volunteer came into the lounge and said "Hi there, John, can your lend me your car so I can go up the island?" I reflected that things had moved on somewhat since I had arrived as a cadet in Northern Nigeria in 1951!

Given our young family, the amount of entertaining we undertook and the potential difficulty, when in the top job, of getting too close to anyone, we decided that we would honour all official invitations but never accept any private invitations. We also decided to avoid club membership and particularly of the one predominantly, if not exclusively, expatriate club. This was probably not much liked by some but made good sense because it kept us clear of the inevitable gossip and fallings out that occur in small communities. We made sure, however, that our children were free to make friends as they wanted, go to their homes and bring them to ours. Our youngest, Ruth, had some good school friends but spent a lot of time with our housekeeper's son who was of a similar age. She became the best Gilbertese speaker in the family. She wandered about Bairiki freely. One day she fell and broke her arm. Some local people picked her up, took her to the hospital and returned her to us, proudly displaying her arm in plaster and sling. She was six at the time. It was just one of many examples of how kind and thoughtful the Gilbertese were but also a reminder that we lived a very public life with all we did under close scrutiny.

We were critical of Rurubao, the primary school, close to Government House, that expatriate children were able to attend. The full time staff were rather laid back New Zealanders, believing that children learned in their own time and at their own pace. Expatriate wives who were experienced UK primary teachers and also employed made a difference but our boys made little progress. They were not put under any pressure and insufficiently disciplined, no doubt in part because of whom they were. They quickly took advantage of that and, consequently, were much less satisfactory pupils than they should have been. I appreciated, for the first time, that the difficulties of fitting them into local schools was one reason why the English landed gentry sent their children away to boarding schools. In the Solomons, where I had been less important and the children younger, we had not had this problem. Sylvester, herself an experienced infant teacher, had taught there and when Gerard began school he was in her class. It worked well. One lunchtime he had asked, "Mummy, do you know what Mrs Smith told us to-day?" Sadly, we decided that the boys would have to go home to school much earlier than we had ever intended, but meanwhile I quietly saw to it that when contracts had to be renewed we recruited, on a joint contract, a UK couple with experience of small rural primary schools in Cumbria. Ruth was able to benefit from their excellent management of the school.

Sending children to the UK to school at the age of seven or eight was devastating. Sylvester stayed at home for their first term but it was never easy. It was a three day journey from Tarawa to the UK. Our replies to their weekly letter home would not reach them for at least two weeks. Unlike in my childhood, when colonial service staff had to pay for their own families' passages, the FCO was extremely generous and it was possible to have the boys out for every long holiday, but we found that, without effective communication in between times, relationships had to be begun almost anew each holiday and carefully nurtured. Although it was a far cry from the days when imperial children were separated from their parents for years on end, it was also a far cry from the present day when mobile phones keep children and parents in daily contact.

One of the perks of living in Government House was the daily arrival of a small group of prisoners to keep the grounds in order. The islands had a high rate of homicide, the result of a strong sense of honour on the one hand, and the fact that most men carried a sharp knife with them for toddy cutting on the other. An insult leading to an argument could easily turn into a fight in which knives were used and end with a fatality. Prisoners coming to Government House were often serving life sentences for homicide. Many of them were also dignified and gracious men of status. One, who had been chairman of an island council, was extremely good with Gerard and Peter, giving them jobs to do and making sure they did them properly. Another, Tanoun, was a famous canoe builder. He had won the Queen's Birthday canoe race my first year, been accused of magic, fought and killed the man who had insulted him. I got him to build me a canoe, which he happily did in the prison. When it was completed he was the captain, I was his crew.

We entered the Queen's Birthday race and came third. Had he had a decent crew, Tanoun told me, he would have come first!

When visitors asked if they might enjoy a sail I always got Tanoun to take them out, my own skill with the outrigger canoe, particularly in tacking when one needed to unship the foot of the spar carrying the leg of mutton sail and carry it to the other end of the canoe, somewhat limited. Our Chief Justice, Jocelyn Bodilly, who visited from the Solomons, was a keen sailor. Hearing that I had a good local canoe he asked for a sail and was duly taken for a spin in the lagoon by Tanoun. On his return the CJ told me how much he had enjoyed the sail and what a good chap my canoe master was, commenting that he seemed familiar. I pointed out that he had sentenced him some eighteen months previously!

Peter, on holiday from prep school, decided that he would like to learn to cut toddy and enlisted the help of one of our prisoners. Morning and evening, Peter and prisoner climbed up the chosen palm and Peter was instructed in the art of tightly binding the fruit-bearing stems together and slicing them very thinly so that the sap dripped into a container. Saturday afternoon came and Peter was looking for his prisoner. I explained that they had Saturday afternoons off. My offer to go up the tree with him was summarily dismissed and Peter set off to the prison, knocked on the door and asked the Chief Warder for 'his' prisoner. He did not know his name so was invited in to find him. Diminutive Peter then came back to Government House accompanied by 'his' prisoner towering above him for his lesson. Prisoners from our humane and well-conducted prison gave us quite a lot of fun. One day, as I walked the few yards between my office and the house puzzling about how to answer some enquiry, a younger prisoner, almost certainly one who had been a seaman, called out to me in English 'John, a penny for your thoughts'. On another occasion John Laurence, who had just arrived, was having a cup of tea with us in the lounge when suddenly a long bare leg came through the ceiling above him and dangled over his teacup before being withdrawn. It was a prisoner who had discovered that access to the liquor store, which had no ceiling, could be easily obtained from the attic into which they occasionally went in order to affect minor repairs. On his way there he had missed his footing on the rafters. When I investigated I realised that only the top shelf in the store had been accessible and the missing bottles were all liqueurs that had rarely if ever been used!

Not surprising then, that I felt rather close to our prisoners and particularly to the lifers. The prerogative of mercy was mine to exercise and when constitutional advance brought the usual expectation of a committee whose advice I would have to accept on its exercise, I argued strongly against its establishment. I remembered an extremely unfortunate case in Northern Nigeria just prior to independence and had no intention of being faced with the same situation. A feud between two families had resulted in an older man of one family being pushed into a well by two younger members of the other. He had died and the two boys had fled to a distant part of the country. Some twenty years later they had returned and had been arrested. They did not know their dates of birth and nobody could exactly date the occasion of the crime but they were almost certainly under the age of twelve at the time. Now as adults they had to be sentenced to death. The judge, convinced that had they been tried at the time, they would have been below age for conviction, suggested that the prerogative of mercy be exercised. The committee would have none of it and the sentences stood. With the Commissioner of Police, and taking advice as necessary, I used to review every life sentence every year and made use of occasions such as the Queen's Birthday or constitutional advance to release prisoners back into their communities if we were convinced that there would be no untoward consequences. Fortunately, most homicide cases were honour killings, the victims of which were adult men and my exercise of the prerogative of mercy never aroused any ill feelings.

When I arrived I inherited a personal assistant and a cipher officer, both permanent FCO staff, from my predecessor. They were coming to the end of their tours and due for leave. Sir John Field had been the first governor and so it had been the first time that any FCO staff, as opposed to Overseas Service staff, had ever been posted to Tarawa. It was to be the last. Both had done a good job but neither wanted a second tour and word had got back to London that ensured Tarawa was not high on the list of desirable postings. I was told that nobody could be found. Latterly in Honiara I had had the services of a New Zealand PA who enjoyed the islands and was of an adventurous temperament. I sounded her out and she was agreeable but the FCO decided that a

New Zealander could not be entrusted with the state secrets to which she might have to be party. I wanted, if possible, to avoid employing a UK expatriate wife. There would be confidential staff matters that it was always much better to keep under close wraps in so small a community where everyone knew everyone else. A niece of mine, born and brought up in the West Indies, a good linguist and with all the right qualifications, was working for a developer in Spain and not very happy in her job. Susan was keen to come and I thought the problem solved. I was mistaken. Susan had been born in Trinidad, where her father was an agricultural officer. He had been born in Tanganyika, where our father had been Deputy Postmaster General. Trinidad and Tanganyika, colonies at the time of both births, were now independent countries and under the latest Nationality Act Susan did not qualify as a British national and did not qualify for positive vetting. I enjoyed sending a telegram saying I found it curious that the daughter and granddaughter of British colonial servants was disqualified from working for her colonial service uncle on grounds of nationality! It seemed to work and Susan, who had a UK passport, arrived. She was soon speaking Gilbertese, got on well with everyone and trained a local successor, Barai, who after independence was an asset in the Foreign Affairs Division of the President's office. Susan and Baireti, a very personable former seaman who I had acquired as my aide when I went on tour, married. Susan worked for KLM for many years and Baireti trained as a pilot. He now works for Micronesian Airlines and Susan has established a successful travel agency in Tarawa.

CHAPTER EIGHT
AN IMMENSITY OF OCEAN

It was once said of the colony that when the tide went out it doubled in size. The small atolls that constitute the land area total only 324 square miles but they are spread over two million square miles of the Pacific Ocean. None are more than a few miles long and often only a few hundred yards wide. Touring was an important part of the job and distances were great. Christmas Island in the east is 2,000 miles from Ocean Island in the west. There are 1,000 miles between the latitude of Washington in the north and that of Niulatika in the south. Airstrips were being built and light aircraft were in use but some atolls were too small and some too distant to be visited except by sea. We were well equipped with vessels but all were small, more akin in size to the boats in which the first pioneers crossed the Atlantic than to the holiday ferries that nowadays ply the English Channel. They needed shallow draughts in order to enter lagoons and seek a safe anchorage across the reef. Inevitably they tossed around in heavy seas but were comfortable enough. On tour they usually served as my living quarters. I would spend all day ashore, return on board in the evening to sail through the night to the next island. Travelling to the Ellice, Ocean Island and Christmas Island took days and, to my regret, I never managed to get to Washington and Fanning because I could not afford to be away for the two to three weeks required.

On one of my first tours a Catholic Sister commented how disappointing it was for the schoolchildren to find that the Governor was just another European in shorts and shirt, of whom there might be two or three because the District Officer and perhaps some other expatriate official usually accompanied me. The Governor was *Te Unimane* so it was presumed that he must be the oldest man. That was not necessarily so. I decided to invent for myself a touring uniform. I already had the military style cap that I had used on arrival and it was easy enough to have khaki uniform jacket and trousers made to go with it, using buttons from my formal white uniform. It was cool, comfortable and different. The usual routine on tour would be for me to go ashore in the morning, to be greeted by everyone on a smaller island and by the whole nearest settlement on the larger atolls. Sometimes the island policeman would be in charge, calling everyone to attention while the national anthem was sung, always in all three verses and always in either Gilbertese or Ellice as well as in English. Then there would be formal greetings from island dignitaries and often handshakes with everyone, men, women and children. Garlands would be presented, usually accompanied by dancing.

Getting ashore varied from atoll to atoll and season to season. I have made the journey in the ship's launch, in one of a whole fleet of canoes, even in a chair carried by four sturdy men hoisted high above their heads. On Vaitupu, the largest of the Ellice Islands, I went ashore in a fleet of canoes but while the others were beached, mine was seized, carried aloft, and finally deposited in front of the reception committee. When Her Majesty received similar treatment some years later her canoe was set aside, never to be used again. Crossing the reef could be relatively easy or really hairy. The best advice I ever received was to ensure that if capsized or thrown overboard I should grab the nearest islander and let him do the rest. I was glad that I was not particularly tall or heavy. I sometimes arrived pretty wet but never had to swim for it.

Once ashore I would visit whatever there was to visit, school, dispensary, radio station, council office, listening to whatever anyone wanted to tell me and watching teachers and others at work. The morning was usually spent this way. I would then change into informal dress and make my way to the *maneaba*, the meeting house. These were always impressive buildings, some of huge size, built with palm trunks as uprights bearing roofs beautifully thatched with pandanus leaves that came so low that one always had to stoop in order to enter. The women would have been decorating the uprights with palm fronds and cooking from dawn or earlier and the entire community would gather. There might be some specific welcome ritual. In one *maneaba* the bones of a founding father were kept high up under the roof and would be lowered with ceremony on special occasions. There would be a feast. The first time I went on tour I was offered a chair to sit on and provided with an enamel plate with a couple of fried eggs and tinned peas on it while everyone else sat cross-legged on mats and tucked into a variety of interesting looking food contained in dishes made from palm leaves. The islanders were excellent cooks and seafood of all sorts was abundant. I made it clear that I would sit like them and eat their food. Who wants a cold fried egg when crayfish is on the menu?

The feast over, dancing would begin. There would usually be two, sometimes more, groups seated opposite each other at the ends of the *maneaba* and they would dance and sing alternately. Traditional dancing was of a very high order and taken extremely seriously. Those watching would be as intent and as critical as a knowledgeable ballet audience at Covent Garden. Children, boys as well as girls, would begin to learn to dance from an early age and behind the stars at the front would be the novices at the back. In the Gilberts many dances were dramatic and exciting to watch especially on the southern islands such as Tabiteuea. The northern islands were more receptive to innovation and after the traditional dances there would be versions of dances from other cultures and finally dances in which all could join. The twist was popular at the time and everyone was delighted when one of ladies invited me to dance. Once on the floor it seemed that I would be expected to go on dancing until it was time to go. I enjoyed it and the exercise was a welcome relief after sitting crossed-legged for a long time. However shy most Gilbertese seemed to be all inhibitions were cast away on these occasions. On tour on Miana with 'Salty' Sellars, the Australian High Commissioner, I was once lifted off my feet by the strapping young lady who was my partner and carried in triumph around the *maneaba* to great applause. I was grateful that no photographer was present!

I wanted to learn Gilbertese but initially found it difficult to find a tutor. After a few months, however, I acquired the services of Baireti Iareta, a ship's steward trained at the Marine Training School, who was awaiting a job overseas following an illness. Baireti, from the island of Makin in the far north, had an easy, out-going, happy-go-lucky personality and had no inhibitions about helping me with my Gilbertese. He used to come over to the office with elevenses and stay for half an hour or so teaching me. So I learned to speak enough Gilbertese to say a few words of thanks in the *maneabas* and that always went down well as did my obvious appreciation of most of the food. The fish was always excellent and I was a particular fan of raw fish marinated in coconut cream. It would have fetched a high price in the best restaurants of Tokyo. Coconut flesh was served in all sorts of ways and both breadfruit and pandanus were excellent to eat. I never, however, became excited by *babai*, to me the rather dull and heavy yam type vegetable that was a staple of the diet. All the fish was wonderfully fresh and ever since I have yearned for freshly caught fish. It tastes so much better.

The first major speech I made in Gilbertese was when I was invited to open a newly built Protestant church. The speech was recorded and subsequently broadcast by the local radio station. My errors and mispronunciations caused some amusement and inspired a new character in a local comic soap on the radio that was modelled on the Goon Show. My Gilbertese colleagues enjoyed it and pulled my leg about it. When the producer was a guest at Government House I talked to him about it and said I was glad to have been of assistance. I asked him when he was going to take the mickey out of the Chief Minister. 'Never', I was told. I was fair game but a minister would be a step too far! I had been pleased to be invited to open a Protestant church, the first of several that Sylvester or I subsequently opened. We were Catholics. The only politics in the Gilberts were religious, some islands, mainly in the north being predominantly Catholic and the others, mainly in the south, Protestant and of the Congregational persuasion. In the Ellice all but one island were Protestant. Mixed marriages were virtually unknown and relationships between the expatriate missionaries of the two communions tended to be formal rather than friendly. On my first tour away from Tarawa, to the island of Abaiang, I was going to be there over a week-end and when the District Officer was discussing the programme with me I said that I would want to attend Mass on the Sunday and understood that I would be able to do so at the Catholic secondary school. Not a churchgoer, he was horrified, assuring me that it was essential that I be seen to be entirely impartial lest some of the most southerly islands such as Tamana refuse to allow me ashore. I stood my ground. Experience of living in Muslim Northern Nigeria had taught me that I was more likely to be respected by acknowledging my faith than by hiding it. And so it turned out. I enjoyed good relations with both denominations. When, in the Gilberts, local leadership of both had replaced expatriate I had no difficulty in persuading them to work ecumenically. They began, with my encouragement, with a Christmas service of lessons and carols. Both the Chief Minister and I read lessons.

Touring the Ellice Islands followed much the same daily pattern but the atmosphere was different and the hospitality could be overwhelming. At some stage in the past missionaries had introduced Ellice ladies to the art of baking. Every visit, however brief, was always accompanied by a break for tea and cake. The tea was always very weak instant coffee mixed with condensed milk and much sugar. The cake was what remained from a recipe for seedy cake without the seeds but enhanced by a rich variety of colouring. The Co-op obviously stocked the latter but not the former. It was usually both hard and dry. Singing in the *maneapas*, virtually the same word in Polynesian Ellice as the Gilbertese *maneaba* with the harder 'b' softened to a 'p', was accompanied not by mandolin or guitar but by wooden drums looking pretty much like packing cases and sometimes a bass made of a single string over an old tea chest. There was a wide variety of Polynesian dancing, some imported from Hawaii, and guests were often invited to join in the traditional dancing rather than wait for the inevitable twist.

Pastors had an important role in island life. Morning and evening prayers, to which everyone was summoned by gongs, were said publicly in the *maneapa* and my presence was expected. On Sundays I would attend the church service that could last for two hours or more. The central feature of every church was a massive pulpit, preaching the main and longest part of every service. Women's clubs also played a major part in the entertainment of visitors. On one island the last call on my itinerary was tea with the ladies' club. After an elaborate welcome, some dancing and singing and the inevitable coffee and cake it was time for me to go. I rose to my feet and said my thanks and farewells whereupon all twenty tons of the ladies' club seized me and tossed me from one to the other as they ran down to the beach where the ship's tender awaited. I hoped at least for a safe landing in it. No way! They ran on into the sea and with shrieks of laughter threw me in and collapsed around me. It was quite the most spectacular farewell I ever had and, if not quite what the protocol surrounding the Queen's representative required, clearly gave everyone a lot of pleasure!

Throughout my governorship airfields were being added so many of the islands could be reached by light aircraft. Our airline used Britten-Norman Islander aircraft that were excellent for the purpose if I was just visiting the one island. Touring by sea was always more relaxing and I was able to take the family with me on one occasion. The boys were really excited by the fishing because as soon as we were in the open sea lines went overboard and everyone, not just the ship's cook, were keen to enjoy a catch. The ships used for touring were the regular inter island communication, taking supplies to the Co-operative stores, picking up cargoes of copra for transfer to a Bank Line steamer elsewhere, carrying government staff on leave or transfer, secondary schoolchildren to and from Tarawa for the term and home again for their holidays, members of the legislature to and from meetings, and helping extended families to keep in touch. The ships were crewed locally and in very capable hands.

Pacific Islanders who live on atolls are natural seamen. Val Anderson, a predecessor Resident Commissioner, had had the foresight to establish a Marine Training School (MTS). It was a huge success with courses for seamen, engine room staff and stewards. Initially staffed by British merchant mariners there were also German staff provided by the German shipping lines operating out of Hamburg that in practice employed the bulk of the school's graduates. The Hamburg consortium was excellent. It employed MTS graduates in groups of eight; seamen, engineers and stewards, so that loneliness was never a problem and there were always sufficient island seamen on board a ship to stand up for themselves when necessary. The training lasted a year. For the final three months, two of which were spent afloat, German boatswains joined the staff, one for each group of eight cadets. These would be the groups' boatswains on their first ship and so they got to know the cadets during the last months of their training. Each boatswain accompanied his group of cadets to wherever they were going to join their ship, and it could be anywhere in the world. It was always the first time any of them would have left the Pacific. Although the British maritime unions took part in the negotiations establishing the school and in the drafting of employment contracts, it was extremely difficult to get any British shipping company to employ our seamen. British seamen's union leaders visited regularly but we never had a visit from a British ship owner. In contrast we got to know the Hamburg consortium owners well.

The sea training of the cadets took place on MV *Teraaka*, the largest ship in our fleet. Built originally as a ferry for use in Scandinavian waters, she had later seen service as President Tito of Yugoslavia's private yacht.

She was a very comfortable ship in which to be a passenger and I made several journeys in her, notably to the uninhabited Phoenix Islands. She was, of course, expensive to run and not all her training voyages could be scheduled to fit in with necessary commercial activity such as the transfer of staff and families working in the phosphate industries of Ocean Island and Nauru. Garth Pettitt, who looked after the economic desk dealing with us in London was a keen birdwatcher, well aware of the interesting bird life in the Pacific and the unique opportunity to observe it provided by uninhabited islands. With his help we organised a tour for a group of ornithologists. All went well while they were at sea, and there were always plenty of birds accompanying a ship. Expectations were high when cadets rowed the group ashore on one of the uninhabited Phoenix Islands. The party went off excited by the large number of nesting birds. The cadets had time on their hands. In their culture birds were not for watching but for eating. They proceeded to catch and cook themselves an excellent lunch. A stream of distressed telegrams followed and such was the upset that we decided that the experiment had better never be repeated.

In most circumstances, however, MTS graduates were good ambassadors for their country and, most importantly, made a substantial contribution to the economy. The majority of them remitted between 70% and 80% of their earnings back to their families. Towards the end of my term of office their contribution to the economy exceeded that of phosphate, which had long been the mainstay. The opportunities the MTS offered for employment and the chance to see the world made it enormously popular with young Gilbertese. The world they saw, unfortunately, was more often than not confined to the red light districts surrounding major ports they visited. When they came back on leave they brought goodies with them such as TV sets for showing videos because there was no local TV service. Some of the films they came with were what they had acquired in the sleazier port areas. I visited a family one evening whose sailor son had recently returned. All generations from grandparents to infants were roaring with laughter at the strange European sexual antics on display! Generally, however, the returning sailors were quickly assimilated back into their culture. Sporting on arrival the long hair and bell-bottom trousers that the mid seventies western world demanded of young men, one would see them the next day with shorn locks and wearing shorts. The guitars, radios and other goods in demand with which they had returned would also have been dispersed around their extended families. The more able and ambitious among them began to ascend the career ladders available in the merchant marine and it was not long before a substantial number had secured promotion and were on their way to becoming master mariners. They were true descendants of those intrepid people who had first migrated across the great ocean in outrigger canoes. When I left the Pacific I was delighted to be able to give my two canoes to the MTS and I am sure that good use was made of them.

I had the good fortune while in Tarawa to get a personal taste of what it must have been like to sail in an ocean going canoe, a *baurua* in Gilbertese. Jim Siers, a New Zealand writer and photographer, had long been intrigued by the canoes of the Pacific. He was convinced that Thor Heyerdahl and the Kontiki had got it wrong. The Pacific peoples, including the Maoris, had come from South East Asia rather than South America. He decided that he wanted to build a *baurua* and see what it could do in terms of a long ocean journey ending in New Zealand, making a film as he went along. In earlier times the British had forbidden the building of ocean going canoes because of the inherent danger in long voyages and the difficulty and cost of searching when things went amiss. So although there was still a great tradition of canoe building for racing and fishing there were few left who had direct experience of *baurua* building or sailing. Jim set up base at Taratai in north Tarawa where he had found Teauba Teakai, a renowned canoe builder with over a hundred canoes to his credit and of an age, when young, to have seen *bauruas* built.

Jim produced the supplies necessary and arranged for the keel to be laid with due ceremony. It was at this point that he was persuaded against his better judgement to build a 23 metre rather than an 18 metre canoe. He learned, too, that Gilbertese ceremonies required substantial quantities of beer! Filming it all, as well as fishing and other aspects of village life, he was content enough, except perhaps with the speed of the work. The great day of the launching arrived. The Chief Minister and I went across the lagoon, clergy from both the churches were on hand for the blessing and Jim had financed a huge feast. Alas the launch was a disaster in which the float of the outrigger was destroyed. Jim persevered and some weeks later *Taratai*, as he named the *baurua*, was ready for sea trials in the lagoon. With two sails and her great length she was a fine sight and it was exciting to sail on her. Jim planned to sail from Tarawa by stages from atoll to atoll to Fiji and then to Tonga and eventually to New Zealand. My offer to sail on the first leg to Abemama, an atoll to the south-east of Tarawa was accepted.

The day for departure came. I boarded *Taratai* from *Kameang*, my launch, giving Jim a chance to film from the launch before, my personal pennant bravely flying, we set sail out of the lagoon into the ocean. Our master was Tenanoa, a native of Taratai with whom Jim had first been sailing and our navigator Peter Barton. Peter was in charge of the GEIDA shipyard. He was a naval architect, a skilled boat builder and an experienced sailor. His advice had been enormously helpful to Jim throughout and he would now ensure that *Taratai* reached her destination. We hit high seas and a south easterly once we left the lagoon. This meant a long tack to the south west, well south of Maiana, another to the north east between Maiana and Abemama and then a final tack south east to our landing. The fewer tacks the better because with two sails to move it was not a simple manoeuvre. We left late in the afternoon and sighted Abemama late the following afternoon. Too dark to negotiate the passage through the reef we anchored off and crossed the reef the following day. It had been an exciting voyage and an interesting insight into the journeys of the original migrants.

They would have had to be better prepared for their voyages. Jim had equipped his crew and taken on ample stores but, alas, their last night in Betio before sailing relatives had come to celebrate and gone off with nearly everything as the tradition of *bubuti* required. If a relative asked for something he or she could not be denied. We arrived in Abemama with very little left of what was necessary to make the passage to Fiji. *Taratai* was also leaking. The pump had been in constant use on the voyage once the heavier seas had been encountered. Canoes are bound together with string made from coconut husk fibre. There are no nails or screws. It works well but the combination of heavy seas and too much sail power had overstrained some of the lashings and loosened them. Jim had several days work on repairs to undertake so I had ample time on my return to Tarawa to send to him some of the things I thought essential if he was to avoid a mutiny, in particular a radio so that the crew could listen in to Radio Tarawa. *Taratai* made it to Fiji but once there Jim decided to build a smaller single sailed *baurua* for the next leg of his journey. He wrote up both journeys and his film has been shown around the world on many occasions.[1]

1. James Siers, *Taratai*, Milwood Press Wellington 1977 and *Taratai II* 1978.

CHAPTER NINE
SEPARATION

The Micronesian Gilbert Islands and the Polynesian Ellice Islands had been administered together since 1892 when the Protectorate was declared. In pre-colonial times there were no central institutions of government linking either the individual Gilbert Islands or the individual Ellice Islands. The first colonial administrators, primarily concerned with controlling European beachcombers and the recruitment of islanders as workers in Australia and South America – blackbirding – assumed the continuation of a large number of individual island 'governments'. It was not long, however, before the Protectorate Government expanded and in 1915 it suited Britain to join the two groups of islands with Ocean Island, where phosphate mining had been established, to form the Gilbert and Ellice Islands Colony. Subsequently and over a long period other atolls, all without indigenous inhabitants, were placed under the colony's administration: Fanning, Washington and Christmas Island, the world's largest atoll, together forming the Northern Line Islands; the Central Line Islands; and the Phoenix Islands.

In the colonial period the population of the Gilbert and Ellice Islands, never more than 80,000, was the equivalent of a onetime English Rural District Council with 25 villages but these villages were scattered over a distance of 1000 miles from north to south, each living pretty much in isolation, separated from its neighbours by seas which, in many instances, could only be crossed by ships of a size beyond island resources to provide or island economies to attract more than a few times a year. To survive each of the 25 occupied islands had traditionally needed to be self-sufficient. Funafuti, the administrative centre of the Ellice (and now capital of Tuvalu), is 830 miles from Tarawa, the former colony headquarters, and there are 200 miles of ocean between the nearest islands of the two groups. In pre-colonial times Nui, the closest Ellice Island, had been invaded by Gilbertese, creating a mixed society. With this one exception, however, the Gilbertese and the Ellice were not only racially distinct but distant neighbours when the British arrived. As late as 1947 there were only 24 Gilbertese in the Ellice Islands and 169 Ellice in the

Gilbert Islands and it was not until well after the Second World War and the first steps in constitutional advance had been taken that the reality of union and of sharing a central administration began to be appreciated. This was in part because the expansion of the role of government and central services provided employment opportunities that the Ellice seized rather more readily and effectively than did the Gilbertese.

During the war the Gilbertese had experienced the evacuation of the British, the collapse of central government, the interruption of education and Japanese occupation of Ocean Island, the pre-war capital, Tarawa, Butaritari and Abemama. The battle to regain Tarawa, albeit short and restricted to the island of Betio, had been one of the fiercest engagements of the Pacific war.[1] The Ellice, however, had not come under attack and there had been no curtailment of education. The use of Funafuti lagoon by the United States fleet had brought prosperity. A few Ellice youngsters were even taken by individual Americans to the United States to further their education. In 1972, when the Ellice numbered 7,000 against 42,000 Gilbertese, it was reckoned that they held 30% of government jobs, were 31% of the merchant seamen employed internationally and 31% of those working for the British Phosphate Commissioners on Ocean Island. The Ellice began to fear that too rapid a move towards self-government could leave them exposed as a minority in a predominantly Gilbertese state. More significant was their concern that Ellice culture was being subsumed. As I experienced myself, each atoll was a very small community, no bigger than a small English village, dominated and rigidly regulated by the elders. Secondary school children coming to King George V School on Tarawa and the families of Ellice Islanders working in the police force, in the hospital and in government offices soon learned to speak Gilbertese and adopted much of the culture. The same was true of Ellice families recruited to work in the phosphate industry on Ocean Island. This loss of tradition upset the elders back home and was especially disliked by the pastors. Unease grew and in 1971 the Ellice members of the legislature called for separation.

---

1. A good account can be found in Vol III of the History of the U.S. Marine Corps Operations in World War II, *Central Pacific Drive*, U.S. Government Printing Office 1966.

It was not a matter that could be ignored. Lord Lothian had minuted in October 1970 that he had 'the uneasy feeling that unless we are very careful, the problems of the Caribbean in the 60s will spread to the Pacific in the 70s. The prospect of the Ellice Islands seceding from the Gilberts at a later stage, if it suited *their* interests, is not a happy augury for the future'.[2] No Pacific Islander would have understood the concern in London lest another Anguilla style crisis be created and they would have been irritated by the arrogance of those, reluctant to accept the concept of mini states and with little sense of the vast distances in the Pacific, who proposed linking the Ellice with Western Samoa and the Gilberts with the Marshall Islands.[3] Sir John Field, my predecessor, toured the Ellice and Mr Anthony Kershaw MP, Parliamentary Under-Secretary, also visited. His brief commented that, 'about all the two peoples have in common is fifty years of British rule and for many years that was hardly apparent'.[4] It went on to say that the prospect of a long-term impoverished and dependent Ellice would at least have the merit of preventing Funafuti 'one of the finest fleet anchorages in the world' from being used by a hostile power. Their tours persuaded both Field and Kershaw of the seriousness of the Ellice petition for separation and the need for a definite policy. The result was the appointment in December 1972 of Sir Leslie Monson as Commissioner to study the relationship of the Gilbert and Ellice Islands. Sir Leslie visited every Ellice Island early the following year and reported in April.

Sir Leslie was quite clear that 'to sever would be to cripple'. He had but recently retired as an Under-Secretary and had spent many years in the Colonial Office. He had the experience of failed federations in Africa and the West Indies. So he also argued that any form of federal or regional government structure would not only be unnecessarily expensive but would merely postpone the day of separation. In his view 'the only practicable alternatives' were 'for the Ellice Islanders to continue as part of a unitary state with the Gilbert Islands, or to separate completely from them'. He recommended that the British Government formally state that it would take the necessary action to

2. FCO 32/683.
3. FCO 32/683.
4. FCO 32/964.

effect separation provided it was satisfied that the majority Ellice opinion was in favour. He also recommended that there be a clear statement of the economic consequences of separation. In their petitions and in discussion, the Ellice had tended to assume that any division of assets would be made on a fifty-fifty basis, despite the fact that they neither represented fifty percent of the population nor occupied fifty percent of the country. Sir Leslie, who had visited every island, also argued that Ellice opinion would best be tested through the ballot box. To ensure that equal weight be given to the views of Ellice Islanders, wherever they were working, he recommended a referendum. His report, never published, was under discussion at the time of my appointment.[5]

My first task, therefore, was to assess things for myself and propose how we proceed so that a statement could be made. While I had no direct experience of the local situation I had but recently witnessed the tragedy of the Nigerian civil war and shared Sir Leslie's views on the dangers of imposing federal government on peoples with little in common other than a few decades of British colonial rule. Although outwardly everyone seemed to get on with everyone extremely well and there were a number of mixed marriages among the better educated, the Ellice concern that as a minority they could always be outvoted and, once the British referee had withdrawn, might be discriminated against was understandable. Isa Paeniu, an Ellice member of the legislature and an unusually independent minded man, and Henry Naisali, the most senior Ellice civil servant were the only individuals to state forthrightly and publicly that they regarded separation as a nonsense that both races would eventually regret. In doing so they shared the views of Sir Leslie Monson who constantly referred to the 'nonsense of separation' in correspondence with the FCO.

The attitude of the Gilbertese seemed the more important to me. I could sympathise with their annoyance that the Ellice appeared to be held in higher regard than themselves and resentment that this was being picked up by the press. In my first few weeks I often heard the glib and unscientific expatriate comment that the 'Ellice are the more intelligent race'. They were also seen as more reliable and more ambitious. I was familiar with equally prejudiced comment in Nigeria

---

5. The Monson Report can be found in FCO 32/982-985

when expatriates compared Igbo and Yoruba with Hausa, though often with a qualification about the dignity and courtesy of the Hausa. It was noticeable that the Ellice tended to enjoy closer relationships with expatriates, with whom the Ellice were inclined to ingratiate themselves. I was startled when Reuben Uatioa, the Leader of Government Business, suggested that I ask Henry Naisali to teach me Gilbertese. Henry was greatly lauded by the expatriate community and was undoubtedly a fine man doing a good job but I personally found him either somewhat ingratiating or patronising. He was certainly not the teacher for me and I told Reuben so, suggesting some names to him. Reuben told me that they would be too awed to correct me whereas Henry would have no worries on that score! Reading papers in the National Archives I noticed that in personal correspondence with the FCO I was quite often guilty of applying the term 'Uncle Tom' to Ellice elders. I never met a Gilbertese to whom I wanted to apply that epithet.

Reuben, himself, was saddened by the demand for separation but not against it. He was no longer in good health and was, indeed, soon to lose his seat in the House of Assembly.[6] The younger Gilbertese politicians and, in particular, Naboua Ratieta, who acted as leader of government business during Reuben's absence through sickness and was to be the first Chief Minister under the new constitutional arrangements, were anxious to see the Ellice issue settled. It was a distraction from what they saw as the real priorities. The constitutional requirement that two of the ministerial portfolios be held by Ellice Islanders was particularly irritating for Naboua because it limited the extent of his patronage and in the new House bright, able and younger members whom he had had to disappoint were beginning to form an effective opposition. It did not take long for me to be convinced that separation was inevitable and that the sooner it happened the better. Before the end of the year I was able to agree a statement by Her Majesty's Government based on the recommendations of the Monson report that should a referendum indicate a majority of Ellice opinion in favour of separation, action to put separation into effect would be taken.

---

6. He stood for a South Tarawa seat. In Nonouti, his home island, he would not have been defeated. He encouraged Ieremia Tabai to take on his mantle there and was clear in his own mind that he was the one, despite his youth, to lead the country.

This was made formally to the House of Assembly in November 1973. It stated explicitly that, with the exception of a single ship, no assets outside the Ellice Islands would be transferred, that the Ellice would have no claim to phosphate royalties past, present or future and that the territory of the new Ellice colony would be confined to the Ellice Islands. This made it plain that the Revenue Equalisation Reserve Fund, built up from phosphate royalties, would remain undivided and that the Phoenix Islands, which some Ellice believed might prove suitable for settlement, would remain part of the Gilberts. My aim, accepted by the FCO, was to try and ensure that the Gilberts was the stronger for separation and better able to become self-sufficient. The Ellice would inevitably have to rely on grant-in-aid but the objective for the UK should be to have responsibility for one pensioner rather than two.

The political decision made, there followed the challenge and excitement of its implementation. I had been on the fringes of a referendum when one was held, under United Nations auspices, in the mandated territory of the Cameroons soon after Nigerian independence so that I had some idea of what was involved. The logistical difficulties were the most daunting. I proposed a rolling referendum, which could be conducted by a single commissioner, moving from island to island on successive days with opportunities for polling on Tarawa and Ocean Island, both of which islands had a substantial Ellice population, and a postal vote for seamen and others abroad. I had, moreover, identified the man for the job. Eric Bailey, formerly a colonial administrator in Malawi, was just completing a contract as census officer. He had done an excellent job, knew the country well having visited most islands, and understood the logistical problems. The referendum would have many similarities to the census. Eric was willing and London agreed to appoint him.

I proposed that an impartial third party observe the referendum. My first thought was that the Australian High Commissioner in Nauru, who was a regular visitor, might be invited but another much more ambitious idea emerged. It was twenty years after Suez but Professor William Roger Louis, whose knowledge of the documents is without parallel, has only recently commented that, 'For at least the next decade, anti-colonialism – so marked a feature of the debates during the Suez crisis – became not only the dominant characteristic of the United Nations but one of the principles for ever associated with the organisation'.[7] The separation statement had dutifully been sent to the UK Mission to the United Nations in order to fulfil requirements with respect to dependencies. These arose from the UK decision in 1961 to volunteer information about development in dependencies. The Special Committee on Colonialism then established, usually referred to as the 'Committee of 24', had become increasingly difficult, its activities, according to Sir Hilton Poynton, a 'disgraceful example of unwarranted international meddling'.[8] The UK had surrendered membership of the Committee in 1971 but relations were improving and it was decided to invite the Committee of 24, now chaired by Mr Salim of Tanzania, to observe the referendum. General Assembly Resolution 1514, guaranteeing territorial integrity, opposed fragmentation, so it was important internationally to avoid any suggestion that Britain was being devious about the creation of another mini state. The referendum provided an opportunity for a controlled visit with a specific purpose but it was a brave decision. Invitations to visit had been avoided since the unhappy experience surrounding the UN mission to Aden in 1967.

I was flattered that the FCO had sufficient confidence in me to allow the Committee of 24 in and pleased that the international interest would help both Ellice and Gilbertese appreciate that what happened locally did have repercussions elsewhere. Welcoming the UN involvement, I diffidently suggested that it would help if there were to be a Commonwealth element in the party to be chosen. Those who had been through the independence process would better understand the constitutional position we were in and might prove useful contacts for our ministers. I also urged that we tactfully try to avoid the inclusion of people with special dietary needs. Fish and coconuts were the staple foods, roots the only readily available vegetables and pawpaw the only fruit. All Pacific Islanders are hospitable and the remoter the island the greater the hospitality. Our visitors would be feasted and pig is the feast food. They would also be travelling on MS *Nivanga*, a small ship with only two good cabins. If someone had to share I asked that the coin be tossed by the UN rather than by me!

---

7. Wm. Roger Louis, *Ends of British Imperialism*, London I.B. Tauris 2006, p688.

8. CO967/434 quoted in BDEEP Series A Vol 5 *East of Suez and the Commonwealth 1964-1971.*

Meanwhile there had been a major educational programme throughout the Ellice Islands, and among Ellice Islanders living elsewhere, in order to ensure that the conditions for separation were properly understood. The necessary Order-in-Council for the referendum was made and Eric Bailey planned his itinerary and got the postal vote underway ahead of the main referendum which would take place in late August and early September. The UN mission was due to arrive on 21 August. On the 19 August I was still unsure about its composition and, indeed, the full details arrived in the bag that came on the plane with them. Given the limited cuisine the *Nivanga* could provide the inclusion of a Muslim and a Hindu raised my blood pressure somewhat, but driving back from the airport with Mrs Joka Bangura, the Mission Leader, who was to be our house guest, my fears were quickly set aside. She was a charming diplomat from Sierra Leone. We not only had West Africa in common but quite a number of friends because her country, with its early start in Western education, had provided many civil servants elsewhere in the region. The other members of the mission were Mr A.F. Al-Masri from Syria and Mr Dilip Lahiri from India. They were supported by a team of four UN officials, led by Mr Richard Wathen, and were accompanied by Mr Tom Richardson from the UK mission.

It was an enormous help having two Commonwealth representatives. I was able to keep my general briefing short because there was so much shared understanding. I warned them that they must expect a great deal of formality on the Ellice Islands which still had a strong whiff of former times, commenting that when they sang the National Anthem on my arrival I sometimes suspected that it was Queen Victoria we were honouring. That evening we held a reception for the visitors and their hosts, the Council of Ministers and all responsible for the administration of the referendum. The next day the team inspected the arrangements for the postal vote and had lunch at the Marine Training School, an institution enjoying UNDP support.

On their second evening our visitors were subjected to trial by *batere*, two and a half hours of singing and dancing, in which they would be expected to join, in the *maneaba*. It was a mild induction. In the Ellice four to five hours would be the norm. There were Gilbertese and Ellice dancing groups so it was a good opportunity for the mission to get some measure of the cultural differences. Mrs Bangura spoke well about the UN and the objectives of de-colonisation. She was listened to in as near to a respectful silence as the insistent gum clicking of the Gilbertese women and children permitted, but abstract concepts such as colonialism were not easily rendered into the vernacular. Colloquially the country was always referred to as 'the Colony', shorthand for the Gilbert and Ellice Islands Colony, which made it all the more difficult for the translator. Attention was, however, mainly directed towards the fact that she was a woman and her obvious calm competence probably did more for women's liberation and Africa than for de-colonisation and the United Nations. There was another novelty, which, to my shame, I never summoned up the courage to explain. Mrs Bangura wore a wig. It had caused great excitement in Government House when Nei Koi, our housekeeper, had seen the wig residing on a stand while its wearer took a shower. Word spread to the *maneaba* and curiosity and incredulity about our distinguished visitor's hair provided a major distraction.

The next day the party set off in *Nivanga* in a happy and expectant holiday mood. Despite some sea-sickness and the cramped conditions on board, especially noticeable to Mrs Bangura, whose last sea voyage had been across the Atlantic in the *France*, the mission were charmed by their reception as they danced and feasted around the Ellice, Mrs Bangura cheerfully receiving several propositions of marriage. They were, however, disappointed in the rather stereotyped response they got to their questions and disillusioned by the ease with which the Ellice assumed the role of mendicants, pleading their weakness and needs. Although one senior Ellice Islander commented to me that he thought it a great impertinence for 'these people, as though they haven't enough trouble in their own lands, to come at all, let alone to tell the mother country how to run affairs when they were so recently her children themselves'. I was, and remain convinced that the UN visiting mission had usefully exposed our ministers to those whose countries had been through the process of de-colonisation and who understood the significance of imperialism on the international agenda. In their turn the UN mission had had an opportunity to gain a genuine, as opposed to doctrinaire, understanding of the problems of the remaining small and isolated dependencies. I was pleased to learn that the mission applauded what I and colleagues were trying to do and Mr Lahiri, who, in particular, had been extremely well briefed on many issues other than separation, especially the British

Phosphate Commissioners, sent me warm messages long after the event. Tom Richardson, who had been an enormous support for me, generously commented that, 'any built in prejudices against colonial governors as such were quickly dissipated'.[9]

The conduct of the referendum went smoothly and, when completed at the end of September, the count revealed 3799 votes for separation and 293 against. Eric Bailey's own report on the referendum made it clear from discussions in the *manepas* that while the Ellice had voted overwhelmingly for separation they had not voted for the conditions that went with it. There was to be a difficult road ahead. The decision having been taken, however, I believed that the sooner it could be implemented the better and the Chief Minister shared this view. We set 1 January 1976 as the target for final administrative separation in the hope that formal legal separation could be accomplished rather sooner.

I made a statement setting out the next steps to discuss the future constitution and form of administration of an Ellice Islands Colony, questions relating to access to King George V School, the Merchant Marine Training School and the Teachers' Training College, to the future employment of Ellice Islanders currently working in the Gilberts and of those employed elsewhere and to the level of UK aid needed to maintain a separate Ellice Islands Colony.

The next stage was a meeting, held in Tarawa in 1975 with Tony Bullock, Head of the FCO Department, and Garth Pettitt of ODM present at which these issues were discussed. I made sure that I chaired the meeting and kept the initiative, in order that any misunderstandings could be quickly and effectively dealt with and that the language used left no doubt as to its meaning. By this stage it had been agreed that Tom Layng, the Deputy Governor, whom I had known in the Solomon Islands and who, in the interim, had been Chief Secretary in the Falkland Islands, should take on the senior job in the Ellice. An undemanding and self-sufficient bachelor, who had proved himself in lonely and difficult jobs before, Tom was the ideal choice for Commissioner as the post was to be named. He was, therefore, able to undertake virtually all the detailed work of preparation himself, leaving me free to concentrate on the Gilberts and, if necessary, fight the occasional battle with London to keep things moving.

9. FCO 32/1049.

Goodwill all round and the easy working relationship Tom and I had not only between ourselves but with our respective ministers allowed us to secure the formal legal separation on 1 October 1975. The one civil service then continued to work for both the governments until the end of December giving time for the establishment of some essential embryonic government on Funafuti and the transfer of staff. Complete administrative separation took place with effect from 1 January 1976, the start of a new financial year for both governments.[10] The opportunity to look back on the successful conclusion of a difficult and potentially divisive exercise was short lived. The separation of the Gilberts and Ellice had been seized upon by the Banabans to make similar demands for Banaba, or Ocean Island as it was then officially called.

---

10. I then ceased to be responsible for the Ellice Islands although I acted for Tom when he was on leave. The Ellice achieved independence in July 1978 as Tuvalu, their own name.

THE
GILBERT
ISLANDS

CHAPTER TEN
BANABA AND PHOSPHATE

Banaba, or Ocean Island as it was called by Europeans after discovery by the British ship *Ocean* in 1804, lies just below the equator some 250 miles to the west of the Gilbert group. Six miles in circumference, unlike the atolls it rises to some 300 feet. Extremely isolated, subject to prolonged periods of drought and lacking easily accessible landing places Banaba was largely ignored until 1899 when Bertie Ellis, a young employee of the London-based Pacific Islands Company, decided to make routine chemical tests on the Sydney office doorstop. It was believed to be part of a petrified tree that had been brought back, a couple of years previously, from Nauru, Banaba's closest and larger neighbour, 160 miles to the west. It contained 78% phosphate of lime. The scrapings from the guano rich islands of the Pacific typically contained about 30%. Ellis had made an exciting discovery.

Nauru, although some distance from the Marshall and Caroline Islands and south of the equator, had been brought within the recognised German sphere of interest in the Pacific and the Jaluit Gesellschaft had been granted sole rights to mine there. The Pacific Islands Company knew that Banaba, which means 'rock' in Gilbertese, had a similar formation to Nauru and, assuming that the Germans must be aware of the potential of Nauru, determined to acquire Banaba for the British. The Resident Commissioner of the Gilbert and Ellice Islands, William Telfer Campbell, was in Sydney for Christmas. His wife was friendly with the wife of Mr Denson, Office Manager of the Pacific Islands Phosphate Company. Before the end of the year Lord Stanmore, Chairman of the company, had received a cable urging him to persuade the Colonial Office to annex Ocean Island.

The High Commissioner for the Western Pacific was disinclined to increase his already over extended responsibilities but Lord Stanmore, himself a former High Commissioner, was sufficiently encouraged by the Colonial Office to decide that Ellis should be sent to Ocean Island. Arriving on 3 May 1900, Ellis lost no time in signing an agreement with a person whom he assumed was the 'King', giving the Company the sole right to raise and ship rock and alluvial phosphate and erect buildings and jetties as required in return for £50 a year.[1] The Company also undertook not to disturb fruit bearing trees and to purchase coconuts, vegetables and fish. Naïve, simplistic and unfair as the agreement now appears, in the context of the time it was better as a business deal than many others entered into in the course of empire. In the Solomon Islands the beads and mirrors, given a century before in exchange for a substantial grant of land for a plantation, had been carefully unwrapped and arrayed before me to the question 'Will the Government take these in exchange for what was once our land?' In fairness to Ellis, £50 was also the standard annual rental being charged for collection of guano from islands elsewhere in the Pacific.

Ellis was to be associated with Ocean Island and phosphate until his death in 1951. He was always warmly welcomed on his many visits and even honoured with a memorial marking his first landfall. Despite the problems that quickly arose from that first agreement, once it was realised that there was no 'King' and that it was necessary to engage in the identification and marking of large numbers of claims by different landowners, Ellis was never blamed by the Banabans, not even when those problems continued in various forms and complexity year after year - even beyond 25 November 1979, the day the final cargo of phosphate left Banaba, four months after the attainment of Kiribati independence. That the phosphateers arrived on Banaba before the British administration and were still there after we left partly explains why this extremely remote corner of Empire was to claim so much public attention during my time as Governor, providing me with the most frustrating and exhausting experience of my entire career. My reading of the history and the documents suggests that while my predecessors may have avoided the public attention, they were equally frustrated and exhausted.

The British flag was formally raised on 28 September 1901 when the master of HMS *Pylades* read a proclamation claiming sovereignty and placing Ocean Island within the jurisdiction of the Gilbert and Ellice

---

1. Maslyn Williams and Barrie Macdonald, *The Phosphateers*, Melbourne University Press 1985 p31. There is a photograph of the actual agreement between pp38 and 39.

Islands Protectorate (which had been declared in 1882). So encouraged was the Pacific Island Company by what had been found that it decided to concentrate on mining. A chance seaboard encounter resulted in the sale of the company's coconut plantations to William Lever and the formation of a new company, the Pacific Islands Phosphate Company to develop mining on Ocean Island, on Nauru as agents of Jaluit Gelleschaft and on Christmas Island in the Indian Ocean. The tonnage extracted grew year on year as did the value of dividends distributed. The phosphate was shipped mainly to Australia, New Zealand and Japan. Ocean Island grew in importance and in December 1907 the administrative headquarters of the Gilbert and Ellice Islands was moved there from Tarawa in order to take advantage of the better communications and amenities that the company was able to provide.

On the outbreak of war in 1914 Australia's intention to seize German possessions north of the equator was thwarted when Japan, an ally, got there first. Britain patched up relations by proposing that Japan operate north and Australia south of the equator. On the 7 November a small Australian force arrived to take the surrender of Nauru. Knowing that the phosphates shipped by the Pacific Phosphate Company were of the highest grade and that, at a time when 5% was a good dividend, the company was giving investors a return of as much as 25%, Australia's Prime Minister, WM 'Billy' Hughes, anxious both to end German commercial interests in the Pacific and to strengthen Australia's defences against the 'yellow peril', determined that Nauru and Nauru's phosphate should be his when German assets were divided after the war. W.F. Massey, Prime Minister of New Zealand, had also been alerted to the opportunities of securing a stake in Nauru's phosphate.[2] Although the Dominions had clearly established their claims to nationhood on the battlefields of France and the Dardanelles, the armistice was arranged without their being consulted. The same lofty imperial attitude nearly kept them excluded from the Versailles Peace Conference as well. Once at Versailles, however, Hughes fought strongly to secure the German possessions occupied by Australian forces. Heated arguments went on

2. An excellent account of the Australian and the New Zealand rivalry can be found in Barrie Macdonald, *Massey's Imperialism and the Politics of Phosphate*, The Massey Memorial Lecture 1982, Massey University Occasional Paper No 7.

within the British delegation for months on end. A complex series of compromises was needed to take account of the ambitions and rivalries involved, including those between Australia and New Zealand. The result was that Britain, the imperial power, was given the League of Nations Mandate over Nauru with Australia responsible for its administration. The three governments of Britain, Australia and New Zealand agreed to purchase the shares of the Pacific Phosphate Company and vest them in the British Phosphate Commissioners (BPC).

The Nauru Agreement setting out the arrangements for the mandate and establishing the BPC, a Commonwealth quango, was signed on 2 July 1919 by Lloyd-George, Hughes and Massey and subsequently incorporated in acts of parliament in each of the three countries.[3] Each country appointed a commissioner in whom all the titles, rights and interests of the Company were vested. All costs of the administration were to be met from the sale of phosphates, which in due course would also repay the cost of the initial investment by the three governments. Phosphate was to be sold to the United Kingdom and Australia, in proportions of 42% each, and to New Zealand in a proportion of 16%, the proportions in which each had contributed to the costs of acquisition. Once the costs of island administration and the development of mining technology had been provided for, the objective of the non-profit making BPC was the provision of phosphate at the lowest possible f.o.b. price to Australian and New Zealand farmers, the justification being that they in turn were feeding the empire. Freight costs and the availability of phosphate from Morocco meant that in practice the UK seldom imported anything like its quota of phosphate and the British government's interest became largely confined to the Treasury ensuring that payments of interest were received as agreed and to the Colonial Office seeking a substantial contribution to the costs of the administration not only of Ocean Island but of the Gilbert and Ellice Islands, which had been formally annexed on 12 January 1916, the Protectorate becoming a Colony.

The majority of the Pacific Phosphate Company's staff at all levels on Nauru and Ocean Island, as well as in Melbourne, were taken over by the BPC. With the three commissioners operating out of their home countries, the general manager of BPC became the key person in terms of

---

3. In the United Kingdom No 8 of 1918.

operational control and development of the industry. The BPC, like the commercial company before it, was a remarkable example of a tight, well-run, patriarchal family firm. Indeed general management was handed on through three generations of the Gaze family, all of whom grew up in the business. Inevitably, the Australian Commissioner, the closest to the action, tried from time to time to exert undue influence. For many years New Zealand's Commissioner was Albert Ellis, who had begun it all with his analysis of the doorstop and whose hands on experience nobody could match. The UK Commissioner was the most remote but, at a time when Britain was still a leading maritime power, played an important role in ship chartering and building. The role was, however, to become both prominent and onerous in the last years of the phosphate operation as the political focus moved to London when the Banabans petitioned for the separation of Ocean Island from the Colony and sued both Crown and the British Phosphate Commissioners in the Chancery Division of the High Court for compensation.

The UK commissioner by then was Sir Alexander (Nick) Waddell, previously governor of Sarawak. He had a respect for and an understanding of Pacific Islanders forged during the war. A district officer in the Solomons when the Japanese invaded, he was commissioned in the Royal Australian Naval reserve and put ashore on Choiseul as a coast watcher together with Captain Seton. At one time they were the target of a Japanese garrison numbering 4,000. Often moving nightly for weeks on end he owed his life entirely to the loyalty of the Solomon Islanders. With their help he was not only able to radio Japanese fleet movements to the allied command but to rescue and arrange evacuation by submarine of American airmen, 23 in all, who had been shot down.[4] He and I were destined to be on opposite sides of the negotiating table. I was glad to be able to get to know him better after retirement and always regretted the circumstances in which we had first encountered one another.

Quite early on both phosphateers and administrators realised that if the full potential of the phosphate rich islands of Nauru and Banaba was to be realised, then it would be best all round if the indigenous

---

4. He wrote an engaging account of his time as a coast watcher, *The Ancient Order of The Rubber Rafters of Choiseul*, privately circulated. The order comprised coast watchers and rescued airmen and was dedicated to inebriation on the anniversary of each man's rescue.

populations could be re-settled elsewhere. It is easy to be critical of such a view but to the end of the twentieth century there were innumerable re-settlement schemes worldwide in order to facilitate water supplies, large-scale agriculture, forestation and industry. In the 1930s, moreover, concern about overpopulation of the atolls, in part the result of the colonial government prohibiting traditional means of population control such as infanticide, abortion, warfare and forced emigration, had already led to a major re-settlement scheme of Gilbert Islanders on the uninhabited Phoenix Islands, acquired for that specific purpose. At an early stage money was set aside from phosphate revenue to provide for the purchase in due course of an alternative island for the Banabans. In 1940 the Banabans themselves petitioned for a new home somewhere in the Fiji group of islands, at that time the headquarters of the Western Pacific High Commission.

In 1942 Rabi (pronounced Rambi), a fertile island in Fiji and ten times the size of Ocean Island, was purchased. In August that year, however, the Japanese occupied Ocean Island and most Banabans were forcibly evacuated to the Gilbert Islands, to Nauru and to Kusaie in the Carolines. Destruction of the phosphate plant and infrastructure by BPC before evacuation and subsequent American bombing to prevent the Japanese from exporting phosphate left the island and mining infrastructure in need of substantial reconstruction at the end of the war. All the Banaban villages had also been destroyed. The by-passing of non-strategic islands by the allied forces delayed the Japanese surrender until September 1945. It was to take several more months before the Banabans, so widely dispersed by the Japanese, could all finally be collected together and temporarily housed on Tarawa.

The priority, a fair one in a starving world, was to secure resumption of phosphate mining as soon as possible. Repair and replacement of plant and infrastructure was the first priority. It was decided, therefore, to re-settle the Banabans for at least two years on Rabi, which had former plantation accommodation immediately available. They were provided with a re-settlement officer to liaise with the Fiji administration, given a month's food supplies and the equipment and assistance to start gardens. The resumption of mining gave them access to their royalty income. Both the administration and the BPC hoped that once they had realised the superior advantages of fertile Rabi they would, in their own interests, decide to stay there, but if not, after two years there would have been ample time in which to provide for their return to Ocean Island.

In May 1947 Banabans expressed their view on returning to Ocean Island by secret ballot. 318 out of a total of 336 adults over 18 voted. 270, 85%, voted to make Rabi their home.[5] Later, when phosphate extraction was well under way again, a few Banabans did return but the majority stayed on Rabi and no major re-settlement of Ocean Island ever took place. Under Lever Bros management, Rabi had produced between 600 and 1,000 tons of copra annually. It never did again, the regular receipt of royalty income reducing the pressure on the Banabans to become effective farmers of their new island. They even employed as many as 80 Fijians to work for them. They grew casual about fishing and earned a reputation as the 'tin openers of the Pacific', their favourite foods apparently tinned salmon and strawberry jam.[6] A tight community living on their own island they made no attempt to integrate with their Fijian neighbours. When Mr Ted Rowlands MP, an FCO minister, visited Rabi in 1975 he was reminded of refugee camps he had seen in the Middle East and commented that even 'after 30 years of occupation the island still resembled a refugee community. Society there was depressed and lacked dignity. Little development had occurred and the Banabans had not become reconciled to living on Rabi'.[7]

That was the opinion of a European, paying his first visit to the Pacific, who had been bombarded with petitions and parliamentary questions arguing the plight of the Banabans and painting a picture of destitution. A British VSO, Richard Allen, who visited Rabi a year earlier on his way home after time spent on outer islands of the Gilberts, offered a rather different perspective. Writing in the *Atoll Pioneer*[8] he commented that, 'the people seem to be extremely happy in their exile and most things seem to be provided. Foods grow in abundance – cucumbers as big as your forearm, bananas, rye as well as *dalo* and *babai*'. After enthusing

---

5. CO 1043.

6. FCO 32/1167 contains a record of an interview that Mr Rowlands had with Professor Maude on 19th September 1975, in which the latter made this comment.

7. FCO 32/1167.

8. *Atoll Pioneer* No 112, 24th October 1974.

about the quality of the Banaban dance group that had performed at the opening of the Sydney Opera House he also noted that, 'there seem to be more Tabiteaueans here than anyone else. Who said that Tabiteueans will rule the world one day?' Tabiteuea, where he had undertaken his VSO assignment is one of the southern Gilbert Islands.

There is no doubt that judged by Pacific standards the Banabans were well-off but over the years they had suffered considerable moral degradation. The disruption they had experienced would possibly not have been so devastating had they not been able to sit back, their remittance status as a community allowing the luxury to nurse what was a genuine grievance. The earliest agreements about mining had not been contracts between equals. The Banabans had not always been well advised or advised at all. Their tradition of landholding made no provision for the concept of community ownership of mineral rights. There had been major agreements when more land was required for mining in 1931 and 1947. The position after 1947 was that BPC, a non-profit making organisation, mined the phosphate on Ocean island and sold it commercially, the proceeds being divided between the Banaban landowners and the government of the colony, 15% going to the former and 85% to the latter. Banaban resentment at the amount that went to the colony festered and attempts over the years to try and settle Banaban claims were inconclusive. Resentment grew all the more as negotiations led to Nauru, which was a lone island and was not part of a larger country, becoming independent on 31st January 1968. It did so under the outstanding leadership of Hammer DeRoburt, who was to become the country's first president. The Nauru Phosphate Corporation took over from the BPC in June 1970. It was an obvious model for Banaba.

The British government, while always accepting that Banaban ownership of the land was not in dispute, argued that there were considerations affecting decisions about granting independence for small dependent territories, including international obligations, so that no commitment could be made. When the Banabans petitioned the United Nations, the Committee of 24, although critical of the administration of Ocean Island and the phosphate industry did not endorse the Banaban demand for separation but recommended independence for the colony as a whole. Invited to London in 1968 to discuss the division of net proceeds of phosphate revenues the Banabans asked for immediate independence. Their request was firmly rejected by Lord Shepherd who in his statement made the point that Britain adhered to 'the principle that the wishes of the people of the territory must be the main guide to action' and that members of the Gilbert and Ellice Islands House of Representatives had made it clear that they would not agree to the exclusion of Ocean Island now or in the future.[9] In 1970 a further Banaban petition was rejected and it was at this point that the Banabans announced they would pursue their compensation claims in the High Court in London. Two writs were subsequently issued, one against the Crown and one against the British Phosphate Commissioners. Work on the pleadings and discovery of documents was proceeding when Ellice separation gave added impetus to the sovereignty issue.

The racial distinction between the Micronesian Gilbertese and the Polynesian Ellice Islanders had been one of the arguments favouring separation. The Banabans argued that they also were racially different from the Gilbertese. Obviously, prior to the start of the phosphate industry, there would have been little regular traffic between Ocean Island and anywhere else but since 1900 there had been a great deal of traffic and although the Banabans claimed to have had their own language nobody spoke it any longer. Professor Harry Maude at the Australian National University was easily the best-informed outsider about the history of Ocean Island and Banaban culture. He spoke Gilbertese, had been Resident Commissioner and, like Grimble, had made a close anthropological study of the islands.[10] He suggested that the Banabans were as distinct from the Gilbertese as the Cornish were from the English.[11] This analogy was useful because it could be understood in Westminster and I was able to argue that the Banaban claim for separate sovereignty should be seen in the same light as would be Cornish claims for a separate state. There were similar differences between the most northerly and most southerly islands of the Gilberts, still noticeable in the 1970s although by then much less obvious than evidence suggests they might have been in earlier times. A United States mariner, Horatio Hale, visiting in 1840, was, for example, surprised to learn that the fair

---

9. FCO 32/82.

10. See *The Book of Banaba* based on the Maude and Grimble papers and other published works and edited by H.C. and H.E. Maude, Institute of Pacific Studies, USP, Suva 1994.

11. Stated in his interview with Mr Rowlands in September 1975 as recorded in FCO 32/1167.

skinned and better nourished people of Butaritari were of the same race as the much darker and slighter people of Tabiteuea.[12]

Although the first arrivals on Ocean Island were Melanesians coming from what is now Vanuatu, for which there is linguistic and archaeological evidence, the next arrivals were from a small group of Indonesian islands (Te Bongiroro), part of the Moluccas, and ancestors of most of the Gilbertese. Later on Banabans colonised Tamana, one of the smallest and remotest Gilbert Islands while at sometime, probably in the sixteenth century, people, probably Polynesians, left Beru, another of the Gilberts, and settled in Banaba. Over-population, prolonged drought and sometimes war were all reasons why Pacific Islanders, over the centuries, migrated. They had developed ocean-going canoes of considerable sophistication. Because the essential need in small and remote communities was for new bloodstock migrants would often be welcome wherever they made landfall. How many perished on these long ocean voyages we shall never know but remarkable navigational skills were acquired and oral tradition kept alive both information and myth.[13] While remoteness and small numbers encouraged the survival of distinct cultural patterns, it can be argued that there was a sense of Gilbertese homogeneity, including Banaba, long before the British arrived. In the 1870s there was a particularly severe drought on Banaba lasting two years and over a thousand islanders were taken to Honolulu and Tahiti by black-birding ships. Maude says that it was generally thought that there were fewer than 50 islanders still in residence by the end of the drought.

With hindsight it is clear that the British administration failed to make the most of the opportunities offered by the physical need to re-settle the Banabans on Rabi, although little was known at the time about the damaging effects too much aid or unaccustomed access to cash can cause.[14] Another missed opportunity was Nauru's independence when new arrangements

---

12. H. Hale, *US Exploring Expedition, Ethnography and Philogy*, Philadelphia 1846 quoted in Betty Schutz's thesis *Pre-Rabi Banaban Experiences with regard to the phosphate industry of Ocean Island* for the University of the South Pacific, Suva.

13. David Lewis, *We, the Navigators*, Honolulu 1975 is a study of the ancient art of landfinding in the Pacific Ocean.

14. When Hurricane Bebe caused devastation to Funafuti in the Ellice Islands in 1973 an excess of aid resulted in apathy among the people that I witnessed myself. Houses had been built but

for mining on Ocean Island could, perhaps, have been negotiated. It was certainly advocated at the time and favoured by Sir Nick Waddell, the British Commissioner.[15] But it must be remembered, in the context of what was happening in the empire as a whole, indeed in the world, Ocean Island was a very small issue, as, for that matter, were the affairs of the Gilbert and Ellice Islands. The bulk of the empire had long since achieved independence before the Banaban affair became for a while the major skeleton in the colonial cupboard. It then achieved a prominence accentuated by the post-colonial guilt common to politicians of all parties, academe and the media, upon which the Banaban advisers played with considerable skill. However much the Banabans complained about Rabi, residence in Fiji had brought them in easy proximity of lawyers, of whom there were none in the Gilbert and Ellice Islands, and later on to media and public relations advisers. Grenville Jones and George Knapp, partners in External Development Services, employed by the Rabi Council, were to become joint secretaries to the Justice for the Banabans Campaign. Jones and Knapp had previously earned their laurels as public relations advisers to Biafra, breakaway Eastern Nigeria in the late 1960s.

Certainly by the 1970s the Banaban network in Westminster was strong and well informed. Sir Bernard Braine, a Tory backbencher renowned for effective championing of causes, constantly asked questions on behalf of the Banabans. When Labour came to power in 1974, the portrayal of the Banabans as 'the victims of unjust, ruthless and sometimes savage exploitation', to quote a petition presented to the South Pacific Forum, was bound to receive much sympathy from a party strongly opposed to colonialism. Significantly for the Banabans, their former counsel, Lord Ilwyn-Jones, was appointed Lord Chancellor. He had drafted the Banaban petition seeking separation. His wife championed their cause and wrote *Treasure Island* under her pen name, Pearl Binder.[16] Any discussion at the highest level in London was, therefore, better informed than it

---

hinges for doors were lacking. When the hinges arrived instead of hanging the doors, well within the competence of many islanders, a request was made for volunteers from New Zealand to come and do the job. In Nauru royalty income resulted in the highest obesity rate in the world, 80% in both men and women.

15. FCO 32/1167.

16. Pearl Binder, *Treasure Island*, London 1977.

would otherwise have been, increasing pressure on civil servants to find a solution. Political connections may also have ensured greater ministerial attention than a minority in a remote corner of the empire would normally have enjoyed. Miss Joan Lestor MP,[17] the responsible minister in the new Labour administration, was sufficiently impressed by Banaban pleading and the attention it attracted to ask that the possibility of separation be looked at again.

---

17. She was later to become a Patron of the Justice for the Banabans Campaign.

CHAPTER ELEVEN
BATTLING WITH THE BANABANS AND THE BRITISH PHOSPHATE COMMISSIONERS

It was at this point that I became involved. It was difficult to avoid becoming totally immersed in the Banaban story. Records in the British National Archives at Kew related to Banaban affairs far outnumber those devoted to all other aspects of the administration of the colony put together. Banaba soon dominated all my dealings with the Foreign and Commonwealth Office, frequently demanding re-assessment of priorities, delaying constitutional progress and absorbing time that could well have been more profitably allocated. The Banaban cause was taken up by all manner of organisations and individuals and I received a steady stream of resolutions and protests from Churches, Trades' Unions, Student Unions, not only from the United Kingdom but from Australia and New Zealand as well, all of which required attention. Parliamentary and public interest kept on forcing Banaba to the top of the agenda but that was not where either the Gilbertese or I felt it should be. There was a country to be governed and developed and a people to be helped towards independence. Reporting on a visit he paid to us Mr Harry Stanley, Assistant Under Secretary in the FCO, commented that we all seemed to treat the Banaban issue as a 'tiresome distraction'.[1] It was fair comment. The Banabans were far away in Fiji and their leaders always endeavoured to deal with London, which they frequently visited, rather than Tarawa, keeping their distance from the Colony Government. Not once did they address me directly either in person or by letter.

A 50/50 split had been agreed on the phosphate revenue to be derived from new leases acquired in 1973 and there was a faint hope in the FCO that if I could secure agreement for a similar split for the remaining years of the operation all might be well. It was also thought that once mining had come to an end the Gilbertese might be willing to release

1. FO32/1154.

Ocean Island in return for a cash endowment. It certainly seemed to me that without the facilities provided by BPC sustaining a population on the island would no longer be viable. Shipping access depended upon deep ocean moorings that required regular and expensive replacement. Making the journey from a ship, cruising offshore, by tender to a small jetty only partially protected from the swell was never easy, often hazardous and could be delayed or made impossible by bad weather. I also doubted whether Banaban sentiment for their home island would remain strong as younger generations grew up with no experience of living there other than as a token presence for a short period.

I was quickly proved to be wrong. The phosphate price improved significantly in the seventies making the Colony Government more conscious of the contribution it made to the economy and providing the Rabi Council of Leaders with even more money to devote to their cause, increasing the media attention that in turn hardened views on both sides. Like many others I had also assumed that money was at the root of both the Banaban wish for separation and the Gilbertese refusal to break up the colony. Feelings went much deeper. Western culture and experience does not prepare one to appreciate the close, spiritual relationship that all Pacific Islanders have with their land. When generations have barely managed to survive on a minute rock in the midst of a huge ocean the intensity of that relationship is all the greater. 'Largely through the activities of the phosphate industry, the Banabans were drawn into a world system, and the people changed mightily. Yet, although transformed, land and blood remained as two focal points in Banaban culture.'[2] The Banabans remained passionate about their lands although now living 1400 miles away.

The Gilbertese were equally passionate about keeping their boundaries intact. They were one people. They not only rejected the claim of the Rabi Council of Leaders that the Banabans were different but resented it. They were able to demonstrate that many, perhaps even most, Banaban families were linked by marriage to Gilbertese from other islands. Among the 1000 who had gone to Rabi after the war 300 were from islands other than Banaba. Nobody in Tarawa regarded the Banabans as

---

2. Martin Silverman, *Disconcerting Issue*, University of Chicago Press 1971, p5. Silverman's study is essentially anthropological but is also a valuable historical account.

a distinct and separate people, the basis of the argument that if the Ellice could break away, so could they. The Banabans themselves accepted that they were closer to the Gilbertese than to anybody else. It was, as Barrie Macdonald neatly summed it up, a question of whether they were brothers or cousins.[3]

The argument about ethnic affinity continued until independence and beyond. It strengthened the Banaban cause as a small nation that had suffered grievously from colonial exploitation. Sir Bernard Braine MP and many others were certainly convinced, but it was never clear to me how far the Banaban leaders carried their own people in wanting to sever connection with the Gilbertese, considering how many of them were linked to other islands by marriage. I was inclined to accept what Reuben Uatoia and others always maintained that kinship links were strong, as proved by frequent visits in both directions. What mattered was to weather the storm and keep options open. So I made sure that at every opportunity the Gilberts government made it clear that Banaban ownership of their island was not and never would be questioned. As landowners they had a right to participate in the affairs of the Gilberts and at independence they would be offered dual nationality, if Fiji agreed, and a seat in the House of Assembly. These statements of intent and others, such as places at the Marine Training School reserved for Banabans and use by the government of Rabi Holdings, a Banaban owned commercial company in Fiji, as agents were set out as fifteen points by the Chief Minister in June 1975 at a meeting in London with delegates from the Rabi Council of Leaders, chaired by Miss Joan Lestor. Gilbertese ministers got scant recognition for these concessions and at times it became extremely difficult for me to hold them to their promise when the Banabans and their advisers constantly rejected overtures from Tarawa and maintained that the Gilbertese were simply obeying orders from the British government.

I also encouraged the Gilbertese to endeavour to keep in contact with the Banaban leadership that was strongly led by Tito Rotan, a substantial landowner on Ocean Island and a man of outstanding character. Land on Rabi had been distributed on the basis of holdings on Ocean Island so he was also a substantial landowner there. He and his sons, especially in my

---

3. Barrie Macdonald, *Cinderellas of Empire*, Australian National University Press, Canberra 1982 p270.

time Pastor Tebuke Rotan, came to dominate negotiations with the BPC and the government. Tebuke spent much of his time in London and was the main contact with lawyers and PR companies. He recognised the weaknesses in his community and understood the need to provide them with a sense of purpose. Reuben Uatoia, leader of government business when I arrived, considered that he had a reasonable relationship with the Rotan family and was optimistic that a solution could eventually be found. He had been instrumental in securing the 50/50 split of royalties arising from the new mining leases in 1973. Some of the younger Gilbertese were, however, less sanguine and were irritated by what they regarded as Banaban greed. Naboua Ratieta, who became Chief Minister after the introduction of ministerial government in May 1974, was among them. Comments from Lord Brockway, Banaban champion in the House of Lords, about 'the appalling suffering of these people' made absolutely no impact.[4] There was a telling letter in *The Times* from Henry Naisali, by then Minister of Finance in Tuvalu (the former Ellice Islands) and not directly involved, when an *ex-gratia* payment was made at the end of the court cases.[5] He commented that the 'ironies of the situation are almost more than we can bear' pointing out that 'the Banabans, by Pacific standards, are a rich, well off people living in a fertile island . . .' He compared their lot to that of the Tuvaluans, 'to us they seem a very lucky people', noting that UK aid to his country had recently been cut and concluded, 'to those that have, more shall be given and Britain does not want to know about those who really are in need!'

With Ellice separation agreed the argument about territorial integrity could no longer be deployed and the Rabi Council of Leaders launched a major offensive. Early in 1975 Bernard Braine and John Lee, a Labour MP who had been a district officer in the then Gold Coast, were invited to visit Rabi and Ocean Island. When I was informed of the visit by the FCO I indicated that it would be taken amiss if they failed to visit Tarawa as well and we made arrangements to ensure that they able to do so, subsequently being accused of hi-jacking their visit! John Lee had been parted from his luggage for some days by the time he arrived and was pleased to find a host able to lend him clothes that fitted,

---

4. FO 32/1403.

5. *The Times*, February 1977.

I being more his size and shape than Bernard Braine. His colonial service background made him the easier visitor. I tried to ensure that they appreciated that from my perspective as Governor helping the Gilberts towards independence the issue was more complex than the righting of an apparent injustice to the Banabans by the colonial power. We talked about other things and got them interested in the Marine Training School and the fact that it was virtually impossible to secure employment for cadets on British owned ships. I like to think that they left with a better understanding than they had on arrival but the Pacific Dependent Territories Department (PDTD) did not take kindly to having them raise a whole set of issues related to the colony and aid on their return to the UK!

Their visit gave fresh prominence to the Banaban issue that had already put a huge strain on PDTD. In those days a parliamentary question commanded a priority that could bring everything else to a standstill. Poor communications did not help. Telephoning London from Tarawa was not practical. There was a twelve hours time difference, our exchange was not open at night when London was at work and in any case the lines were poor. The diplomatic bag came and went weekly on the same plane so there was always at least a week's delay in response to any query. I had lived with this sort of communication delay throughout my career and thought nothing of it and got used to telegrams being the mainstay of communication. Even telegrams did not always prevent delay. In the FCO people sent off telegrams before 'close of play' on a Friday (Saturday morning in Tarawa) in the hope that replies would be on their desks by Monday morning. I often did not see the telegrams much before then because the week-end had intervened and there was a limit to the amount of traffic our somewhat primitive equipment could handle. There might also be need for several exchanges in cipher at 'personal to governor' level before there was an agreed draft that could be sent *en clair* to the colony government. The result was irritation at one end or the other that a response to some query had taken so long. Any Banaban or Gilbertese or, indeed, academic critical of colonial government, reading papers in the archives might be surprised by the tone of some of my exchanges with the FCO. I sometimes found 'back seat driving' by the PDTD intolerable. For example, when the Gilberts government, with ministers in control, decided to have an independent survey made of the phosphate operation with a view to confirming the size of the remaining deposits and assessing the most economic rate of extraction, the UK helpfully provided technical assistance but, then, instead of keeping well clear, PDTD began to deal directly with the contractors and even insisted that their report be classified as confidential without any consultation. It was exactly how not to deal with the government of a colony on the brink of independence.

The British government was undoubtedly in an unenviable position and PDTD bore the brunt. It carried all the opprobrium about exploitation and colonialism, never easy with a Labour administration in office, yet had to try and broker agreement between the Rabi Council of Leaders and the Gilberts Government, between both and the BPC, between Fiji and the Gilberts, all without upsetting either Australia or New Zealand, partners in the BPC, with their own agendas and playing a much more active role in the Pacific than the UK ever could. PDTD, moreover, was staffed by diplomats, most of whom probably found it an unwelcome interruption of their mainstream career, especially at a time when Empire had become a dirty word and there were exciting new interests such as the European Community. It was not easy for them to accept that I was not their man in Tarawa looking after British interests. My primary duty was to the people of the Gilbert Islands and, as constitutional development progressed, local ministers increasingly called the tune as my position moved towards that of constitutional monarch.

PDTD was, of course, often extremely helpful. I had been reluctant to see resources diverted to counter the Banaban public relations onslaught in London but Tony Bullock, then head of the department, very helpfully put us on to Michael Rice and Associates. One of whom, Maurice Chandler, took us in hand and did the Gilberts proud. After independence he was appointed Consul General and continued to serve them well for many years. His contacts were remarkable and brought home to me one great disadvantage of an overseas career. It was not only all too easy to lose contact with contemporaries from school, university and army as paths diverged and one grew older but all of one's work contacts were made overseas. However well known I might be in Nigeria and the Pacific, I was unknown in London. When I went on leave in the summer of 1975 Maurice organised lunchtime meetings with MPs and the media that I could never have arranged myself to give me an opportunity to explain the Gilberts' view of the issue. There was an excellent response that led to other useful encounters.

Separation was not, of course, the only issue. Understandably, given the terms of original acquisition and the colonial situation, Banabans argued that they had not only been exploited, their island ravaged and themselves forcibly moved but that they were still impoverished. In the High Court, Rotan Tito and other landowners were suing the British Phosphate Commissioners, by name because BPC was not incorporated, for replanting of certain land or damages in lieu, damages for the wrongful removal of phosphate from a certain area and for damages in respect of unauthorised removal of sand. Rotan Tito and the Rabi Council of Leaders were also suing the Attorney General in connection with the compulsory acquisition of 150 acres in 1931 and the voluntary acquisition of two larger areas in 1947. On both occasions the plaintiffs claimed that the Crown stood in a fiduciary position towards them. Compensation was sought to make up for a royalty fixed at a less than proper figure in respect of the 1931 acquisition. In 1947 it was claimed that compensation was due because the Crown had not disclosed that phosphate was being sold at less than its true value to Australia and New Zealand and had failed to provide information about the sums being paid by BPC to the colony government.

The Gilbertese were at one with the Banabans in wanting to see a higher proportion of phosphate revenue remaining in the islands rather subsidise Australian and New Zealand farmers. This conflicted with the Australian and New Zealand objective of obtaining cheap phosphate. Where Banabans and Gilbertese did not agree was over the division of phosphate revenue between them, the Banabans believing that they should have it all. Whatever the actual wealth of the Banabans, to the ill informed outsider the split, understandably, seemed unfair. Few appreciated that while the Banaban 15% was a royalty payment, completely free of tax in both the Gilbert Islands and Fiji, the 85% paid to the colony government was in lieu of all other taxation. BPC paid no company tax, BPC employees paid no income tax and were exempt from all licence fees. No import duties were levied on Ocean Island. The arrangements may once have made sense but with a colony heading for internal self-government and independence it was an unhelpful anomaly. As I pointed out in a despatch proposing a change in legislation, 'although the amount of money involved is small, the principle of an individual employee having the cost of his dog licence debited against the share of net proceeds due to the government is unacceptable and probably unique in taxation arrangements anywhere in the world'.

It was unfortunate to have the precedent set by the taxation arrangements agreed for the country's major industry at a time when the government was promoting joint venture fishing enterprises to fill the gap when phosphate would cease. The taxation arrangements even meant that BPC was not obliged to submit any accounts to the government. With such a system, too, government staff got no experience of examining the accounts of a major enterprise and it was not surprising that there was little understanding of what legitimately constituted costs of production. This situation contributed to the poor relationships between the colony government and BPC that I found on arrival. There were other factors. Whatever might have been the case when it was the colony headquarters, by 1973 Ocean Island was a company island. In nearly every way BPC was a model employer. Staff housing was of a high standard for everyone, as were health and welfare services. BPC provided a store, sports facilities and a cinema. Transport to and from home islands was provided for families as well as for workers. Schools were BPC financed and staffed. BPC supplied power and water. It was a BPC port and the harbourmaster a BPC employee. There was little left for government to do. The district officer, supported by a small police detachment and an occasional visiting magistrate, was insignificant by comparison with the island manager.

I had lived in the mining area of Nigeria so I was used to government taking advantage of company infrastructure, such as electricity supply, and keeping in close contact with a major revenue provider and employer, but I was unprepared for such overwhelming company domination. For example, BPC insisted on keeping Melbourne time not Gilbert Islands' time and the government had to fall in line in order to avoid two time zones on a small island. The schools followed an Australian syllabus, kept to the Australian school terms and were inspected by the Victoria State Department of Education. Health links were also with Australia. There were those on my staff who pointed out that this all made good sense and saved resources. The arrangements had not been so much discussed and agreed as simply fallen into place over time and then been accepted as the norm. As Governor, I still needed BPC's agreement to visit and once there I was behoven to BPC for accommodation. Permission was never withheld and the Island Manager was always hospitable but to me it all shouted 'colonialism', which I was in the business of ending, and on my first visit I sensed that I had slipped back a couple of decades in time. Barrie Macdonald commented, 'From the outset the BPC became a law unto itself, a secretive body intent on preserving its power and privilege. Its overbearing presence became the obsession of more than one Resident Commissioner or Governor who knew that its advice often carried more weight in London than his own. The phosphate industry and those who ran it played a decisive part in shaping policies for the Colony from 1900 until independence.'[6]

My feelings were readily shared by Ted Rowlands, who, accompanied by Nick Larmour, an assistant under-secretary, visited Ocean Island with me in September 1975. Rowlands, on his first ministerial visit, who had been pleased with what he had seen of Tarawa and had much enjoyed the voyage to Ocean Island, was taken aback. He agreed that things could not continue as they had been allowed to do for so long and he and Nick Larmour were to be extremely helpful. His predecessor, Miss Joan Lestor, had not visited and had only met Gilbertese leaders a couple of times as opposed to many encounters with Tebuke Rotan and Banaban advisers. It was a relief to have a helpful and open-minded minister with whom I was able to develop a good personal relationship and an equal blow when he was moved to other duties in the FCO and was replaced by Lord Goronwy-Roberts who never visited and got to know the Banaban lobby much better than ourselves.

In terms of relationships with the BPC it was too late in the day to achieve anything as effective as had been done in Nauru where an indigenous corporation had taken over control of the phosphate industry, contracting services out to BPC as necessary. The Ocean Island phosphate deposits had a finite limit and it seemed almost certain that at current rates of extraction the operation would be wound up about the same time as the Gilbert Islands achieved independence. Given the position taken by the Rabi Council of Leaders and with their strong support in Westminster even unravelling the anomalous tax position

6. ibid p 275.

147

would almost certainly prove impossible but I lobbied hard for some kind of involvement of the Gilberts Government in determining the rate of extraction and other matters, arguing also for Rabi Council representation. I demanded access to BPC accounts. They were laid on the table of the House of Commons but not sent to Tarawa. After Rowlands' visit the FCO supported our efforts to achieve a more adult relationship with BPC and a visit by the UK commissioner and the BPC general manager helped. Unfortunately difficulties in arranging its timing when we only had one flight a week resulted in both the Financial Secretary and Roniti Tewaki, the member whose constituency included Ocean Island, a graduate and a critic of the arrangements, not being able to return in time from meetings elsewhere in the Pacific.

Rowlands had met with BPC in Melbourne and with the Australian British Phosphate Commissioner but getting the latter to see that relationships needed to change was difficult. The Commissioner maintained that BPC had no need to deal with the colony government, that was the job of the UK. He seemed to have the support of his government in that approach. By the mid seventies Ocean Island was a very small part of the total BPC operation. The main interest, particularly for Australia, was the extraction of phosphate from the Indian Ocean Christmas Island. Little change was achieved but in time I did manage to establish regular meetings between BPC and the government that certainly helped to ensure the exchange of accurate information and a better understanding by ministers of the complexities of phosphate mining and marketing. There were, however, still innumerable incidents that hindered rather than helped relationships. For example, the Island Manager, licensee under the liquor ordinance for the BPC store, was summoned for selling liquor to under age youths. There had been a bout of drunken misbehaviour among Banaban visitors who had nothing to do and too much money in their pockets. The police had felt it necessary to act. Of course the Island Manager had not been personally involved but as licensee was responsible in law. He took umbrage but instead of seeking advice from colony officials complained to his General Manager who, in turn, took the matter up with the UK commissioner who got on to the FCO. The first I knew about it was an angry telegram from the FCO. The solution was for the Island Manager to plead guilty in the local magistrate's court (the district officer), where he would have received a caution, and to discipline his store manager. It could have been done quietly. Instead he insisted on being tried before the senior magistrate, who, for other reasons, put the case down for hearing in Tarawa. That increased the annoyance. Sorting out a trivial issue such as this took an immense amount of time and upset an incredibly large number of people, all of whom felt that they had a principle to defend and could not see the larger picture. Tony Bullock complained that I treated BPC as though it were another United Africa Company. I riposted that UAC, at an equivalent stage in political and constitutional development, had been light years ahead in terms of understanding and localisation. I pointed out that, 'phosphate and Ocean Island not only dominate our life but are fundamental to forging the attitudes of our politicians, nearly all of whom have worked for BPC at some time or another.'[7] A prudent BPC would have ensured long since that a local manager had been trained and positioned to take on duties such as that of licensee. Fortunately a change of island manager saw a marked improvement in relations.

As public interest in the Banaban issue increased it was inevitable that Fiji, where they lived, became more involved. The Banabans sought the mediation of Ratu Mara, the Prime Minister. He was an aristocrat of considerable physical presence and of great status within the Pacific. The Gilbertese ministers were prepared to let him chair a meeting but not to mediate. The FCO was at first wary and I warned that whatever came out of the meeting it was likely to involve a solution that would be unacceptable. The UK High Commissioner in Fiji, Stanley Arthur, thought it was important at least to give Ratu Mara the opportunity and I persuaded ministers that it was worth a try and would ensure that Ratu Mara heard their views at first hand. Tarawa hosted the meeting lasting over three days, in October 1975.

I met them all socially but took no part in discussions. The meeting was certainly friendly and to that extent did some good. Ratu Mara proposed that the separation and exploitation issues be dealt with separately. It was agreed that talks about the former should continue. As compensation was being sought through legal action, that matter should be left to the courts. He argued that the Gilbertese were not to blame for the past and that both sides should agree that the return from phosphate

---

7. Letter to Tony Bullock in FCO 32/1208.

in the last years of operation would not be sufficient to secure the future of either the Banabans or the Gilbertese. They should mutually agree on a sum and negotiate with UK, Australia and New Zealand to get it. He warned that they would probably have to settle for 75% of what they asked for. I sent the two resolutions agreed to London:

> *We and the Banabans are concerned for the future well-being of our respective peoples when the phosphate mining on Ocean Island is exhausted in two to three years' time. We also recognise that the beneficiaries have been in the main the partner governments that comprise the British Phosphate Commissioners. We strongly feel that the partner governments have a deep moral obligation towards both of us for our future economic survival as a people. We therefore resolve that negotiations between us and the three partner governments be commenced without further delay to determine the extent by which some satisfactory and amicable solution can be arrived at so that each may properly discharge their respective duties towards us both. We believe that negotiations should be conducted on a government to government basis and should start immediately.*
>
> *The Gilbert Islands Council of Ministers and the Rabi Island Council of Leaders resolve to continue discussing the constitutional relationship of their islands pending the settlement of the question of financial provisions of their future. The form and type of their constitutional relationship will be determined by the financial provisions available from the proceeds of the remaining phosphate resources and any contribution that may be forthcoming from the Countries which have benefited from the exploitation of the phosphate resources over the last 70 years.*[8]

A subsequent meeting, to discuss figures, was arranged. It was to be held in Nauru but not under Ratu Mara's chairmanship. There was a flood of telegrams and letters from the FCO expressing dismay and

---

8. *Atoll Pioneer* No 163 of 16th October 1975.

urging me to steer ministers away from claims for compensation. I replied somewhat intemperately, an indication of the strain that the Banaban issue put us all under:

> *I appreciate that you don't like the result of the Ratu Mara meeting but what else did you expect? These meetings we have encouraged cannot work miracles. For over a year I have pointed out that the common ground between Gilbertese and Banabans is dislike of the BPC and belief in past exploitation, and I have named the price to be paid if both sides are to be satisfied. There is no question of ministers being steered away from thoughts of compensation or assessing the size of the cake at the Nauru meeting this month when Ratu Mara's prompting of the meeting was for this precise purpose. What else can you possibly imagine they might discuss? They are certainly not going to shed tears for the partner governments and agree to drop everything.*

Ratu Mara had produced the very solution the UK government least wanted. It became even less wanted when the Nauru meeting, held in December, produced a figure of 140 million dollars, 80 million for the Banabans and 60 million for the Gilberts. Ratu Mara had commented to me on a social occasion that the 'Pacific way' was 'getting good value for your money without actually spending any'! While the High Commissioner in Suva kept on reminding the FCO that he was under pressure to inform Ratu Mara what decisions had been taken in response to his initiative the months passed by as we all stumbled around looking for some sensible next move. The court cases were over, judgement was expected and we all hoped that it would provide a helpful cue to further negotiations and a settlement.

Other things were also happening, however, and arrangements were going ahead for the achievement of internal self-government. Informal constitutional talks were held in London in July 1976. The Rabi Council of Leaders was deliberately not invited in order to provide the opportunity to explore all options with the Gilberts ministers informally and without the presence of legal advisers. Talks included discussion to confirm and to refine the constitutional provisions, set out previously in the Chief Minister's 15 points, that they were prepared to make for Ocean Island and the Banabans. It was an unusually hot summer and it was extremely unpleasant being cooped up in the Foreign Office. Offered a room when we needed to consult among ourselves, I suggested that we adjourn to St James's Park. Jackets, ties and shoes were quickly discarded as we sat island style under the shade of a plane tree. Tourists and office workers passing by scarcely gave us a glance unaware that a cabinet meeting was taking place! That occasion is one of my fondest memories of my governorship and I still occasionally return to the tree to give it a friendly tap. The outcome of the talks was agreement that internal self-government would be introduced on 1st November. This would mean the replacement of the Financial Secretary with a minister of finance in time for the budget meeting of the legislature in November. At the same time I would relinquish chairmanship of the Council of Ministers in favour of the Chief Minister.

Back in the Pacific, Ratu Mara was becoming increasingly irritated by the lack of progress in reaching any settlement of the Banaban issue. He also felt that he had not been thanked appropriately, namely by a minister, and that rankled. He used the constitutional talks, reported in the press, to complain that the Rabi Council had not been consulted. He was told that internal self-government would have no effect on the status of Ocean Island or the Banabans. Their future would be fully discussed at the Independence Constitutional Conference. Still angry, Ratu Mara said that he would no longer act as a mediator but would in future speak and act on behalf of the Rabi Council. The Council meanwhile had canvassed support from trades unions and succeeded in preventing all aircraft movements out of Fiji to Tarawa for over a month. The unions also interfered with the carrying of diplomatic bags, causing yet more problems with communications. It was a difficult time and a flight carrying Lord Goronwy-Roberts, who intended to make amends for the discourtesy to Ratu Mara, was prevented from landing at Nadi. Ratu Mara flew to Wellington to see him and relations were restored but in the process Ratu Mara urged that self-government be postponed. Keeping Ratu Mara sweet was important for Commonwealth considerations that had nothing to do with the Pacific, possibly at that time in connection with the situation in Southern Rhodesia. It was on this occasion, I suspect, that Ratu Mara informed Lord Goronwy-

Roberts that my removal would resolve the Banaban problem. For the rest of my term of office I was *persona non grata* in Fiji.

Fortunately I had warned the Council of Ministers that given the Rabi Council demand for separation and association with Fiji, combined with their ability to finance protest, there might be problems in connection with the achievement of self-government. Now the Rabi Council lawyers produced a legal opinion arguing that self-government be postponed. HMG's legal advisers countered with a provisional order reserving to me the power to carry out any instructions from the Crown flowing from any order the judge might make following on from the court cases. I was confident that we could live with that and as delay was still a possibility I agreed to an earlier proposal that we stage the process, something I had originally opposed. What really mattered was that a minister of finance, rather than an official, presented the 1977 budget at the November meeting of the legislature. I would also ask the Chief Minister to chair the Council of Ministers, which I could do under the existing constitution because there was no longer a deputy governor. This way it would not matter unduly if the full order came into force some months later. This is what happened but, unfortunately, the telegram announcing the formal postponement of internal self-government explained that this was on Ratu Mara's advice in order to give the Rabi Council more time to consider the proposals. A personal telegram to me from Lord Goronwy-Roberts saying that Ratu Mara 'in effect delivered an ultimatum to me that, if I did not make some move to meet the Banabans over the date of implementation of self-government, he would publicly abandon his efforts to help find a solution' arrived too late for me to urge that Ratu Mara's name be kept out of the announcement.

I now had to face a very angry Council of Ministers. The knowledge that Ratu Mara had played a crucial part in the whole business really annoyed them. In a letter I sent to Tony Bullock on the 20 October I said that 'I have never before seen ministers so united, so talkative and so angry. The Chief Minister was actually shaking with rage during several hours of discussion'. There followed angry debate during the House of Assembly meeting in November on a motion introduced by the Chief Minister expressing deep concern 'that as a result of the intervention of another country Her Majesty's Government has seen fit to delay the operation of the order granting internal self-government . . . ' and seeking an assurance 'that neither the country concerned nor any other body will be allowed to interfere further in the affairs of the Gilbert Islands without the knowledge and consent of the Gilbert Islands Government'.

Reported in the press, this further infuriated Ratu Mara. Meanwhile Tebuke Rotan in London lobbied for changes to be made in the internal self-government order providing for separation of Ocean Island along the lines of Ellice separation. It was back to square one. The two month delay in internal self-government did nothing to bring the parties closer together or to get nearer the 'generally agreed settlement' that was so easily talked about. I had the stickiest weeks of my governorship but played things as though internal self-government was already in force and the letting off of steam in the legislature helped ministers to cool off.

It was during this period, in December 1976, that judgement in the cases was finally given. The action, years in its preparation, had eventually got under way on 8th April 1975. I had been asked if the Attorney General could be available in London. I asked for an estimate of the time involved and was advised 30 days each for two actions. We decided that he should not go unless and until he was required as a witness on a specific point. It was just as well. The cases made legal history by being the longest on record: 106 court days for the one and 100 for the other with an additional 15 days spent on a court visit to Ocean Island. Mr J R Macdonald QC was a month opening on behalf of Rotan Tito. Judgement by the Vice Chancellor, Mr Justice Megarry, took a week to deliver. It was, indeed, as he said, 'litigation on a grand scale'. As it was our Lands Officer, Dick Turpin, had to spend over six months in London, most of the time twiddling his thumbs, bringing to a halt all lands cases because we had nobody to replace him.

Many of the days in court, and I attended a few of them while on leave, were taken up with detail about the various land transactions, jurisdiction against the Crown, arguments about esoteric legal matters such as the meaning of 'trust' and 'beach' and the citing of other cases thought to be relevant. Legally it was clearly fascinating and, no doubt, 'Ocean Island 1' and 'Ocean Island 2', as they came to be known, will in turn be quoted down the ages. But their surfeit of days in court did not meet the expectations of Rotan Tito and his people. Damages claimed against BPC for failure to replant land after mining, for over-mining and for unauthorised removal of sand resulted in only a very modest sum being awarded, $A11,000 in respect of re-planting. It was derisory against the $A1.25 million that had been offered for an out of court settlement. The case against the Crown in respect of its fiduciary position in the 1931 and 1947 mining agreements was dismissed as was the claim that royalties paid to the colony government should have been paid to the Banabans.

The Rabi Council of Leaders could, however, claim a moral victory. The judgement made clear that while the Crown had not been in a fiduciary position it had had governmental obligations that had not been honoured. The 1932 arrangements for fixing the royalty to landowners was severely criticised because it was left to the Resident Commissioner to determine with no process of arbitration and no basis of valuation laid down. The Resident Commissioner at the time was Arthur Grimble and the Vice Chancellor had been outraged by a letter he had written to the Banabans urging them to accept the deal offered by the BPC for the acquisition of further land for mining. The letter, written in 1928, and read out in translation into twentieth century English did indeed sound awful. Grimble wrote not as Resident Commissioner but as their 'long standing friend and father' and warned that they must chose between 'life and death', that if they chose not to sign the agreement the land would 'be compulsorily acquired for the Empire', that 'the limits of the compulsorily acquired lands will not be known' and that they would bring shame on the King. It was this letter that the media took up with such relish.[9]

The Vice Chancellor very fairly stated that he thought the letter out of character and called attention to the circumstances in which it had been written. Grimble was ill, separated from his family and awaiting a long delayed leave in order to try and achieve an agreement. The Vice Chancellor concluded, however, that, 'with every allowance made, it is impossible to read the letter without a sense of outrage'. As a colonial administrator I considered that remark unfair. I could sympathise with Grimble, clearly frustrated after months of tiresome negotiations with the Banabans entirely on his own and without any effective support. I had had many letters over the years exhorting me as 'father' to right some wrong, some written by Nigerians long after their country had achieved

---

9. Law Reports, Chancery Division, 1977, 159-162, 235-237.

independence. Deference was universal in the 1920s and the monarch did then symbolise the Empire. The life and death analogy was also one that would have seemed normal in the more flowery language in which Grimble was writing. He knew the Banabans as nobody else did at that time. He was, I am convinced, simply trying to ensure that they got a better deal than they would do without his support and his language was chosen so that they would understand that. Nobody was less likely to try to do down the Banabans than Grimble. Sadly, Grimble, long since dead, who had written so charmingly about the island people he called 'princes of laughter and friendship and poetry and love', and whose anthropological notes are to this day an important resource for scholarship, became a convenient scapegoat. His *Pattern of Islands* had been a text for 'O' level English Literature for several generations of British school children and must surely have been the most widely read account of colonial administration. He was a fallen idol. It was especially hurtful to his daughter Rosemary who had collected together and illustrated some of his papers.[10]

Judgement was delivered in early December. On the 6th January 1977 BBC Television showed a film entitled *Go Tell It To The Judge*, about the Banaban story. Presented by James Cameron, the well-known journalist, who had already written extensively in favour of the Banaban cause, it made a considerable impact and was widely reported in the press. When the production team passed through Tarawa on their return from Ocean Island we offered every facility, emphasising that there were points of view other than those of the Banabans. When the producer, Jenny Barraclough, came to see me she expressed surprise that she had just been able to walk in and had not been interrogated by a police guard. She obviously subscribed to the usual anti-colonial prejudices of the time. I made sure that she called on the Chief Minister so that he could express the views of his government. Naboua Ratieta was a man of somewhat swarthy appearance. She noticed the sunglasses on his office desk and making an excuse about lighting astutely took him outside for the interview to be filmed. Before going out into the sunlight Naboua put on his sunglasses, making him look very much like the popular concept of a Mafia gangster. I was on leave and able to see the hour-long film. Sylvester tells me that

---

10. Rosemary Grimble, *Migrations, Myths and Magic from the Gilbert Islands*, London Routledge, Kegan Paul 1972.

she has never seen me so angry in our entire married life! I certainly fumed. Grimble was depicted as an absolute ogre. In a reconstruction he was shown dragging away screaming Banabans clutching onto their coconut palms ! It was extremely unfair and one-sided.

Back in Tarawa we produced a small leaflet entitled *Go Tell It To The Judge – But Tell It True*. It pointed out the one-sidedness. The Chief Minister had been given less than thirty seconds in which to explain the views of his government. The film stated that the Banabans had no relationship and no cultural or emotional bonds with the Gilbertese, so the leaflet stated the fact that 152 of the 337 male settlers on Rabi came from islands other than Ocean and that while since 1947 there had been 30 years in which the Banabans and Gilbertese had not shared common experience they still both spoke the same language, danced the same dances and shared the same myths and customs . Fiji had even legislated to allow the Banabans to retain the Gilberts tradition of land tenure on Rabi. The film raised an old chestnut by saying that the government had made Ocean Island a closed district and prevented Banabans from landing there. The order had, in fact, been made as a preliminary to the removal and repatriation of some 200 non-Banaban squatters who had no right to be on Banaban land. The ordinance expressly exempted natives from its provisions. Against the film's portrayal of Ocean Island as 'a sort of Eden' the leaflet quoted Professor Maude's description of it in 1900. It also pointed out the failure of the film to mention the 1947 referendum or to explain that the money received by the government from BPC was in lieu of taxation.

Maurice Chandler ensured that the leaflet, taking less than five minutes to read, received wide distribution in London. How much good it did is hard to say but it clearly upset a few people. The Director-General of the BBC took offence at the imputation that the film had not told the truth and I embarked on a stately correspondence with him, achieving no more than the statement that we would not be able to convince one another. I had watched the one-sidedness of BBC television coverage of the Nigerian civil war (in complete contrast to the fair and impartial reporting by the BBC World Service) and I had good friends at the BBC who I knew were often unhappy with much of the television reporting of the time. Learning that Jenny Barraclough was a Limehouse neighbour of David Owen, who in early 1977 had become Foreign Secretary, I avoided involving the FCO as much as possible.

While on leave in early 1977 I worked hard to persuade people to speak up for the Gilbert Islands. The combined effect of the judgment, or rather the judge's moral condemnation, and the impact of *Go Tell It To The Judge* had, however, lowered morale in the PDTD. Trust between minister and civil servants had been badly damaged and I felt extremely sorry for Harry Stanley and Tony Bullock. Their master was not easy. I always found that Lord Goronwy-Roberts did all the talking, convincing himself that I, who was forcibly silent most of the time, had agreed to his propositions. On one occasion when the Chief Minister and I had been especially summoned to London, Naboua said to me after we had had an hour with the Minister, 'was that really worth a week of our time and many thousand of miles air travel?' When I first saw Lord Goronwy-Roberts on the 7th January I thought that he was ready to hand over Ocean Island lock, stock and barrel to Fiji there and then. A couple of weeks later, however, he was more relaxed and made two statements to me that were reassuring. The first was that the Gilberts would not suffer financially whatever the decision about Ocean Island and the second was that if Ocean Island were to be removed there would a be substantial price on its residual value.

Although there was the possibility of Rotan Tito and the Council of Leaders appealing against the judgement, the opportunity to pull both the sovereignty and compensation issues together and make some substantive offer was now available and Lord Goronwy-Roberts, prompted by a parliamentary question, appointed Richard (Dick) Posnett as a personal emissary to go to the Pacific and sort things out. It was a good move and Dick, who had been in the colonial service in Uganda and Governor of Belize was an excellent choice. Carrying no baggage from previous attempts at finding a solution, he could be seen as genuinely independent. The time was also right. BPC and the partner governments were anxious after the interminable and costly court proceedings for a solution before Gilberts' independence and the end of phosphate mining.

Posnett was soon in the Pacific and during February and March visited all those concerned. He had particularly difficult talks with the Australian and New Zealand partner governments but by April had produced a clear and straightforward report. On the sovereignty issue he recommended that the Banabans have four representatives at the Independence Conference, one from each of the four traditional villages, and on the compensation issue he recommended that the partner governments invest $A7million in a trust fund, the capital of which should be kept intact and the interest devoted to projects of benefit to the Banabans. His report was decisive. On 27th May 1977 David Owen made a statement in the House of Commons. No final decision on Ocean Island would be taken before the pre-independence constitutional conference but the premise was that Ocean Island should remain part of the Gilbert Islands with discussion continuing about additional guarantees and safeguards for the Banabans, which would also be discussed with Ratu Mara. The partner governments were also prepared to make a once and for all *ex-gratia* payment of $A10million to establish a trust fund for the Banabans on condition that there would be no appeals against the High Court judgements and that no further claims would be made on matters arising from past events. This payment was eventually accepted but not until 1981.

Posnett came too late to prevent some unnecessary angst and expenditure on what were really foolhardy ideas. On the Banaban side there was a formal request to Fiji for incorporation of Ocean Island and talk of basing a fishing industry there. There were plans to embark on a replanting scheme, in August 1977 even talk of an 'invasion'. The Gilberts government commissioned Kleinwort Benson, London merchant bankers, to examine the phosphate operation and, persuaded by Geoffrey Pimm, the Attorney General, instructed Lord Goodman to advise on the sovereignty issue.

In March a group of Gilbertese private citizens, concerned at the collapse of good relations and encouraged by Posnett to do so, visited Rabi. Reuben Uatioa was the leader. Tebuke Rotan deliberately absented himself and the visit was inconclusive. Reuben returned sad and disgusted. Through the year discussions revolved around the concept of autonomy and there was genuine goodwill on the side of the Gilbertese. In November a meeting between the government and the Rabi Council of Leaders produced the Bairiki Resolutions[11] that, among other things, proposed a referendum, to be supervised by the United Nations and funded by HMG, of all the islands about the future position of Banaba

---

11. They can be found in a written answer in Hansard of 24th November 1977.

and rehabilitation of Banaba by the partner governments. The Rabi Council of Leaders subsequently declared that the resolutions were a take or leave it package. This was denied by the Gilbert Islands Government, on reflection aware that some of the resolutions went too far, and nothing further was heard of what was the last attempt to find a solution before the independence conference.

One of the problems was that Tebuke Rotan always avoided attending meetings. He argued that he because he was not a member of the Council of Leaders he had no status. In practice, however, he was always the voice of Banaba to the rest of the world, confident and at ease in London and New York. In his report Posnett wrote of Tebuke, 'I conclude that he has by his family position, force of character and outstanding ability imbued his people with his own views to the extent that the two are not easily distinguishable. They are happy to follow him, to accept his advice and to abide by his decisions.' His position of authority was soon to come to an end. In 1978 the Rotan family was ousted from the Rabi Council of Leaders and from Rabi Holdings. The latter had long been mismanaged and was soon to be in the hands of receivers.

My own involvement also came to an end in 1978 when I completed my five year term of office in May. Before leaving I had the privilege of overseeing the pre-independence election and the formation of the new government with Ieremia Tabai elected nationally as Chief Minister. His attitude to the Banabans was more conciliatory than Naboua's and he had not had to experience the humiliation and the bad press that Naboua had suffered at the hands of the Banaban lobby. The Rabi Council of Leaders had representatives at the Independence Conference in November and December 1978.[12] After trying to delay the conference until the following February, despite having had the same notice of the intention to hold it at the end of 1977 as had everyone else, at the opening session, which was attended by the press, they demonstrated by walking out, led by Sir Bernard Braine, one of their advisers before Lord Goronwy-Roberts had even had the chance to open it. They returned, without comment, the same afternoon for discussion of the future of Ocean Island but when on 28th November, no compromise position having been reached, Lord Goronwy-Roberts ruled against separation of

12. Conference briefs are in FCO 32/1460 and the report in FCO 32/1459.

Ocean Island and its association with Fiji, they walked out again and did not return. The Justice for the Banabans Campaign issued a statement repeating the usual inaccuracies relating to the 'sordid and shameful story of the commercial and financial exploitation of the Banabans by successive British Governments.' One new point was made. The Banabans, loyal subjects of the Queen of Fiji, would be forced to sever their links with the Crown on Banaba against their will when the Gilbert Islands became a Republic on independence.

Constitutionally the Banaban legacy left hurdles to overcome. The Labour government by this time lacked a parliamentary majority. It became politically important to try and accommodate the substantial number of parliamentary supporters of the Justice for the Banabans campaign, far more Labour than Conservative members. The Gilberts government was at one stage pressed to accept the terms of a treaty that would have given a quasi-colonial authority to the UK as guardian of Banaban rights on Ocean Island. It was, perhaps, fortunate that the Independence Bill was before the House of Lords when Mr Callaghan offered his resignation on 29th March. After the general election the Conservative government re-assessed the situation, after it had been discussed in private by the parliamentary party, Sir Bernard Braine putting forward the case for the Banabans and Mr Peter Tapsell MP the case for the Gilbert Islands government. The Independence Bill was re-introduced to parliament without any embellishments despite a final appeal to Mrs Thatcher from Ratu Mara.

Independence was finally achieved on 13th July 1979, thanks to the Banabans, a year later than Tuvalu. At first the Banabans made no use of the provisions safeguarding their rights and giving them a seat in the legislature. It was to be many years later, when death or retirement had removed all the principal actors from the scene, before good relations were restored and effective use began to be made of the constitutional provisions. It was a classic story of how unexpected and unaccustomed wealth can so easily destroy the best in people. For the greater part of the twentieth century many profited, directly and indirectly, from Banaba and the Banabans with little thought of the damage being done to the people whose island home had chanced to be a phosphate mine. Resources put into effective resettlement in 1947 might have saved all the subsequent upset and mistrust and the Banabans might have been able to settle happily in Rabi and have contributed effectively to Fiji, in much the way that the Gilbertese communities in the Solomon Islands, unencumbered by wealth, had done.

CHAPTER TWELVE
EXTERNAL AFFAIRS AND SECURITY - THE GOVERNOR'S SCHEDULE

External affairs and security remained reserved subjects until independence. Most of the time neither were significant. External affairs that mattered were mainly regional affairs and rightly the concern of ministers. One important exception was the need to resolve before independence the long-standing question of United States claims to a number of islands. Apart from an occasional scare about Banaban 'invasions' of Ocean Island security only became important domestically prior to independence when the Chief Minister, Naboua Ratieta, decided that he wanted a defence force. In my safe, for my eyes only, was a secret file entitled reinforcement plan. Every second year or so, a junior officer in the Ministry of Defence would visit to discuss and update the contents. There was no military presence of any kind. The police force had an armoury with a hundred .303 rifles which they used for the ceremonial occasions on which they mounted a guard of honour: the Queen's Birthday parade, the opening of the legislature and the High Court sessions. Some of the police were trained to shoot but there was no formal riot squad or armed response team. Were the need to arise the plan was reinforcement by a frigate at fourteen days notice. When one morning we woke up to find a substantial Russian fleet of so-called research vessels anchored in the lagoon I wryly reflected that a frigate at fourteen days notice would not have been of much help. It could only have been useful had some local insurgency taken place that the police were unable to control or if, indeed, the Banabans had accepted armed help, as Tebuke Rotan maintained was on offer, from either Libya or the IRA. As it was we occasionally reinforced the police detachment on Ocean Island as a precaution but it was never needed.

The cold war was still in full swing when the Russians arrived, supposedly to water but no doubt to improve their knowledge of the facilities. The captain of the fleet did not call, as diplomatic protocol demanded, but invited me to lunch. I declined and passed on the invitation to the Chief Minister who was happy to accept. While on board he agreed that crew would be welcome ashore and they came steadily, always in threes, throughout their stay. The problem was that they had no money of any kind. They wanted to barter using tins of condensed milk of which they appeared to have an endless supply. David Harrison, the General Manager of the Co-operative Wholesale Society, Berititala Neeti, the Commissioner of Police and myself agreed an exchange rate, reducing it as the week-end went by and more and more Russians, at least half of whom were women, came ashore. On the Sunday when the family went across to Bikeman for a swim we found a hundred or so Russians enjoying our sandbank, looking somewhat sinister in their wetsuits. They were uncommunicative but that evening after the last tender had returned to the fleet I used Kameang, my launch, to deliver three Russians who, the worse for wear after drinking sour toddy, had been left behind. I was relieved that, fearing the punishment awaiting them, they did not seek asylum!

Alas, we never saw a British naval vessel during my term of office but we entertained two fisheries patrol boats from Papua New Guinea (PNG) and, less willingly, a French warship. At the time the French were very unpopular in the Pacific because of nuclear testing at Moruroa. The PNG navy would, I hoped, persuade ministers that if any defence was needed after independence it should take a maritime form although the costs of that would inevitably have been a stumbling block. Unfortunately Naboua was convinced that he wanted a Gilbert Islands Defence Force. The idea had originated with an expatriate administrative officer, Mark Adkin, who had had a short service commission in the army and hankered for a military career again. Writing some time later Naboua argued that what he wanted was:

> '. . . a disciplined group of people, peace-time soldiers, to undertake projects such as the construction of airfields, which in fact the Royal Engineers built on many of our islands and to help the outer island councils in their various construction programmes.'
> But he also added, 'and, of course a defence force would provide us with an insurance against acts of violence. The Banabans, for example, are not going to go away. Their experience in Fiji

has taught them about demonstrations and the use of protest.
What will we do if they decide to adopt more violent means to
achieve their goals?' [1]

This suggests genuine concern lest the Banabans actually acquired the armed support Tebuke had boasted was available to them but at the time I suspected that he was more aware of the fact that it might be more difficult for indigenous political leadership, should it prove unpopular, to sustain authority with the very limited security available to me and to my predecessors.

Defence was my concern and a reserved subject. It was, however, perfectly reasonable that ministers should consider what they felt might be necessary after independence. I also had no wish to antagonise the Chief Minister. I suggested that he bring a paper to the Council of Ministers. He won the day. I then intervened and said that I thought we ought to have some more expert advice than Mark Adkin could offer and this was agreed. I suggested to the FCO that it would be helpful to have somebody from a smaller Commonwealth country whose approach would not be too grandiose. It was arranged that Colonel Barnes, Military Attaché at the Jamaican High Commission in London should visit. Father of John Barnes, the footballer beginning to make a name for himself in England, he was a charming guest and while, as a professional soldier, he was obviously in support of a defence force his report proposed something along very modest lines.

This had all delayed things for a while but it now became necessary for us to go ahead with planning. My approach was to keep things moving but slowly because I sensed that the Chief Minister did not have much real support at grass roots and even some ministers were beginning to express mild opposition. The next stage was to provide a barracks and training area. Because defence was a reserved subject I was able to make sure that planning at every stage was done in such a way that land and buildings could be converted to some other use if necessary so that expenditure would not be wasted. We also began the slow business of seeking a commanding officer on secondment from the British army to

---

1. Naboua Ratieta, *The First Gilbertese Government in Politics in Kiribati*, University of the South Pacific 1980, p18.

set things up and pull together a training team. Fortunately, we had not got too far before the pre-independence general election took place in February 1978. The defence force became a major election issue as I had hoped it would be and it was clear that Naboua's popularity elsewhere than on Marakei, his home island, was falling. There were also younger and better educated candidates than in the past, a number of them former civil servants. Among them were the much respected Babara Kirata who had been Permanent Secretary in the Ministry of Finance, Taomoti Iuta, who had been the most senior Gilbertese working in the Development Authority, and Ieremia Tabai, graduate of a New Zealand university and a recently appointed accountant. The election for Chief Minister was held nationally, as proposed by the Constitutional Convention, and when the House of Assembly met to put forward not less than three and not more than four candidates for national election these three were among five nominated. Naboua and Roniti Tewaki were the other two. Naboua secured the lowest numbers of votes and so was eliminated. Ieremia Tabai, who was subsequently elected Chief Minister, was opposed to the concept of the defence force and had no difficulty in putting paid to it. Nobody had been recruited and the buildings at the embryo barracks were allocated to the recently formed fisheries department.

Although we never had a call from a British warship, every year we would enjoy a visit by a detachment from the Royal Engineers or the Royal Army Ordnance Corps who would attend to the battle detritus that had accumulated since their last visit. Just occasionally there would be an emergency visit if a large unexploded device had been come across in the course of building work. Tarawa had been a major battlefield and it was quite common, for example, to come across mines on the reef that been exposed after a storm. As always, the military did their work speedily and effectively with complete professionalism. Their presence broke the routine as did the splendid explosion that accompanied the last day of their visit! One year the Royal New Zealand Navy undertook the duty, arriving, alas, not by sea but by air. It was a training exercise for them and they stayed some three weeks throwing an excellent party on their final evening. One of their objectives appeared to be to get the Governor drunk. Fortunately I spotted the tampering with my glass and was able to leave with dignity but I was not very well the next day! The Royal Engineers had over the years done an excellent job that in recent more environmentally enlightened times might not be approved of: blasting passages through the reef to make easier, safer and quicker access to outer islands.[2] Whatever the ecological impact I, as were many others, was always extremely grateful to them every time I crossed a reef. A call for their return was a constant refrain.

External affairs were mainly regional affairs and although technically I was responsible this was clearly an area where it was important that ministers should play their part. When I was Financial Secretary in the Solomons I had attended meetings of the South Pacific Commission (SPC), a body that brought the metropolitan powers and the Pacific countries together. The assistant under-secretary and head of PDTD attended as the UK representatives. As countries started to gain independence the SPC had politically been supplanted by the Pacific Islands Forum. The Forum was established by and for independent Pacific nations. Australia and New Zealand were members but France and the United Kingdom were not. Dependencies were allowed observer status and membership came with internal self-government. Naturally the Chief Minister attended meetings and it was important that he did so in order to meet and get to know his colleagues from other countries. Usefully for the education of those attending meetings, they were held at the capitals of the independent nations. It was rare that overseas travel gave ministers and officials a chance to see anywhere in the region other than Fiji, the communications hub. Almost inevitably, after the Gilberts obtained internal self-government, the Banaban issue resulted in Ratu Mara trying to prevent the Gilberts admission to membership. Fortunately he not only failed but the attempt secured little in the way of publicity.

Although not strictly speaking a matter of external affairs membership of the Asian Development Bank (ADB) had some obvious benefits and it seemed important that the Gilberts join ahead of independence. Having secured entry for the Solomon Islands while there I took the lead. I remembered the problems the bureaucracy associated with an international development bank had caused. The bank's assessment team of six specialist economists had all expected counter-parts and I recalled how the team leader had come to express his indignation that his

---

2. Dan Raschen, *Don't Step on a Stonefish*, London 1993 is an account by a Sapper of the work the Royal Engineers did on the reefs and gives a vivid picture of the islands in the 1960s.

accommodation in the Mendana Hotel was exactly the same as that of the rest of the team. I pointed out that all rooms at the hotel were identical and there was only the one restaurant. Pacific islands did not have the facilities of a metropolitan capital. In the Gilberts we had one recently qualified economist but the assessment team was less demanding. Lessons from the Solomons experience had perhaps been learned. Once admitted to membership, however, sacks of mail arrived by nearly every post. I had them sent to my office. All members were treated alike and the agreement was that tender documents for any ADB financed project would be sent to all members. The specification documents for a major dam could run into hundreds of pages. It proved impossible to prevent the flow of paper flooding into a country without a single engineering contractor of any sort! I used to take a quick look myself to pull out anything that was relevant to our position and the rest was consigned to waste.

There had been a somewhat similar situation with the last census. We had sought and obtained UN assistance that was extremely helpful in all but one aspect. The printed census report had to comply with a standard used internationally. The final result was a report with page after page of columns of zeros because small atolls with a handful of fishermen simply did not have anyone to fit the employment and other categories worth recording in more developed economies. Handling small nations is a dilemma for international agencies. There must be parity of esteem and equality of treatment, but to reap effective benefit from membership a flexible approach to implementation of routine procedures is needed. The census report, for example, could have been more cheaply produced and been far more accessible to those consulting it had the more sophisticated data been confined to one cover sheet for the whole country with a more simplified analysis island to island. It was, after all, dealing with a population of thousands not millions.

Dislike of French policy in the Pacific, which ensured that independence was not on the menu for New Caledonia and other dependencies, was a motive behind the creation of the Forum. France was universally disliked and nuclear testing in the region during the seventies added to the disapproval. This attitude towards France caused the one major external affairs incident during my tenure of office. There had been further nuclear tests in the early part of 1974. When the MV *Coriolis*, a French scientific research ship, sought permission to water at Ocean

Island on 19th July that year, the Council of Ministers saw an opportunity to demonstrate their condemnation of nuclear testing actively rather than passively. They objected to what would normally have been a standard request. I informed the FCO that I had refused permission except in an emergency because I had no wish at that early stage in constitutional development to quarrel with ministers. As *Coriolis* could easily water in the New Hebrides, some three days sailing from Ocean Island, I thought that that would be the end of the matter. Mr Wilson, the Prime Minister, was, however, due to visit Paris in July with a view to improving Britain's terms of membership of the European Community. The FCO, concerned about UK relations with France in these circumstances, asked me to intervene. I explained that the whole Pacific community, including Australia and New Zealand, whose news agencies were setting the pace, were angry about the testing and that ministers did not want to be seen to be out of step or to have their dependent status high-lighted. Pointing out that the port at Ocean was private, owned by BPC, with Australian management, I also warned of the risk of a strike or demonstration on Ocean Island if the ship were to moor. If any incident did occur it would almost certainly attract attention to the Banaban issue.

The FCO accepted my advice and found a sensible formula to put to the French Embassy in London. In Paris, however, the British Embassy was firmly told that Ocean was in a British Colony and it was up to the UK to take a decision and to prevent any incident. Our embassy in Paris, understandably, became anxious lest the affair cause a note of discord on the eve of the Prime Minister's visit. I decided to use my reserve powers and grant permission for watering on condition that nobody was allowed ashore and that nobody was allowed on board except for the purpose of mooring. I reminded the FCO that I could not instruct BPC to moor the ship or to provide water. I commented that further resentment might be provoked from 'the French being the cause of my having to bare my constitutional teeth, something British governors do less readily than French'. *Coriolis* did not show up on 19th July, the actual day Mr Wilson went to Paris. It was just as well because that same day the Australian radio had reported another nuclear test on the 18th July so that a demonstration might well have occurred. Then without any warning *Coriolis* appeared on 2nd August, taking on ten tons of water and leaving within two hours. There were no difficulties. The two week delay suggested to me that she had already watered elsewhere but called nevertheless to make a political point. The incident was not, however, forgotten in Tarawa and quoted right up to the time when self-government was declared.

The most important external affairs matter in my view was the United States claim to the eight Phoenix and six Line Islands. Only Christmas Island in the Lines was inhabited by Gilbertese and of immediate significance. British atomic testing had taken place there and as a result it had substantial infrastructure. The largest atoll in the Pacific, about the size of the Isle of Wight, it had several coconut plantations and the Development Authority was establishing tourism based on excellent deep-sea fishing and bird watching. Canton, in the Phoenix, was also inhabited but as a United States military base. The Gilbertese originally settled there had been resettled in the Solomon Islands. Canton and Enderbury, also in the Phoenix, were formally constituted as a United States and United Kingdom Condominium in 1939 but there had been no British presence there for a long while.

The history of US claims is interesting. American whalers had been active in the Pacific from the eighteenth century but any attempt to acquire islands for the United States was always disavowed or disregarded by the government. When Congress enacted the Guano Act of 1856 it did no more than seek to protect American citizens in the trade. The Act used rather ambiguous phrasing saying that any guano islands occupied 'may, at the discretion of the President of the United States, be considered as appertaining to the United States.' Even when, in the late nineteenth century the Germans and the British, encouraged by Australia and New Zealand, began to take an interest in the acquisition of islands, the United States seemed content to leave matters as they were. The guano deposits had mainly been worked out during the early years of the twentieth century but then a new interest arose as air travel was developed. Seaplanes were used to make the long haul across the Pacific from the US west coast to Australia. Canton in the Phoenix with a placid lagoon at its centre was ideally located for development as a refuelling stop between Honolulu and Sydney. Imperial Airways established a hotel there where passengers could overnight. The Americans realised the potential and in 1939 the Condominium was agreed with an exchange of notes between the Foreign Office and the State Department. It is significant that three of the seven terms of the brief agreement refer to civil aviation and communications. After Pearl Harbour, of course, the value of Canton as a military base was immediately apparent and it remained important in the early stages of the Cold War, although by the seventies advances in technology were beginning to make a base there unnecessary. There was a certain amount of rather pointless secrecy about the US base. The Russians could not have failed to know all about it but we were, for example, required to exclude the base from the census!

The Condominium agreement was due for renewal after fifty years, namely in 1989. I was anxious that decisions were not left until then but were reached before independence not only about the agreement affecting Canton and Enderbury but about all the other claims as well. It seemed wrong to leave a very small and newly independent nation with a potential territorial dispute with the most powerful nation in the world. Initially both the FCO and the State Department were unhelpful, the attitude being that it would be best to 'let sleeping dogs lie'. I, on the other hand, was aware how important fishing rights in both territorial waters and economic zones around the Phoenix and Lines might prove to be. At the time, too, there was considerable speculation about the possibility of mineral exploration on the ocean bed. It was also possible that the infrastructure developed for the base on Canton might enable resettlement of the island, providing a useful safety valve for population pressure.

Nobody was available who had ever visited Canton. We had no means of direct communication and I got the impression that everyone was rather surprised to be reminded of the existence of the Condominium agreement. I decided to visit. Berititala, Commissioner of Police, came with me. Together, both in uniform, I thought we might be able to impress the military command at Canton. Sailing in MV *Teraaka*, the MTS training ship, we were able to visit all the Phoenix Islands. Some were extremely small with limited vegetation, no palm trees and no obvious fresh water. The ecology could be delicately balanced. The islands were important nesting places for seabirds and some of the larger ones for turtles. Ships calling over the years had left rats. Going ashore barefoot I found myself treading carefully to avoid either stepping on booby eggs or rats. The rats ate the eggs that the boobies continued to lay. Boobies look pretty stupid but it was obvious that a balance had been reached that satisfied both parties.

Wading across the lagoon on one of the larger atolls I was attacked by a shoal of black-tip shark, much to the amusement of Berititala, who pointed out that they were attracted by my white legs and not by his. He was a keen fisherman and had brought a circular throwing net with him. At lunchtime with one throw he had a net full of milkfish. The cadets who had rowed us ashore lit a fire, prepared the fish and grilled them. In twenty minutes from start to finish the best fish lunch I had ever had or would ever have again was ready. As we cruised along, lines were overboard all the time and there was a constant supply of good fish on board as well. It was obvious to me that these remote atolls held great promise in terms of fishing opportunities and rights.

It took us some time to establish our credentials when we arrived at Canton. I donned my white uniform, swan feathers and sword. We had to anchor offshore and cadets, in their best uniforms, rowed us in. The Commandant declared himself unaware of the Condominium agreement but took my word for it and we were all entertained to lunch. While Berititala and I were shown some of the facilities the cadets were entertained by television in the canteen. We were there soon after the death of Elvis Presley and the cadets had been entranced by film of his funeral and by programmes re-capping his life. Rowing us back to *Teraaka* I was asked if the Americans could be invited to take over Tarawa! I subsequently paid a visit to the State Department and learned that the Canton base would soon be abandoned having served its purpose. Before I finally left things were beginning to move but it was not until after independence that the United States formally gave up their claims and the Condominium agreement was abrogated.

The Christmas Island infrastructure encouraged the Japanese to establish a down range tracking station there as part of their space programme. It was extremely helpful because the Japanese wanted to be able to change their staff regularly as well as to ensure that they were properly supplied. That guaranteed the viability of regular flights, a necessity if there was to be a future for tourism. For a brief while flights between Tarawa and Christmas Island, using an elderly propeller aircraft, were tried but there was insufficient traffic to make it worthwhile. The easy and quickest route to Christmas was from Honolulu. Travel from Tarawa required a flight to Nadi in Fiji and from there to Honolulu.

A problem with an international flavour arose towards the end of my term of office. We were seeing Gerard and Peter off at the airport on their way back to Britain and school in September 1977 when I noticed Dr Teimone Flood, the Chief Medical Officer, consigning a medical looking flask for despatch. I asked him what it was and he told that he was sending material to the Communicable Diseases Centre in Atlanta for analysis. He thought it possible that there were cases of cholera in the hospital. When he told me that it would be a week or more before he heard the results of the analysis I suggested that we meet later in the morning in my office together with the Minister of Health and the Secretary to the Chief Minister. Teimone explained that there had never been a cholera outbreak in our part of the Pacific so he had to be cautious but from the fuller information he was able to give us at the meeting and because I had complete confidence in his experience and diagnostic skill I decided that we should treat whatever it was as cholera until we knew better. I insisted that we go public immediately both in order to stop its spread and to ensure we obtained everything that might be needed without delay.

The patients he had in the hospital were all Tarawa based and there were no reports of cholera- like symptoms from any of the outer islands. It was a simple matter to forbid all traffic between Tarawa and the outer islands and ensure radio announcements to this effect. The hospital was short of the saline drips and other drugs required. What Teimone needed to do was to be able to discuss the international precautions that had to be taken and the availability of drugs required with the regional World Health Organisation (WHO) officials. The telephone system was not good. Lines were often interrupted and audibility was poor. We decided to use the excellent radio link established for use by the extension services of the University of the South Pacific. It was not secure because anyone could listen in if they had a radio and knew the wavelength in use but we had to take that risk. I also sent a flash telegram to London, copied to the High Commissions in Australia, Fiji and New Zealand.

That afternoon I visited the hospital and met all the patients with suspected cholera. The staff had rigged up coconuts above their beds to provide drips of coconut milk, a completely sterile and vitamin rich fluid to replace the saline drips, the supply of which had already been exhausted. Making my own analysis of the patients I noted that there was not a single civil servant, policeman or student among them. They were all people living on local food, not on store food. Tanoun, my canoe builder and now, out of prison, my fisherman, was among them. We all shared the same mains water supply that had been installed a year or two earlier, supplied from wells in North Tarawa. There were, however, still local wells in use so it was possible that it was these that were contaminated.

All this happened on a Thursday. By Friday things were really buzzing. On the positive side Australia was despatching all the tetracycline we needed to provide prophylactic preventive doses and vaccine for hospital staff. New Zealand was sending an army field hospital and medical supplies by plane on the Saturday. WHO were assembling a team to come to assess the situation and determine the cause of the outbreak, if indeed it was cholera. On the negative side airlines and postal authorities were questioning whether they would continue to handle Tarawa traffic. The Air New Zealand aircraft, flying from Fiji to London and carrying our sons and other UK bound schoolchildren from Tarawa, had been diverted to a remote corner of the airfield on arrival at Honolulu for refuelling. Armed National Guard, wearing masks, had come on board and segregated passengers from Tarawa. They were taken for medical examination. On arrival at their prep school in Wales two days later, the local medical officer of health and his team were waiting to give our sons another health check. It was not until then that the boys learned what was afoot because they had left Tarawa ignorant of any cause to be alarmed.

As soon as the tetracycline supplies had arrived we arranged for the entire population of Tarawa to be dosed. It was not as difficult as it might sound. There was a road from end to end of South Tarawa and everyone lived within a few yards either side of it. Radio announcements told everyone when to assemble and medical teams drove from one end to the other handing out tetracycline that had to be taken on the spot. The whole operation was completed in a day.

By the time the WHO epidemiologists arrived we were pretty certain that it was cholera and they had the equipment to prove that that was so. They were convinced that the water supply must be the cause. Everyone had been warned to boil all drinking water and the mains supply was chlorinated. Local wells were tested and the well in the Catholic Bishop's compound was contaminated. One of the priests had recently returned from a course in the Philippines. Cholera patients seemed to be mainly

Catholic and for a while it looked as though cholera was a Catholic disease that did not affect Protestants! Our own investigations discovered that there had been a Philippines fishing boat in port for repair recently that could have been the source of the epidemic. I pointed out to the epidemiologists that all the patients to date had been people who did not live on store food and that it was common practice for shellfish to be caught and then corralled in shallow water in the lagoon until needed. Reef latrines provided sanitation on the island. Called *kai-nako-tari* in Gilbertese, plank-over-the-sea in English, these were all supposed to be on the ocean side of the atoll but over-population had led to many being erected on the lagoon side as well. These were often only feet away from shellfish corrals. I was assured that the cholera virus could not survive in salt water. Years later browsing in the library of the London School of Hygiene and Tropical Medicine, where I was treasurer, I came across an article about the Tarawa outbreak showing that it had revealed that the virus could indeed survive in shallow salt water. I remain convinced that shellfish rather than water was the initial medium of infection, spreading to wells and the water supply later.

The Minister of Health, Nei Tekerai Russell, was a strong advocate of traditional protocol. On the Saturday morning I went to the airport with her to meet the New Zealand Royal Air Force Hercules bringing in the field hospital team. Dressed in camouflage denims, doctors and nurses jumped out, drips at the ready, as though they expected to find bodies scattered all over the airfield needing attention. A line of pretty island girls, dressed in grass skirts, singing and bearing garlands greeted them. Everyone had to be garlanded before they were allowed into transport to go to the hospital. Once there they were taken to the hospital *maneaba* to be formally welcomed and feasted before being allowed to see a single patient. It was a test of their patience unlikely to be of much military training value! It was, however, a great gesture by New Zealand and with the epidemic under control the team was able to return home two weeks later, having been an immense help. Inter island traffic was also allowed again after two weeks on condition that doses of tetracycline were administered, at police stations, for three days before a journey.

During the epidemic the Island Manager of Ocean Island, where the BPC doctor held nineteenth century views about cholera, had refused to allow any traffic, even mail, from Tarawa. There was nothing the district officer could do about it. The Island Manager was in charge of the port and, on his doctor's advice, he said no. This remained the position over a month or so after the outbreak, which had been completely contained. Under 500 cases had been treated, fatalities numbering 18 in all. There had been a few cases in North Tarawa and on three other outer islands, two of them close to Tarawa. The outbreak had been contained on them all. It seemed that the only way to break the deadlock and get normal communication with Ocean Island going again was for me to travel there in person. Sylvester, Ruth and I duly went along to the police station for three days running and took our tablets to the applause of interested onlookers. On arrival at Ocean Island, the doctor came aboard and begged us not to land. I had to be fairly heavy handed and eventually he agreed, provided that we again took a huge doze of tetracycline! The whole business had been an eye-opener into the unreasonableness and primitive approach of so many as soon as they thought they might be at risk. Cholera is serious but the later half of the twentieth century had the means at its disposal to contain an epidemic effectively. It was relatively easy to do, given a well disciplined and caring people and the very small numbers involved.

The plane that had taken our sons back to school had brought Peter Tapsell MP and his wife, Gabrielle, on a visit. I had been scheduled to attend a dancing festival of one sort or another on Betio on the Saturday the New Zealanders arrived. I asked the Tapsells to deputise on my behalf. They bravely agreed. It was Gabrielle's first visit. By the time I met them again in the evening for dinner both had had enough island dancing to last them a lifetime and then I had to break the news about the reaction to cholera and the possibility that the plane they were due to leave on might not arrive! Fortunately by the time they left sense had prevailed and they were able to get away. Peter was visiting in his capacity as a partner in James Capel, London stockbrokers. His presence was the result of my interfering in matters not strictly within the Governor's schedule but I had been a permanent secretary of a state ministry of finance in Nigeria and Financial Secretary in the Solomon Islands, both jobs where I was managing deficit budgets with nothing to invest. The Colony I now governed was rich in comparison because phosphate revenues provided for a substantial surplus each year. A predecessor had wisely established the Revenue Equalisation Reserve Fund (RERF). Its purpose was to provide income against the day when phosphate was exhausted and the revenue from it might not have been fully replaced from other sources. The fund was managed by the Crown Agents in London in return for a fee. I was discussing the poor performance of the fund with Pat Reardon, the Financial Secretary, with whom I got on well, and I asked how much we were involved in investment decisions. He explained that once a year somebody from the Crown Agents overnighted (it was at the time when we still had a weekly DH Heron flight, arriving one afternoon and leaving the next morning) to discuss the investments but otherwise there was no consultation and he, as FS, played no part in the active management of the portfolio.

We agreed that we should do something about it. Phosphate prices were high and parts of the stock market were doing extremely well. I was about to go on leave and Pat agreed that I should seek advice while in London. Once home I called a good friend in the city, Peter Tapsell. We had been in the army together and had shared a tent for many months in the Egyptian Canal Zone. We lunched and I sought his advice about merchant banks. Peter pointed out that stockbrokers could provide a similar service without the fees we would be paying a merchant bank. James Capel partners were stockbrokers to the Queen and he personally was the partner dealing with the governments and central banks of the new Commonwealth countries. Capel's record was impressive. He doubted if we could do better than entrust them with our investments. He invited me to his office and his colleagues put on an impressive presentation. What particularly appealed to me was their insistence on the need for some of them to visit at least once a year for at least a week to get the measure of our needs and knowledge of the place and people, and on the need for an investment committee to determine investment policy.

On my return Pat Reardon agreed that this looked like being a sensible way forward and he put a paper to the Council of Ministers that was accepted. In no time at all Peter, accompanied by Jim Church, a partner who specialised in government securities, appropriate for what was in essence a trustee account, visited. They were a great success with everyone and were duly appointed. The partnership quickly grew the investments substantially and diversified them effectively, taking note of our Australian dollar currency. It was decided to protect the capital of the RERF and legislation to this end was enacted. The RERF proved its value as an important device years into independence and the capital has not been raided. James Capel offered excellent advice and management. They were also very good at looking after ministers and officials when they were in London, giving them a helpful insight into the world of investment.

Peter was a regular and welcome guest, always happy to join in any activity, sailing with me on one of the trials of Jim Siers' *Taratai*. He occasionally gave me tricky tasks. On one visit he was travelling on to Nauru, where he was to be the guest of President Hammer DeRoburt. He had learned that the President had recently lost turtles from a pool in his garden. A few days before Peter's arrival, he sent me a telegram asking me to have a male and female turtle ready for him to take on to Nauru. Turtles were no longer common on over populated Tarawa and I nearly telegraphed him to suggest that he try Harrods! With help from local friends, however, two turtles were secured although whether there was one of each sex to ensure the future of turtles in Nauru I was never sure. It was only an hour's flight to Nauru and Peter was travelling first class on Air Nauru so we had no difficulty in persuading the crew to let them fly alongside him and, no doubt, share his champagne. Had Nauru followed the Gilberts' example and engaged James Capel and heeded the good advice they would have received, their finances might not have suffered as severely as they were later to do.

It was obvious that Kiribati, as the Gilbert Islands would be known after independence (Gilberts spelt using the local alphabet of thirteen characters that has neither 'g' nor 'l' and 'ti' denotes 's') would not be able to afford high commissions or embassies anywhere. Very sensibly it was decided that the permanent secretary responsible for foreign affairs should be accredited wherever it seemed most useful. I had talked to the Commonwealth Secretary General about the need for the smaller countries that would shortly be joining the Commonwealth to be linked with a larger nation, sharing similar problems and aspirations. They could then be effectively represented at important international conferences, such as those on the Law of the Sea. It would be impossible for tiny states such as Kiribati or Tuvalu to be able to afford the expertise necessary. If the Commonwealth stood for anything, it should come to their aid. While there is an effective Commonwealth technical assistance programme the obstacles to achieving partnerships to assist smaller countries are formidable.

I also privately urged the United Kingdom not to establish a High Commission in Tarawa. Space was at a premium and there really would be little enough for a high commissioner to do. There would come a time when an economy drive would force the closure of small High Commissions and that would be more damaging than never establishing one in the first place. What was needed, was a regular visit from an enlarged High Commission somewhere else in the region. My advice was ignored and it came to pass as I had foreseen, the High Commission being closed in 1999.

Chapter Thirteen

Constitutional Development and the Path to Independence

By the 1970s, well recognised paths had been trodden many times before along which the executive, legislative and judicial institutions in most British dependencies would travel during the transition from colony to sovereign independent state. The usual outcome of this journey in constitutional development was an independence constitution following the Westminster model, retaining the monarchy and the procedures of the Mother of Parliaments for at least an initial period. The Westminster model was an almost inevitable outcome of the process of constitutional development starting from the typical colonial base of executive council, legislative council and judicature. In some dependencies anything other than the Westminster model, complete with mace and Speaker dressed in horsehair wig, would have been viewed as opting for second best. It might even have been seen as an insulting indication that the indigenous population was insufficiently advanced to be able to handle the democratic processes established in Britain. The Westminster model was, moreover, what we British knew, or thought we knew because few of us were aware how much the British constitution continues to evolve and, for my generation, how substantially it would do so in our lifetimes. We relied on a vague knowledge of Bagehot and the availability of a copy of Erskine May to verify parliamentary procedures but were ignorant of the 'hidden wiring' of Britain's unwritten constitution we were trying to emulate.[1]

We were also less aware than we ought to have been that colonial government was in many ways an unsatisfactory training for the Westminster model with its executive responsible to an elected legislature and an opposition providing an alternative government in waiting. Much the greater part of the colonial experience was an inevitable, if unintentional, preparation for a Tudor rather than a constitutional monarchy, and all too

---

1. Peter Hennessy, *The Hidden Wiring*, Victor Gollancz, London 1995.

often in post-colonial states dictatorships and military governments have indeed become the norm. We assumed that apparent consensus was at best a manifestation of benign despotism and would never have expected that fifty years after independence an experienced and respected Nigerian politician would comment, 'An opposition to us is an enemy. If you have a multi-party system, you will end up with glorified tribal organisations as political parties'.[2]

On my arrival the Gilbert Islands had begun to follow the traditional path towards independence, with which I was familiar from Nigerian experience. But I had remained in Nigeria for ten years after independence and in that time had been a participant in the change from dominion status to republic, the failure of the independence constitution, *coups d'etat*, public disorder over constitutional issues and civil war. In the Solomon Islands I had experienced the Governing Council system, favoured in the 1970s after the poor performance of the Westminster model in the new African nations. It drew inspiration from the way committees were used in English local government and had been modelled on the Donoughmore constitution used in Ceylon prior to the transition to independence. As seen in Chapter 2 it had not proved satisfactory in the Solomons. An historian by training, these experiences determined me to try and do better for the Gilberts. As I gained in knowledge and experience I realised how important it would be to seek an independence constitution that suited both scale and culture so that it stood a better chance of survival than had the Westminster model in many former dependencies.

At first, however, my main concern was to keep constitutional development moving and I decided that, as far as I legally could, I would generally act as though we were already at the next constitutional stage. When parliamentary pressure about Banaba forced London, at short notice, to postpone the attainment of internal self-government by two months, I was able to take the pressure off by simply acting as though it had already been granted. Had I not done so, the situation might have become difficult. It was unlikely that the government would have resigned, although some individuals might have done so, but I anticipated

---

2. Alhaji Maitama Sule reported in an interview with Tom Burgis in the Financial Times *Nigeria at 50* supplement published on 30 September 2010. Maitama and I worked together on the 1952 Kano census.

a refusal to co-operate in the formal transaction of government business. The Civil Service would have been put in an impossible position.

Well before that crisis I had progressively shed the Tudor mantle as much as possible. When I arrived I presided in the legislature, the House of Assembly. In addition to the Chief Secretary, Financial Secretary and Attorney General, several heads of department, all expatriates, were members. An elected member was leader of government business and some of his colleagues had a portfolio interest, but no real authority over departmental heads. English was the normal language of business with translation into Gilbertese and Ellice. Elections were due and at the next constitutional stage I was able, in my discretion, to make a number of changes. As soon as I could I identified a local person of standing to preside in my place as Speaker. The heads of department were removed from the legislature and I made sure that Gilbertese became the language of the House with translation into English as necessary. I also made sure that an effective ministerial system was introduced. There were those among my colleagues, often supported by their professional advisers in London, who thought that it was possible to satisfy local demand for recognition with the title of minister and the appointment of a well meaning and usually well-liked expatriate secretary while leaving all executive authority in the hands of expatriate heads of departments. This was a battle that had to be fought time and again in dependencies despite the evidence of what had happened elsewhere. If ministerial government was going to mean anything, heads of departments had to be subordinate to their ministers.

I was conscious that we were planning an independence constitution for the equivalent of the population of a small English town scattered in hamlets between twenty remote islands, with limited resources, and set in an immense ocean. The culture was homogeneous and egalitarian with a premium placed on diffidence. There were no political parties and there was considerable concern about their possible appearance. Custom expected you to take your turn at exercising community responsibility when chosen but never to demand privilege or reward. It was, for example, noticeable at elections that electioneering as we know it in Britain did not take place. In particular, a sitting member standing for re-election would keep a low profile, lest he or she appear too presumptuous. Calling on Reuben Uatioa a couple of days before the 1974 election I expressed surprise that he was not out and about in his constituency. 'Do you want me to lose my seat?' was his response.

The country had acquired the usual colonial executive council and legislature as recently as 1972 when a governor was appointed for the first time and the link with the Western Pacific High Commission severed. So there was little experience upon which to build and my touring had demonstrated that there was considerable tension on the outer islands between the traditional *maneaba*, controlled by the *Unimane*, and the recently introduced elected local government councils. It would have been interesting to theorise about the structure of government that might have emerged by trial and error, and without foreign interference, to suit the unusual environment to which the Gilbertese people had adapted so well but we had to begin from where we were. A programme of education seemed the best way to start. Under the guidance of Professor David Murray of the University of the South Pacific, seminars were arranged to engender confidence that the Gilbertese were perfectly capable of working out what they wanted in a constitution. Professor Murray often reminded participants at the seminars that constitutions were not solely the responsibility of legal boffins; their own people had already fashioned the constitution of the Gilbert Islands Protestant Church. Participation was by invitation and the seminars were an instant success. They gave local leadership an opportunity to appreciate the variety of constitutional options that existed and how they operated with the aim of achieving a better understanding of possible solutions that might better suit local aspirations and circumstances than the Westminster model. Professor Murray prepared a series of papers about aspects of government that were used as discussion documents by participants among themselves and with others. For a wider public, every weekday for four weeks, I made a five-minute evening broadcast explaining in simple terms what independence would mean, why a Constitution was necessary and what matters a Constitution needed to cover.

The usual de-colonisation route, step by step, began with a report of a select committee of the legislature, which would then be debated by the whole house. Negotiation between colonial government and Whitehall would follow, with the final meeting usually taking place in London at Lancaster House, after which legal draftsmen would fine tune the agreed proposals into a constitutional Order-in-Council. Prior to internal self-government and independence, the British government required general elections to be held and these were regarded as referenda in favour of the major constitutional step about to be taken. The whole process could take place without much effective public debate, the majority of the population being little aware of what was afoot other than what was conveyed by slogans such as 'freedom' and 'whiteman go'. The Macpherson Constitution in Nigeria, introduced shortly after my arrival there, had been an exception with widespread consultation and Nigeria was blessed with a lively nationalist press.

I was anxious that the Gilbertese should have a similar chance for an effective airing of options before decisions were reached. The intense interest aroused by Professor Murray's seminars encouraged me to propose a constitutional convention. A formal constitutional convention would be a novelty in a dependency and the Chief Minister was not enthusiastic about departing from the usual routine. Potentially it could be difficult for him and, understandably, he was more concerned with the immediate than the longer-term future. Some expatriate civil servants were also uneasy, worried about the unknown and unsure about where their loyalty lay. But I managed to command support in the Council of Ministers. It was appreciated that without greater involvement of everyone of influence it was unlikely that the country would achieve an independence constitution that drew upon the great strengths of the traditional way of life. For example, there was a generally held hope that the legislature could be seen to be a national extension of the *maneaba*, the meeting house in every community where the elders met, in public, to discuss mutual concerns, where everyone's opinion was respected, where there were no parties and where it was the custom always to achieve consensus.

The Convention, with some 160 members, met for four weeks in April and May 1977.[3] It included the elected members of the House of Assembly, Presidents of Island and Town Councils, representatives from Island and *Unimane* Associations (the elders), Co-operative Societies, the Churches, Unions and Staff Associations, Women's Clubs, local senior civil servants

---

3. Roniti Tewaki, *The Constitutional Convention and the Gilbertese Culture, in Pacific Perspectives* Vol6 No2 1977 gives a good account of how the Convention was regarded locally.

and local managers of the Development Authority. I welcomed them and took no further part. The Speaker of the House of Assembly presided, assisted by Reuben Uatioa, former leader of government business and President of the local council in whose *maneaba* the convention was held. The only expatriate present was Professor Murray. He was on hand throughout to answer questions and explain issues but not to make recommendations.[4] The Convention met in public. No specific matters were formally put to the Convention for discussion but it was guided by a list of questions that had been widely circulated for several months. There were 52 of these, some basic, such as whether membership of the Commonwealth should be sought, others reflecting matters about which concerns had been expressed in recent years, such as whether both political and civil service heads of ministries were necessary and should ministers be appointed or elected. I had drafted the list (see Appendix C) in support of my broadcasts, when asked for some sort of paper that could guide discussion. I had not intended that the list become a formal agenda but some of the *Unimane,* who had used the list in the course of their local discussions insisted that the questions on it and only those questions and in the order they were presented should be discussed. Thus the list of questions became an agenda and to this extent I could fairly be accused of having unduly influenced the outcome.

The Convention produced a short and simple report to assist in drafting constitutional proposals. Thirty paragraphs covered the name of the country, citizenship, the legislature, the executive, the public service, the police, the judiciary; the control and audit of public finance, fundamental human rights and membership of the United Nations. The Convention has been criticised in Kiribati for being 'benevolent manipulation', on the grounds that the list of questions I had provided were leading questions to which 'unsophisticated islanders' reactions' could be anticipated.[5] I can understand that criticism made by Naboua Ratieta. I am less sure that others present would support his contention that 'had it not been

---

4. Professor Murray wrote about the Convention in *Constitutional Instruments in Kiribati and Tuvalu: a Case Study of Impact and Influence,* in (ed) Hiery & Mackenzie, *European Impact and Pacific Influence,* I.B. Tauris London 1997.

5. Naboua Ratieta, *The First Gilbertese Government,* in *Politics in Kiribati,* University of the South Pacific 1980, p20.

for the patience and understanding of the government of the day the Convention would have just been a political fiasco.

The Convention was in some ways a wake-up call to pay attention to the views of outer islands. This was understood by Naboua's successor as Chief Minister and the first President, Ieremia Tabai:

> 'The relative success we have had in governing ourselves since independence is due in large part to the way our basic institutions in government have been functioning. They are similar to those of any other democratic country, but there are differences that reflect our cultural and traditional values. Prior to independence we spent much time and effort working out what form of constitution would be appropriate for Kiribati. These efforts culminated in a Constitutional Conference that was held on South Tarawa and involved prominent I-Kiribati from throughout the country. A number of ideas that we believed were relevant and appropriate to our needs came out of that meeting and were incorporated into the Constitutional Document. One of these is the way the president is elected, which is by popular vote. This is more acceptable to the I-Kiribati way of thinking than a straight Westminster parliamentary system in which the prime minister is simply the leader of the strongest party or coalition. This constitutional procedure helps to make for stability in the overall system of government. Because the people are involved and participate directly in the election of the president, they are more likely to be supportive of the policies of that government.'[6]

It has also been argued that 'the procedure employed was essentially as laid down by Britain' and that the Kiribati constitution had many characteristics of the Westminster model.[7] Inevitably the constitution took into account the form of governance in place which was British in style and of which the Gilbertese had practical working experience.

---

6. Ieremia Tabai, *The First Twelve Years* in Howard Van Trease (ed) *Atoll Politics*, University of the South Pacific 1993.

7. C.J. Lynch, *Three Pacific Constitutions: Comparisons* in The Parliamentarian Vol. LXI No 3 1980.

Its final form was also an Order-in-Council following British legal forms and, in terms of some detail, the drafting precedents of other constitutions which, in law, had been conferred by the United Kingdom. Many of the Convention's key recommendations, however, ignored the Westminster model. A single chamber legislature was favoured, election to which would require the support of more than half of the voters with a system of alternative voting used when a majority was not obtained at the first ballot. The life of the House was set at four years. The decision to reject the first past the post ballot was significant as was the introduction of a member's recall if a majority of voters in his or her constituency so petitioned. The Westminster model of a Speaker who remained a member representing constituents was rejected in favour of a Speaker elected by members but who would not be a member. To meet the exceptional logistical problems of Kiribati, the Convention proposed that the timing of bills and policy proposals should provide an opportunity for members to return to their islands to discuss matters with constituents before final decisions were made. This was typical of the issues that bothered the population on outer islands but was unwelcome to those in office and their civil service advisers who were anxious to despatch business quickly.

Among neighbouring Commonwealth states, Nauru had an executive presidency while Fiji had retained the monarchy. Nauruans were fellow Micronesians and many I-Kiribati worked in Nauru. Micronesia does not have the developed chiefly systems of Polynesia and a colonial governor is a better model for an executive president than for a figurehead governor general. There was concern that an eminent person with little to do other than preside at the occasional ceremony might well be tempted to interfere in matters not the responsibility of a Governor General. On very practical grounds once it was known that the Queen would not provide the cost of a figurehead governor general the Convention recommended that the chief executive combine the functions of head of state and head of government. While some expatriates were aggrieved at the loss of the monarchy I came across no evidence that it was an issue of much concern to the Gilbertese. It was, indeed, unreasonable to expect people without a chiefly tradition of their own to sustain loyalty to a monarchy thousands of miles away on the other side of the world, however great the pleasure shown when the Prince of Wales visited in

1970. The Queen, as Head of the Commonwealth, provided sufficient continuing attachment. In fact, by that stage in the dissolution of empire, the Palace had intimated that Her Majesty would rather not be head of state in smaller states, although I do not recollect that I was aware of that at the time. I do recall in my first months, however, when talking about the future with the then head of PDTD, that in response to my comment it would be best if they opted for a presidency, he commented 'the Palace would never take it'. Both the Solomons and Tuvalu retained the monarchy in their independence constitutions.

The Convention recommended that the president be elected nationally from among members of the legislature immediately after a general election, again a major departure from the Westminster model. Some of those in office would have preferred the easy option of election from within the legislature but the feeling was strong that the nation as a whole should have the opportunity to choose its leader. The legislature would be required to put forward not less than three and not more than four candidates. There were no political parties but there were two main churches, which to some extent reflected geography with Catholic islands in the north and Protestant islands in the south. The provision was a prudent endeavour both to avoid there being one candidate from each denomination or there being too many candidates. Once elected, if the president came from a single member constituency, the Convention, following the same lines as it did with the speaker, proposed an immediate by-election so that constituents felt they had a member who could represent them effectively, if necessary by criticising the government. The chief executive was, accordingly, exempt from the recall provision but could be removed from office by a vote of no confidence in the legislature, a provision that has subsequently been used.

The President's term of office was limited to two terms. This was helpful to younger presidents because they could leave office without being seen as a failure and embark on another career. Ieremia Tabai was only 29 when elected. The Westminster model was followed in respect of the appointment by the President of ministers with departmental responsibilities from among members of the legislature.

After the Convention had met, the usual procedure was followed with the Convention's recommendations forming the basis of the report made by a select committee of the House of Assembly. Political reaction to the

Convention had been so favourable that the government appreciated that it would be imprudent to try to go counter to the bulk of the recommendations made. The FCO was remarkably tolerant of the whole business. The Banaban issue and the problems it caused in London was always their prime concern. The constitutional convention had been my initiative and its success was such that nobody sought to argue against any of its recommendations.

Some of the Convention's proposals were introduced before the pre-independence election held on 1st February 1978. A constitutional amendment increased the number of elected members from 21 to 35, for the first time making every one of the twenty inhabited islands a constituency as well as providing for more than one member in the more heavily populated constituencies. An electoral law provided that to be elected a member must have an overall majority of the votes cast and in 15 constituencies a second election had to be held a week later. When the newly elected House met its first task was to decide whether or not to bring into force a constitutional amendment providing for the national election of the Chief Minister. It was unanimously decided to do so, members showing their commitment to the moral authority of the Convention and their support for a nationally elected head of government.

The Independence Constitution was finally drafted in London in the form of an Order-in-Council, the British government accepting the provisions for Kiribati to become a republic, for national elections for the president, for alternative voting systems and for the principle of recall.[8] I had hoped that we could finish up with a fairly simple and short constitution such as Nauru had in the vernacular. The final drafting took place after I was replaced as Governor in May 1978 and in the event it was helpful for the government to take advantage of the legal draftsmen in the FCO but the final Order was much more elaborate than had ever been intended. Fortunately, Professor Murray was still able to advise the government, providing important continuity from before the Constitutional Convention. Inevitably the Banaban issue dominated the final constitutional conference in London. Provision was made for Banaban representation in the legislature, at the time not wanted by them and at the time reluctantly agreed by some in Tarawa.

---

8. Kiribati Independence Order (Statutory Instruments 1979, No 719).

Initially it was not taken up but many years later proved its value when a younger generation of Banaban leadership was ready to enter formally into the relationship that had always existed informally. The Banaban issue also dominated the final debate in the House of Commons and, indeed, resulted in the Gilbert Islands Independence Bill, then before the House of Lords becoming a casualty of Mr Callaghan's resignation in 1979. The bill was re-introduced in the new parliament. Because there were Conservative members opposed to Gilbert Islands independence, without provision for Banaban separation, there were further delays. Mrs Thatcher, the new Prime Minister, did not want to introduce a government measure that would call attention to party indiscipline in the first weeks of her administration. The difficult passage of the bill can be measured by the many inches of its report in Hansard, in contrast to the short and easy passages of bills introducing independence for much larger and more important dependencies.

The Independence Constitution survives. More important than its content, the people of Kiribati felt that they had been involved effectively in its drafting. They have owned it and they have cherished it. I was honoured and humbled to be awarded *Ana Tokabeti Kiribati* by the President in recognition of the part I had played in the formulation of the Constitution on the thirtieth anniversary of Independence in July 2009.

The grandest arrival of all : coming ashore on Vaitupu in the Ellice Islands

Gilbertese girls ready
for the dance

Male dancer in a
Tabiteauea maneba

Welcomed on arrival at Bonriki Airport by Reuben Uatoia
- Leader of Government Business, and his wife, Nei Marie

Government House, Tarawa - our home for five years

The family in the garden of Government House soon after our arrival

GH staff with Ruth :
Nei Koi - housekeeper
Tatake - cook
Nei Amata - laundress

Toddy cutter

Tonoun building my canoe in Bairiki Prison

My canoe sailing - Baenete at the helm and
Baireti crewing with a visitor, Anna Craven

Saluting the Royal Standard at the Queen's Birthday Parade

Butaritari Brass Band

Inter-island shipping in Betio Harbour

Arriving on Maiana with the Australian High Commissioner, 'Salty' Sellars

A fine maneaba, village meeting house, on Tabiteuea

Outside accomodation
prepared for me on tour with
village dog in attendance

On a fishing trip and wearing
the traditional fisherman's
pandanus leaf hat

Mv Teraaka - the Marine Training School ship

Jim Siers ocean-going canoe Taratai
- ready to sail for New Zealand

The United Nations observers on arrival : Mrs Joka Bangura, Mr
Al-Masri and Mr Dilip Lahiri - I am next to Mrs Bangura and
Naboua Ratieta, Chief Minister is at the end on her left

Mrs Joka Bangura with Sylvester, Peter and Ruth

The Gilbert Islands House of Assembly after the 1958 election -
Ieremia Tabai, the new Chief Minister and first President after independence, is on my right

Phosphate being loaded at Banaba (Ocean Island)

Banaba (Ocean Island) landscape after phosphate mining

Tom Layng, HM Commissioner for Tuvalu, being carried ashore

Our final farewell at Bonriki Airport seen off by ministers with cadets
from the Marine Training School singing us 'sabo' - farewell

Epilogue
REFLECTIONS

Attitudes to empire have changed hugely since my decision to join the Colonial Service and continue to change. The only criticism I faced in 1948 was from fellow undergraduates who were less concerned with empire than with the Civil Service. After my retirement from the Overseas Service and my move into university administration, my son Gerard, by then a teenager, was anxious lest his classmates learn that I had once been a Colonial Governor. Post-colonial guilt was probably at its most noticeable in the eighties and, with regard to the Colonial Service, ridicule not far behind. But by 1999, when some of us organised a commemorative service in Westminster Abbey to mark the end of the Overseas Service, graced by the presence of the Queen, and followed by a good party spread over no fewer than three royal palaces, the event attracted hardly any media attention at all. Those final years of the twentieth century saw the publication of the excellent Oxford History of the British Empire and in 2002 the Museum of British Empire and Commonwealth was opened to considerable acclaim. Empire is now essentially a matter of history, but a history about which many still feel uncomfortable and in which the word 'exploitation' plays a major role.

How could I have wanted to be part of it? When I was appointed in 1950, I believed I was doing the right thing by helping the colonial empire follow the Indian empire into independence, a major world event of my undergraduate years. It did not occur to me then that in later life I might be regarded with suspicion, on occasions with distaste, as an imperialist and be assumed to hold all manner of prejudices – not so much in the countries where I served but in Britain. My study of history has confirmed the instinct I believe we all share; that no human being is ever willingly subject to another, even if circumstances make it inevitable. The British Empire, right or wrong, and however acquired with whatever motivation, was a fact, as had been and still are other empires, but its time was over. The earlier empire of settlement had long since moved on, the Indian empire of rule had shown that imperial shackles could be shed and African independence was an aspiration I could readily share. The clearly stated objective of the post-war Labour Government to 'guide the colonial territories to responsible self-government within the Commonwealth' was one I wholeheartedly supported. I did not question what that statement actually meant to those in power. Had I been told that 'the British aimed to control their own destiny, presiding if possible over the rebirth of the Imperial system rather than its dissolution'[1] I suspect that I would have thought in terms of a self-governing Commonwealth sharing values and defence obligations, and offering preferential trading terms. In that I would not have seen a conflict of interest. The Commonwealth bond had been greatly strengthened by the war. The United Nations was still in its infancy and untried. While United States economic and military power was evident, it was not until after Suez that US world political domination was really brought home. To that extent Britain's role as leader of the Commonwealth and still a significant world power was something I took for granted. I certainly felt no guilt about it.

There were, of course, other, more dominant factors involved as, like any young man, I considered the options open to me in my final year at university. In the 1940s we thought in terms of lifetime careers. Youthful exposure to Kipling, Baden-Powell and Arthur Ransome encouraged me to look for something active, outdoor, adventurous and fulfilling. The Colonial Service offered that as well as opportunities for responsibility and travel that I did not see as part of any career available to me in England. In February 1951 the *Sunday Express* even had an item headlined 'Sanders of the River: Still the Best Job for a British Boy'.[2] Besides, I had grown up with empire, so it seemed a natural thing to do. My father had worked in both Nigeria and Tanganyika in Posts and Telegraphs. He had been killed before I was seven and I only ever met him once, when he was on leave and I was five, but there were photographs, the seaside bungalow where we lived was named *Sai Anjima*, Hausa for 'until we meet again', our family language included a few words of Swahili because my elder siblings had been born in Dar-es-Salaam, and it was

---

1. Wm. Roger Louis, *The Dissolution of the British Empire* in Vol IV of the Oxford History of the British Empire. There could be no better succinct analysis of the end of empire.

2. Quoted in Anthony Kirk-Greene, *The Colonial Service in the Novel* in (ed) John Smith, *Administering Empire*, University of London Press, 1999.

there that my cherished Post Office Savings Account had been opened. (An aspect and advantage of empire to the individual few will recall!) As a schoolboy I had regularly visited the Imperial Institute in South Kensington and felt drawn by the dioramas depicting ways of life, strange and yet familiar. On our mother's side we came from farming stock and my elder brother, after reading agriculture at university, had joined the Colonial Agricultural Service.

By my teens I had read sufficient to know that it was colonial administration that appealed. I was unaware then what the statistics show: that recruitment to the administrative service was mainly from a background of public school, Oxbridge and the Church of England. I enjoyed none of these labels but was not lacking in self-confidence. After graduation in 1948 I ignored advice from the University of London Appointments Board suggesting that the Education Service should be my aim, Administration being the reserve of Oxbridge candidates. Interviewed at the Colonial Office I was less directly given the same message by being urged to undergo National Service usefully in the Education Corps. I made sure that I gained a commission in an infantry regiment.

The training on the Colonial Service Probationers' Course at Oxford (the Devonshire 'A' Course) did not appear to have a hidden agenda. It was designed to prepare us for the particular country to which we were posted in the context of current political development. Even Lugard, whose attitudes to race and language belonged to an earlier age and who, understandably, these days gets a bad press,[3] had coined the dictum that 'good government is no substitute for self-government'. To that I could subscribe, however dated and comic I, and my contemporaries, later found some of the instructions in Lugard's *Political Memoranda*, occasionally collecting dust on a shelf in a district office, but certainly no part of our course. When talking of empire it is important to remember how much our own society in Britain had moved on in the fifty years between the raising of the flag in parts of Africa and when I joined the Colonial Service. There had been dramatic social change after the First World War and by the end of the Second there was little nostalgia left for

---

3. Olufemi Taiwo, *How Colonialism Preempted Modernity in Africa*, Indiana University Press, Bloomington 2010 is strongly and refreshingly critical of Lugard.

the remnants of an earlier age that could still be glimpsed in the twenties and thirties. My generation, maturing in the forties, was particularly scornful of Victorian and Edwardian attitudes.

Historians are inclined to dismiss the concept of progress from Colony to Dominion as a myth, even if it sometimes has to be conceded that there may have been sufficient good practice and dedicated colonial administrators to keep the myth alive.[4] The fact is that I always assumed that my career would be in de-colonisation. That played a part in why I chose it, a decision I have never regretted however much the mood of public opinion has changed, and that is why, when I had completed my commission as a colonial governor I declined the offer of an appointment in Hong Kong, where independence was not on the agenda. My first night in Nigeria, wheeled in before Sir John Macpherson, the Governor, at a reception for new arrivals, I was asked how long I thought I had. I replied a certain five years, a possible ten and a lucky fifteen. Sir John assured me that I had a full career ahead of me, which indeed I did, but half of my eighteen years in Nigeria were serving the independent country, and I then had the privilege of helping three other dependencies to achieve Independence in the Western Pacific, the topic of this book.

We cannot avoid being the product of our age and I like to think that my generation was well prepared for the challenge of de-colonisation. We had grown up in the shadow of the Great War in which our fathers and uncles had served, our families had felt the affect of the great depression and we were directly involved in the Second World War. The 'never again' factor applied not only to our own society but to the Empire as well. We had a unique opportunity to address past wrongs by helping to bring the dependencies into the wider world as viable, independent states, hopefully compressing into decades the trial and error of the centuries our own society had experienced. We made many mistakes and were far too optimistic about what could be achieved in the time and with the resources available. It is easy now to blame those of us in the Colonial Service for much that has since gone wrong in former colonies but unfair to question our intentions or commitment. Although it is not my place to say it, I believe that

---

4. Bernard Porter, *The Absent-minded Imperialists*, Oxford University Press 2004, p280.

the latter day Colonial Service would have taken for granted the seven principles of public life listed in Lord Nolan's report.[5]

With hindsight I accept that the concept of a 23 year old Englishman, as I was when I first arrived in Nigeria, being sent out to 'rule' thousands of Africans in an area larger than an English county seems ludicrous. In practice, of course, I wasn't 'ruling'. I was doing little more than showing the flag and, as best I could, making sure that the indigenous systems of governance functioned. I was also learning about the country and its peoples. And they had the chance to teach me what I needed to know if I was to be acceptable to them and be of use in the future. For people living at subsistence level and before the era of literacy and easy communication the issue of who ruled them beyond their immediate village community neither made much difference nor mattered all that much. One master was usually as bad as another and best avoided. In Northern Nigeria as late as the 1950s there were many communities hardly aware of British colonial rule, by then in its last decade. Government in person was the Village Head and, perhaps by reputation but rarely in the flesh, the District Head. So there was never any question of my feeling guilt about being a 'ruler'. Equally, when frustrated by extreme incompetence or truculence I chalked it up as fair pay back, reminding myself of our part in the slave trade and the easy, and in earlier times common, racial arrogance of many Europeans towards Africans.

At Oxford on the Administrative Service course, my understanding of what lay ahead was reinforced by having Africans as fellow students, by the occasional talk we had from African nationalist politicians and by access to the outspoken West African nationalist press. I was struck by how Dr Francis Ibiam, a doctor working in a mission hospital, a leading nationalist and before long to be appointed the first Nigerian Governor of Eastern Nigeria, defined our role as stewardship. He gently reminded us that there was more than one view about how the present position had been reached but the district officer was a fact of colonial life, doing a job that needed doing and needed doing well. The district officer must understand that he was transitory, trusted to look after things as best as he could until the time came for local people to take over. I have never forgotten that talk, the most useful hour of the whole course. It

---

5. *Standards in Public Life: First Report* p 14 , quoted in Peter Hennessy, *The Hidden Wiring*.

helped me to begin to appreciate how much I would need to learn from the Africans with whom I would be working. It was the first glimmer of something that was to grow stronger as my career progressed, an appreciation that I was engaged in a two-way process with as much to gain as to give, a process in which both parties were equal.

I was lucky that my upbringing had unconsciously prepared me for this approach to what I was embarking upon. My boyhood had, after all, been in an age when Africans were usually referred to as 'natives' and when anti-Semitism was widespread. We were exposed to crude racist propaganda about the Japanese during the war and I had witnessed racial segregation within the United States forces stationed in Britain. I had learned to accept that this was how things were but not how they should be or had to be. The three dominant elements in my formation were my schooling, scouting and National Service. My London Catholic grammar school was unusually multi-national for the 1930s. A Spanish friend was strongly critical of Franco and I viewed the Spanish Civil War, my first conscious interest in international politics, more objectively than I might otherwise have done. There were refugees from Austria and Czechoslavakia and an English friend, brought up in Italy, all with first hand knowledge of fascist regimes. There were Irish boys who, as the war drew closer and then began, became more aggressively anti-English, a few in the dark days of 1940 even relishing the thought of British defeat as just desert for our imperial record in Ireland. That taught me that when other peoples have different points of view they usually do so with good reason. The fun I got from scouting as a boy would probably now be seen as evidence of patriotism. Maybe; and I spent the school holidays in the summer of 1940, as the Battle of Britain was fought overhead, making fire brooms with which to protect the harvest, but the international brotherhood of scouting was for me part of the appeal.

In the army I came into contact with young men who had not only had a different childhood to my own but with whom there were not the links that attendance at a grammar school implied. There were some who, although far from being illiterate, had never had the need to write a letter. Spotted as 'being handy with a pencil' on my first Sunday afternoon in uniform I found myself writing letters to the girl friends of fellow recruits whose beds were near mine. There were also public school boys. I began to distinguish between those who felt they were a cut above the rest of us, usually from the least significant schools, and those who mixed easily. At Officer Cadet Training Unit I met sons of ancient and aristocratic families. Destined for the Brigade of Guards it was unlikely that any of them would rub shoulders with me again but I enjoyed their wit, their disdain for military idiocies and their invariably good manners. Having grown up without a father and having spent my teen years in wartime I had plenty to learn. I had never been to even a minor league football match. I had never played darts, billiards or bridge. When, as a platoon commander, I had my own soldiers to look after and in whom to take an interest it was immensely rewarding. Many of them knew much more about human relationships than I did. With this kind of formation it was, perhaps, just as well that I was posted to West and not East or Central Africa. That may well have been discernment on the part of the recruiters but I sometimes speculate on how I would have responded to a posting to Kenya or some other white settler colony and, whether indeed, I would have remained in the Colonial Service.

Harbouring no regrets about my choice of career, how do I assess our record? Of course, I have plenty of regrets about things I did or failed to do once in the job. Some have been noted in the previous pages. I also regret aspects of the colonial legacy. Jack Straw, when Secretary of State for Foreign Affairs, complained that most of the problems he faced were the result of empire governance. That was an unfair exaggeration but a legacy underlying many of the problems in new nations has been their colonial boundaries. More often than not, these were arbitrary, the consequence of compromises patched up between the great powers of the nineteenth century with little if any thought for the peoples directly affected. Of the four countries in which I served two have had difficult times since independence. Both, Nigeria and the Solomons, inherited the burden of unsatisfactory boundaries. That they did so, however, was more the responsibility of Jack Straw's predecessors in office than of those who administered empire on the ground. Systematic re-ordering, not only of external frontiers but of internal boundaries as well, in order to keep cultures intact, might have prevented some post-colonial conflicts, but it would have been difficult to have attempted to do this much after the end of the 1920s. Then, however, it was not only believed that there was ample time available but that substantially sized nation states were the only viable option. A Europe that had seen the unification of both

Germany and Italy in recent history was unlikely to advocate the creation of small states. I was able to preside over the separation of the Gilberts and the Ellice only because by the mid 1970s many of the former convictions about the impossibility of launching a myriad of small states on the world had been set aside. Policy had been modified by experience.

We were naive in our expectation that stable nationhood could be achieved after a few decades rather than over centuries and that others would readily learn both from our example and from our mistakes. People really only learn from their own mistakes and however good the intentions of our successors both the pressures and the temptations they faced from the moment they took over were substantial. Human weakness is more easily taken advantage of when individual loyalty is towards extended family rather than a recently born and somewhat unnatural new nation. In colonial days theft of farm produce was extremely rare and seen as a heinous crime, in keeping with centuries of tradition, whereas embezzlement from the public purse, a recent and imported concept, was undertaken lightly and carried little stigma. That attitude survived. My direct personal experience in post-independent Nigeria made me well aware of the activities of present day international exploiters, including arms dealers, only too ready to take advantage of inherent weaknesses in new states, of untried systems, of checks and balances and of the universality of Acton's dictum about the corruption of power.

So should we have stayed longer? Views differ on the question of whether we could have done a better job of preparation for independence had we had more time. Many of my former colleagues feel that Iain Macleod, in particular, let us down by forcing the pace. His time as Colonial Secretary affected the East and Central African dependencies rather than any in which I served, but I support his policy. It is easy to demonstrate the lack of readiness for independence but once the process was under way, further time would not necessarily have been devoted to better preparation. The chances are that it would have had to be spent on dealing with political agitation, recrimination and the disruption of infrastructure and services as those demanding political independence became increasingly impatient and espoused violence. The final years had to be a two way process, mutually agreed, with a timetable that met local political aspirations and kept goodwill intact. Inevitably we were going to hand over to a small elite. The longer we stayed the greater the opportunity to antagonise that elite. And that elite, rather than ourselves, was always going to have the prime influence on the next generation. The fact that, with very few exceptions, the Union Jack could be hauled down in an atmosphere of celebration and in the presence of royalty is something to be applauded, whatever has since happened.

More time would probably not have made much difference to our major fault: neglecting to provide sufficient skilled human resources for the management of a modern state. We failed to put sufficient resources into the provision of local qualified personnel early enough. It was not simply a matter of money. Too often we failed to recognise the need or appreciate the urgency. Where local culture was strong, as for example in Northern Nigeria, Western education could be unpopular, even at the primary level, and especially for girls. So we became complacent, all too readily accepting the easy route of not pushing too hard, believing that things would sort themselves out eventually as understanding of the advantages of education grew. We thought we could wait until local demand forced the pace. Elsewhere, in the Pacific for example, education in the early days was left to the missions, whose first priority was to satisfy their own needs for pastors, catechists, teachers and nurses. We were also guilty of underestimating both the time involved to produce fully qualified professionals, for example, it takes twenty years from the first year of primary education to produce a doctor, and the numbers that would be required to meet population growth and demand as society became more sophisticated. As late as 1935 only 23 out of 45 colonial territories had education departments, many of which were still small and rudimentary.[6]

There were reasons for the lateness in promoting education. In many colonies we were only just getting established when World War I distracted attention, then there was the depression followed by World War II. Despite what was happening in India, there was an assumption that there was plenty of time elsewhere. The nature of empire also meant that it was relatively easy to fill immediate skill gaps with Asians, as happened in East Africa, building up substantial problems for later solution. More significantly, our approach reflected the age and the society in which we had been brought up, something that applied right to the end of

---

6. Clive Whitehead, *Colonial Educators*, I,B, Tauris, London 2003.p.85.

recruitment to the colonial service. Percentages of children completing secondary and university education in Britain in the 1920s, 30s and 40s were extremely low. That was our norm. Our sights were set low. I think this a better explanation for the failure to promote education than the supposed preference of colonial administrators for 'the noble savage' and dislike of mission educated 'savvy boys'. That we did not face up to the need until very late in the day is, in my view, the most serious indictment of the service. I have, of course, nothing but praise for those who did their best with very limited resources to get education and training going.

Did we have sufficient resources to do a worthwhile job? The answer is undoubtedly 'no'. Britain was mean in administering its Empire. Colonies had to be self sufficient, aid only becoming an effective factor after the Second World War when the political process speeded up and de-colonisation was on the agenda. On balance, however, that may have been helpful. The need to balance budgets ensured that costs were better understood and that the numbers of British personnel were kept low.[7] Had funding been more generous it might have resulted in far more expatriates and even less pressure to produce local counterparts.

Exploitation is a common charge and there is no doubt that economic motives played a considerable role in the acquisition of empire, as has been recorded in these pages with respect to Banaba and phosphate. The view that economic motives remained dominant, however, ignores the evidence. Britain certainly wanted to retain beneficial economic relationships but these did not determine policy locally. I was never going to try and develop fishing in the Solomons with the UK White Fish Authority! The need for a dependency to be self-sufficient, and in the run up to internal self-government the need for development, made us aware of the importance of achieving as much local added value as possible. We were aware that political independence would be meaningless without economic independence. That was also understood by many of the companies, British and otherwise, that had traditionally traded and exported primary produce but began to manufacture locally to provide

---

7. In 1939 there was a total of 7,566 Colonial Service personnel of all categories and grades serving a population of 43,114,000 in the East, Central and West African colonies. Of that number 1,123 were administrators. Table 2.8 in Anthony Kirk-Greene, *On Crown Service*, I.B. Tauris, London 1999.

import substitution. Logically, too, the prospecting, exploration and marketing that economic development requires could only be provided initially by foreign companies. It was by no means all exploitation. My experience with establishing Solomon Taiyo made that clear. Getting the economy going was just as significant in the final decades of empire as the maintenance of law and order and it was done with the territory's interests in view, not those of Britain, but if the two coincided, as sometimes they did, all the better.

Despite our failures and aside from the inherent fault of imperialism of one people being subject to another, the legacy had and continues to have benefits. The popular assessment of law, language and liberal democracy as the legacy of British Empire has merit. Empire governance also helped the spread of football, cricket, golf and tennis across the world and we need not be guilty about that! Pride of place must, of course, be given to access to the English language. Latin was a legacy of the Roman Empire that survived as a language for scholarship and science into my lifetime. My generation could not matriculate without Latin. English, the international language of the present day, has given former dependencies access to the modern world and its technology and the opportunity to participate within it on equal terms. Some sense of the rule of law as a goal has also prevailed, even if often set aside. Liberal democracy is more often an aspiration than a fact but that it is an aspiration is important. I like to think, too, that the personal example set by the Colonial Service had some effect on its direct successors. The popular image tends to be built around pomp, parades and plumes. In fact after the Second World War the vast majority of the Service were ordinary professional people pursuing their jobs as teachers, doctors, nurses, engineers, surveyors, agriculturists, foresters and so forth.[8] They were the same sort of people as those doing similar jobs in Britain, laying foundations and engendering values for the future post-colonial states. While they certainly lived at a standard more elaborate than that of most of those they served, by the standards of their contemporaries in the United Kingdom their living conditions were often elementary and unlikely to be envied. They were adequately but not especially well paid.

---

8. Professor Peter Marshall called attention to this in his keynote lecture, *The British Experience of Imperial Rule*, at the Administering Empire conference at the University of London in May 1999.

Family life was often subject to long separation and loneliness. It says much that the fondest memories for many of them are of the camaraderie of small stations. Many enjoyed close relationships with local people that led to enduring friendships. A vital component of liberal democracy is that of public servants doing a good job honestly and fairly.

The Administration had a longer history during which it acquired a certain awe, but was not all that much different to the professional services. I have learned with the hindsight gained from second and third careers in England that the Colonial Service, in all its branches, was unusual in terms of loyalty, respect, affection and hospitality. We enjoyed our work and were deeply committed both to it and to one another. Trust played a major part in all we did, trust in one another, trust in the people we served and their trust in us. We all had our faults as human beings but honour and duty were unspoken concepts we shared. That is one reason why suggestions that we were devious and dishonest, deliberately rigging pre-independence elections in order to suit British Government policy are so wide of the mark.[9] As a wise senior said to me early in my career, 'our job is to keep people out of prison, not to put them in', and we often had to accept misdemeanour in those to whom we hoped to hand over responsibility. But tolerance of faults in those of another culture rarely resulted in our becoming casual about integrity ourselves. Quite apart from the character of the people involved, however, rigging of elections nationally would have required logistics and secret procedures of a sophistication that simply did not exist. On these occasions everyone was willing to lend a hand and a huge number of people were involved. Any attempt at rigging would quickly have been exposed.

It is not, perhaps, generally appreciated how different the Colonial Service was in practical ways to the home Civil Service. A lot of the time we worked in relative isolation. We were used to being on our own and taking decisions. Frequently we were fighting on behalf of our district, province or colony against the views of higher authority. It

---

9. For example, the BBC Radio 4 broadcast of Monday, 30th July 2007, *The Gift of Democracy*, in the Document series, in which Professor David Anderson said: 'It would not be unfair to say that in almost every single colony, the British attempted to manipulate the result (of elections) to their advantage. Indeed, it would be surprising if as colonial power they had not done so'.

was common sense to get on with as much as one could locally without involving anyone else. Reading files in the National Archives I now realise that the reverse was also largely true. Policies were debated in London and issues argued between ministries that we never heard about. Absorbed in our limited environments we often ignored what must have been hugely pressing matters for the UK government of the time. Only in recent years has it dawned upon me that the key years of de-colonisation took place at the height of the Cold War. Primitive communications, still pretty poor even when I was a governor, added to the isolation. I telephoned the FCO only five or six times and I only once placed a personal call. When I first arrived in West Africa, a radio powered by car batteries was beyond my resources to buy, carry around and maintain when I had no permanent house and my means of transport was horse, cycle or foot. For news of the wider world I relied on copies of the *Manchester Guardian Weekly* and *The Listener*, which I read two to eight weeks in arrears.

It was only with the advent of the transistor radio that African villages and Pacific atolls really became part of the world. This was brought home to me one day in the sixties. I was taking John Macintosh MP, a good friend whom I had met when he was teaching political science at Ibadan University, around a relatively remote Nigerian village to get a feel for the local political situation, then in some turmoil, and about which he was writing. Speaking Hausa, I introduced him to the village blacksmith as an MP from England. Without looking up from his work the blacksmith immediately enquired, 'Tory or Labour?' and on being told asked a pertinent question or two about current UK political issues. Five years earlier the exchange would have been inconceivable. The transistor radio now brought the Hausa programme of the BBC World Service into the remotest village. In the Pacific, reception was less good, but local broadcasting services relayed the world news once or twice a day. Sadly, but perhaps inevitably because we no longer have confidence in ourselves, Britain has allowed this superb service, in which huge numbers of the most influential people worldwide had trust, to decline. At the very end of the twentieth century I picked up an old Nigerian friend at Heathrow. On the journey home he asked if he could listen to the news. I tuned into Radio 4 on the car radio. After a few minutes of the news he asked me why hadn't I got the proper BBC!

My impression is that some academics, reading the archives and used to the instant communications of the present day, fail to recognise how deeply immersed in our local concerns we were and how limited was our intellectual exchange with our UK contemporaries and contacts. Colonial administrators must often appear to have been unaware, ignorant and stupid, but as my ten years experience in university administration re-assures me, no more unaware, ignorant and stupid than academics often are about the affairs of faculties other than their own! A colony was very much like a university faculty, having some common factors with other faculties but strong in its own culture and tradition with its own objectives and problems dominating.

At no point in my career was I in the mainstream, except for the week-end in January 1960 when Harold Macmillan stayed at Government House, Kaduna where I was Private Secretary to the Governor. No 10 came with him. Within seconds of their arrival I was asked by David Hunt 'to get Salisbury on the phone', a feat I did not expect to achieve given the rare occasions on which we had tried to telephone London! This was the tour that was to end with the famous 'wind of change' speech in South Africa and, with hindsight, I realise how apprehension about its reception lay underneath some of the tensions I discerned between senior members of the party. What we did day to day rarely caused ripples elsewhere. Nigeria, one of Britain's largest colonies and subsequently one of the largest African nations only made world news for the Queen's visit in 1956 and independence in 1960, and in the next decade for *coup d'etats* and mayhem ending in civil war. During my time in the western Pacific only the Banaban issue generated interest in the UK media.

Discussion on the matters that primarily concerned us, other than with our immediate colleagues, was best provided by the exceptionally talented group of newspaper correspondents who reported on the transition of power in Africa. Alas, there was no equivalent in the Pacific. Inevitably their living depended on reporting bad rather than good news but talking to Colin Legum, Anthony Sampson, Bill Kirkman, Patrick Keatley, Walter Schwarz, Bridget Bloom and others over the years I sensed that they had a much better understanding of what we were about than many a politician, FCO diplomat or academic. How helpful it would have been had one of them followed the path that Peter Hennessey was to take in later years in respect of Whitehall, moving from the role of trusted and exceptionally well-informed journalist to a leading and highly respected academic with a chair in contemporary history.

Looking back on my life in old age I rejoice that I had the good fortune to pursue the career that I did, a career unique to the twentieth century and available for only a brief few decades. The peoples for and with whom I worked added huge richness to my life and I learned much from them. I like to think, too, that in some small way I was able to help them fulfil their aspirations. Despite the tragedy of civil war in Nigeria and of the events leading to it, my memories are essentially happy ones and I treasure the friendships gained and sustained to the present. The British Raj in India in an earlier century may have had different motivation but in the last decades of empire it was neither money nor glory that encouraged us. We knew in our hearts that it would be difficult to find another job that gave so much responsibility and satisfaction in equal measure at so early an age, or a life that was as rich in enjoyment as it was rewarding in fulfilment.

APPENDICES

APPENDIX A
HANDING OVER NOTES ON DEPARTURE OF J.H. SMITH
20 MAY 1973

I regret that, as usual, these notes have been produced in a last minute rush and will prove inadequate. There is also the problem that I am unsure for whom they are written. So much that can be left unsaid or needs to be said depends upon a successor's background. It is also a time of change in the Solomons. A general election is in progress and there are proposals for constitutional advance. Many staff changes have taken or are about to take place that affect Finance Branch and departments. I have tried to indicate what I have been up to and what needs to be done. Most of the current issues will be well known to John Yaxley, the DFS, who will be acting meantime and who will be able to show you the ropes in person.

CONSTITUTIONAL AND POLITICAL STATUS

The constitutional status of the FS is laid down in the British Solomon Islands Order 1970. You need to master this and the Functions of Committees Directive. Both can be found printed in a stiff covered handbook. The constitution gives the FS a key role and one bringing him closer to the politicians in some respects than either the High Commissioner or CS. The FS is the Chairman of a Governing Council Committee which associates him with the other chairmen, all of whom have in recent months been elected members, and is responsible for a portfolio which not only brings him into daily contact with other portfolio holders and their secretaries but one which currently attracts rather more popular interest than does the CS's portfolio of reserved subjects. I have accepted this political role and used it to advantage. For the time being FS is both Minister and Permanent Secretary. DFS is taking over the perm-sec duties increasingly but it will be hard to achieve a complete split even if desirable which I doubt in so small an organisation.

There are constitutional proposals currently under discussion that would introduce a ministerial form of government. FS would then take his place in the cabinet that would then handle business currently dealt with by Finance Committee. Proposals can be read in the report of the Special Select Committee.

The general election now under way will result in a larger Council with at least half of the members new. The atmosphere may be different but the old hands will exercise a lot of influence initially.

GOVERNING COUNCIL

Private Meetings. Ex-officio members have played private meetings formally but in low key but the FS has to present some of the more controversial business such as tariff changes which can lead to sharp exchanges. I have looked for compromise, never dug my toes in to the bitter end and, above all, never worried about what the FCO might have to say. We have, for better or for worse, an elected majority and if it is to mean anything there must come a point beyond which one doesn't hold on. In general I have found the response not unreasonable although, of course, I have often had private reservations about the wisdom of a particular decision. Past papers are in a bound volume. It is a matter of judgement whether to submit memoranda in draft to CS and HE.

Finance Committee. Finance Committee has recently been composed entirely of Committee Chairmen and has been fairly responsible. You should look at the bound volumes of F papers presented since its formation to get a hang of the kind of business dealt with. Meetings are fairly informal and it has been my custom after the closure of business on the agenda to encourage general discussion of a broader nature to try and obtain some sense of cabinet *esprit*. There is a long way to go. I have incidentally always spoken for and voted for a Finance Committee decision in a private meeting of Governing Council after I have been outvoted in Finance Committee. My colleagues, however, have never felt the same obligation towards collective responsibility (which is not imposed by the Constitution) and you must expect the disconcerting experience of finding that a member who has backed you in Committee reverses his views subsequently in private or public meetings.

Finance Committee has established precedents which set a somewhat different routine to the other committees. Because of the easy availability of members, meetings have been called when needed rather than at set periods and in general I have avoided holding meetings during the crowded week of the month when all elected members are in town for the Private Meeting. I have also tried to push out papers as ready and only to put on the agenda matters that require urgent decision. Members are very careless about papers and often lose them but at least they cannot complain of lack of opportunity for prior discussion and briefing. (Senior Assistant Secretaries need to do much more to help their Chairmen function effectively.) It has also been the practice, because of the composition of the Finance Committee and its status under the Public Finance Law, for some matters to by-pass the private meeting. We do not put annual estimates before the Private Meeting, although members will have seen those parts which refer to new proposals relating to the portfolio of the committee on which they serve. I have also usually managed to put finance bills for publication straight from the Committee. Much of it is technical and nobody has objected. But where a major new policy is involved, e.g. currency and the NPF, I always make sure that there is a Govco direction under my belt before commencing but prefer to keep to general principles rather than detail. The Council when re-convened may act differently.

Public Meetings. Public Meetings of Governing Council – that is Governing Council as a legislature – may change in character with the new house. It is not easy for the FS to get the feel slowly as there is so much business to present. My guiding rules have been to give way gracefully when needed, never to be ashamed to admit error and always keep my temper – sometimes just a little hard! The Chairmen expect you to back them up at question time when facts and figures are needed. They were getting much better and the last couple of meetings I was on my feet far less often than in the early days. Members like to be able to understand the budget speech and they are more interested in this than the budget, which, however, they really get into in Committee of Supply when it is essential to be well briefed. A glance at Hansard will give you an idea of what comes up and members have always been kind to me by warning when an attack of strength is to be launched on a particular department or topic. Private Members Day is rather a strain. FS can come off lightly but some motions are yours for reply and on others you simply have to come in to salvage things. But I have unwisely sometimes joined in when it wasn't really essential and I have always regretted it afterwards – if only because I missed my lunch! After the first few occasions I tended to play motions off the cuff. If you are too prepared you can miss the feel of that day or even moment – and this does vary enormously from meeting to meeting and day to day. It is much better to respond to the mood of the house if you can. I always have by me the Abstract of Statistics, the current Estimates, Development Plan and reviews and any other key documents which suit the debate. I can then if need be do some rapid homework when a member talks about something quite unexpected.

Procedure is standard Commonwealth with the usual problems of small countries, namely that you can't get up and leave the chamber very easily and business is squashed up so one can report three Bills and then move third readings in a row. The physical constraints are considerable. It is very hard to get officials in easy reach without causing a disturbance. I think you must insist on your staff backing you up. The younger generation often seem to regard it all as a waste of their time. You had also better be prepared to write your own speeches! Most Finance Committee and Private Meeting papers are drafted lower down, however. I insist on seeing them in draft. Again there is a tendency to feel that if one has drafted a paper then the man on top has no right to change it. But this has got much better and F staff know my feelings on the subject.

LEGISLATION

It is always worth having an informal meeting with members to explain a Bill which isn't routine or minor. Most drafting has been done by myself. There is no spare man around and if passed down legislation tends to get put on one side on grounds of difficulty and time. The FS is about the only person who can ignore pressures of other business which easily overwhelm. There are three pieces in the pipeline: a banking bill, and amending bills for the Public Finance and Exchange Control Ordinances. A currency law will be needed in due course. A first draft is available. It is essential to persuade the law officers to have a final look. There is a tendency for one to disagree with the other which results in a lot of time consuming and paper wasting last minute changes.

STATUTORY DUTIES

The FS has a number of statutory duties under a variety of Ordinances. These should be exercised personally as no delegations have been made and are not always permitted. The laws establishing statutory corporations are concerned, as are Forestry and Fishing Ordinances as well as the more obvious laws covering activities for which FS has direct responsibility, e.g. the Customs and Excise Ordinance. Whenever the statutory duty falls within the portfolio of another Chairman, I have insisted upon the recommendation to exercise the statutory duty coming from the Chairman or as a decision of his committee. I have never declined the advice offered. These duties are something of an anomaly and will become more so in the next Constitution. It is a matter which needs looking into.

OFFICE PROCEDURES

Secretariat procedures are laid down by CS and Chapter 0 of General Orders is relevant. PA to FS is your local expert and knows better than anyone the procedures for handling legislation, committee minutes, etc. The office of the Clerk to Govco is weak in this respect and very prone to lose papers.

ORGANISATION OF FINANCE BRANCH

Finance Branch consists of the FS, DFS, SASDand ASS Planning which currently include an economist, a manpower planner and a generalist with bias towards rural development; SEOF, a registry clerk and the FS's personal assistant. The DFS and other staff share the stenographic and typing pool of the Secretariat. CS always discusses senior staffing but Establishment Branch moves clerks and executive officers without consultation which is embarrassing.

There are two registries, one open kept by the Clerk and one restricted kept by the PA to FS. I keep one or two hot files in my safe. A joint file register is kept which needs bringing up to date from time to time. You will see from a perusal what kind of subjects we handle. File numbering is part of the Secretariat series. Open files are kept in accordance with the Manual of Registry Procedures on the commercial back to front basis with all papers placed on the right hand side. This system was introduced in 1972 to replace split files. Restricted files, to suit my own personal fad, are kept as book files reading from left to right. I find it much easier to follow a story through this way but I don't think anyone else much is in favour (except DCS who shares my preferences) and having two systems is, of course, confusing. You will need to lay down guidelines when you achieve a new amalgamated department. Personally I find our numbering system unnecessarily restrictive. I can see no merit at all in all files being confined to a 400 series or in placing files in the archives just because the series has been overtaken without consideration of the desirability of keeping those papers to hand. Several vital instructions are contained in the 200 file series now in Suva!

As far as possible I leave the basic running of the Branch to the DFS. More frequent meetings of all staff than I have held would be valuable. DFS and I are in constant touch and I see others as need be but have perhaps been a bit too remote from SASD. I hope to get the Economist and Manpower Planner on the top floor after the election which will help contact.

Mail circulates and DFS marks it. Some mail comes addressed personally to FS and there is a danger of keeping this to one's self. As far as possible I initial and pass direct to DFS. Occasionally it is necessary to pass to DCS, CS and HE although I sometimes do this on file.

Mrs Vitorovic has been in F Branch a long time and is a fund of knowledge about papers. She also has the ability to spirit up copies of reports etc. which usually take weeks or months to find. You will find your laws and committee papers etc. kept meticulously. How you arrange these is up to you. Mrs Vitorovic will show where they are currently all are. We bind Finance and Govco papers annually. I have not bound papers of other Committees, but I doubt if anybody else has either so they may be hard to obtain.

SEOF is Clerk to Finance Committee. I insist on immediate production of minutes in draft. PA to FS prepares all papers and issues them. I have been passing extracts of conclusions for action but this ought to be done at a lower level.

There is a fair amount of contact between DCS and FS. I attend CS's Monday morning prayer sessions, but let DFS handle the business. I have found it very useful to have a discussion with HE of a general nature from time to time. This helps keep HE in the picture and provides me with an opportunity to sound out views and float ideas. I always try and give HE fair warning of impending disaster.

Traditionally FS has had an overlord function in respect of natural resources, communications and works and commerce and industry while CS has the same kind of role in respect of social services and internal affairs. I have deliberately weakened this role because of the possible friction it can bring between oneself and a chairman. The natural links are, however, strong, particularly with natural resources and commerce and industry. I see a lot of the SASS and their Chairmen. Exactly how you play this is very much a matter of personal judgement and will depend to a certain extent upon the personalities involved. Without a Cabinet there is undoubtedly a co-ordinating job to be done and the demi-official method of writing to the FCO also keeps one involved.

DEPARTMENTS FOR WHICH FS IS RESPONSIBLE IN LEGISLATURE

The FS is responsible for the Treasury, Inland Revenue, Customs and Excise, Stores and Statistics Departments. The FS is not a head of department and finance branch is part of the Secretariat and FS is responsible to CS who is the Head of Department. This produces some curiosities in administration. F heads of departments can approach CS directly and will issue circulars and instructions without consultation with FS. I have tried to bring relationships much closer and there is now good personal contact and very little exchange of memoranda. This has worked well with the Treasury and Customs and Excise. I would like to work off their files where authorities are concerned but distrust of the Secretariat is still so strong that I have not been successful. I do, however, work off submissions submitted directly to me, e.g. for remission of custom duties, and returned by me direct to the head of department. Relations with the Commissioner of Income Tax remain formal but there is very little day to day contact. Statistics has been no trouble with a volunteer as head of department and we do most of our business over the telephone, Mr Callan often joining in as a member of the Planning Unit. The Treasury takes over the Stores on 1st July. You should get around and meet F departments first and quickly. You'll have to take the initiative.

It is proposed in 1974 to amalgamate the F group of departments into one department. Ultimately this could become a traditional type of ministry of finance. Proposals are in RF.46/1/1/5. Establishments are very much involved. Things are going quite well but because physical integration will not be possible in 1974 it may be a year or two before much in the way of savings becomes apparent where staff is concerned. ES accepts this.

Stores accounting staff will move into the Treasury building but there isn't room for anyone else. DCS, with whom you must keep in close touch, is co-ordinating moves all round and the position is too fluid to make comment worthwhile. I have personally been prepared to move out of the Secretariat building into inferior accommodation to obtain physical proximity which is essential to harmonious and effective working relationships between the heads of divisions in a larger department or ministry. You should make sure that the Planning Unit stays close to you. There are, of course, advocates of separation of economic policies and planning from fiscal policies and financial administration. All I can say is that my experience elsewhere under both systems makes me 100% in favour of a joint operation, the more so in a little economy such as this. This does not mean that I would oppose a planning committee under the direction of a chief minister or of his secretary. Such a body would, after all, be but a committee of the cabinet which ought to take the decisions. But I do think that those responsible for putting forward economic policy proposals in an overall way and for implementing them need to be part and parcel of the agency which is responsible for the supply of money, taxation, public expenditure etc. A planning unit tucked away by itself may develop separatist tendencies or illusions of grandeur, or both.

All round amalgamation will greatly help effective financial management and control. It will also, of course, mark a further step towards the end of the colonial secretariat in which the FS's role as third in command sometimes assumes greater significance than his role as financial manager.

STORES AND QUEEN'S WAREHOUSE

We have agreed that the Ports Authority should build a store with an office block to accommodate the government Stores, the Queen's Warehouse and the Customs Long Room. The building will be at Point Cruz close to the wharf. Rental will be around $A20,000 per annum and we have agreed on a long term lease. This will overcome the need to look for development aid for this type of building which might be rather hard to justify. It will also enable us to move the Stores to the wharf and avoid the present high costs of handling and transport. It is essential to replace the Queen's Warehouse, which is very old, and provide accommodation for the Long Room away from the Treasury building. All round savings will cover the costs of the rental. As the need for stores accommodation declines, moreover, we will be able to sub-let areas to the private sector.

Relationships with Heads of departments other than F Departments

The FS attends meeting of Heads of Departments and I recommend that you get around and visit them as soon as possible. You will see much more of some than others. The most regular visitors are the Directors of Agriculture and of Education, both of whom like to go to the top. The former can be a bother with his habit of discussing some matters in passing very casually and leaving your office straight for SAS(D) or somebody else and announcing that the FS has agreed to a lot of things which were not discussed in those terms at all! The Director of Education is more anxious to discuss approaches and ideas and does not take advantage of the situation. I find the Conservator of Forests comes along every couple of months and keeps me in general touch but also bellyaches at length about his problems – usually with establishments about which I can't do much to help. He has some strong views on organisational matters. I hold him in very high regard and only wish more departments got on so effectively with the business of development. The Director of Geological Surveys also comes along and we discuss mining and prospecting as the need arises. I have had good and close relations with Information and Broadcasting but see very little of other heads of departments except on specific matters or at meetings. DFS tends to see more of them over estimates etc. but perhaps links should be closer. It is surprising how different interpretations of development plans and policies can be!

I would like to have seen more of the district commissioners. Direct links of an institutional sort are very few. I have visited districts and have tried to do a little touring in depth, e.g. walking along the weathercoast of Guadalcanal, to give me an insight into the country. For an outsider this is vital and I am only sorry that my stay has been too short to permit more. It is also very helpful to have a good look at logging, plantations, cattle, etc as opportunity offers. Everyone is always delighted to see the FS, believe it or not.

PRIVATE SECTOR CONTACTS

FS attends a quarterly meeting with private sector representatives chaired by CS which SAS(C&I) organises. I have also kept in fairly close touch with the managers of the big concerns but much of the private sector here is small beer and casual social encounters are probably sufficient contact without arranging anything special. I see a great many visiting businessmen (and academics) but SAS(C&I) can increasingly reduce the load. Much will depend upon your own personal contacts and interests.

I have made it a rule to accept any invitation to speak about or discuss development etc. I have always learned enough to make the time spent well worthwhile and often this has been my only way to get into any kind of dialogue with Solomon Islanders outside the political and senior civil service group I meet regularly. I have found the secondary schools and training college occasions especially useful and have enjoyed talking to Church groups and meetings arranged by the University of the South Pacific.

MANAGEMENT OF PUBLIC FINANCE

Public Finance (Control and Audit) Ordinance
The basic document is the Public Finance (Control and Audit) Ordinance. This is fairly standard and is in process of amendment after a couple of years' operation. It was first drafted by a person who wanted us to head for an exchequer system and a little of this was left in but with amendment all should be well. The retiring Accountant General likes to have everything spelled out. I don't, and the Director of Audit is on my side. I cannot, for example, agree that it is necessary either to issue treasury warrants each year or to give accounting officers letters of appointment. The approved estimates can serve both functions perfectly well and an operation which is purely clerical in content but carried out at high level is avoided.

The FS is required in most cases to exercise his powers under the law in consultation with Finance Committee. You might want to consider the establishment in due course of a capital development fund. It would help locally but ODA is very rigid about development aid accounting in dependencies and I have not, therefore, pursued matters.

Financial Instructions

Following on from the introduction of the law, Financial Instructions have been revised. These are about to be finalised. Interim Instructions have been in use since February to try out and test, and the Accountant General Designate is carrying out the final revision. The new Financial Instructions have been drafted by myself in conjunction with the Accountant General and the Director of Audit. On the whole we have ironed out all disagreements but there are one or two points where the Treasury has not had its way and may try to come back. It is essential to keep the Audit involvement which I have found invaluable. My own criticism of the finished product it that it is too long and unnecessarily detailed on matters which concern very few – e.g. the duties of the Accountant General, but I have accepted this in the interest of good relations. I am also critical of some of our procedures which seem to be unnecessary or weaken control. Revision of FII has enabled plenty of change but some areas merit further investigation. For example, centralised payments make good sense (e.g. Solair bills) but a better system could be devised because I am convinced that liabilities are not properly accepted and there is a tendency for people to spend other peoples' allocations. Everyone denies this but from the messes which occur, it must happen. I am also unhappy about the departmental warrant system which is inflexible and misused. Instead of annual allocations, departments tend to make them monthly or even to meet a single payment. I prefer authorities to incur expenditure which can be passed up and down the line without limit and which are treated as expenditure or credits in the vote books. Our vote books are now much better but still far from the simple control document which is needed. They provide for massive analysis upon which some departments waste immense efforts, possibly a hangover from the days of innumerable items in subheads. While progress has been made there is still much to be done. I have arranged the format of FII so that it can be used as a training manual.

Stores Instructions: A first draft of Stores Instructions is available, but a lot of work is needed. It was next on my list but I have not even begun.

Estimates: Estimates procedure is laid down in FII. I have altered the format of Estimates over 1972 and 1973 and there are other changes to be included in 1974 so that proper analysis is available. It is really a matter of bringing in extra columns for actual expenditure and percentages. Those concerned know the form. The cleaner look has made the Estimates a much more consulted document. The government Printer is very cooperative and year by year there is room for improvement in design and layout.

The numbering system may seem rather excessive for so small a budget but I went for head numbers which give flexibility so that there is room to introduce new heads in a logical sequence without having to change all the number allocations. I also wanted to ease matters for machine account operators and checkers. All head numbers are three figures, recurrent and capital revenue and expenditure clearly defined by hundreds. With a move to fewer departments or ministries one could perhaps manage with tens but I doubt it. Revenue heads have been firmly removed from the traditional functional groupings and made the responsibility of departments. There are a few oddities because of convenience but in every case those who collect revenue know broadly what they are responsible for and can be called to account about.

In 1974 we are trying to get away from too much functional division of heads into parts. This helped analysis but greatly increased accounting, often to no advantage. Functions can still be indicated but I can see no reason why the estimates must allocate T&T to the livestock, fisheries, extension services, headquarters etc of Agriculture. This is the job of the accounting officer, not the legislature. Analysis in building up the estimates is, of course, needed. The object is to finish up with a reasonable sized subhead so that it is much easier to refuse applications for virement and supplementaries, to reduce opportunities for misallocation and to get everything to a sensible size.

District Commissioners, for example, dislike receiving allocations on a departmental warrant instead of having a head in the Estimates. With my background in a big territory I find this hard to take. It all makes for interminable committee of supply, the wrong kind of detailed probing by the legislature and fruitless accounting.

In general I have encouraged effective subheads. But there are still some for as little as $A20 in the small departments which need watching. The new service structure should eliminate them in due course. FII now lay down common subheads and the Estimates memorandum indicates their use. People are still very childish about this and one needs to check each year to see that 'magazines' are included as well as 'newspapers', for example, otherwise much time and temper will be lost over audit queries or just plain nastiness in some departments. I have refused to allow items within subheads. A few years ago we had all items and hardly any subheads. As we didn't account for items the constant need for virement was a complete farce. The authority was inevitably down-graded and it provided a jolly game for the executive grade to play, resulting in a mass of useless paper and wasted man hours every year. My principle has been that if items are really necessary then there should be a subhead.

Audit is a little unhappy about the institutional 'operating costs' subheads but these are no worse than the PWD maintenance subheads and in practice far less likely to be abused. My argument is that contract doctors and principals will have little patience with government procedures and often stay too short a time to learn much about them. It is much better to let them administer one omnibus vote which covers those things needed and not provided for in the common subheads.

I have retained a detailed Personal Emoluments subhead 1. My experience is that this is much simpler to administer than establishment warrants and, of course, a lot more politics is about jobs than most civil servants care to admit. It is, therefore, better to give the legislature the opportunity to argue and make points about localisation etc. without the suspicion that something has been concealed from them. Establishments have been very helpful in preparation of PE.

I have kept statutory expenditure in the head concerned which is simpler administratively. (In 1971 we had it all in one head controlled by the Accountant General.) The summary page to each head makes this clear. There has been a mix up over the High Commissioner's salary and this must appear as statutory expenditure in 1974.

I have eliminated special expenditure on the grounds that minor replacements should be handled from recurrent subheads, if necessary centralised – e.g. office furniture now handled by Stores on a centralised basis with a reasonable annual provision but formerly special expenditure as required department by department – and that major replacements should be part and parcel of longer term planning and included in the development plan and capital estimates. There are some anomalies as a result – e.g. elections expenditure this year, but the discipline has been salutary.

Capital expenditure subhead numbers are identical to development plan project numbers. These are five figures but there is no need for the machinists to use head numbers at all – not that I have succeeded in putting this over to the Treasury!

Draft estimates have been distributed to departments as well as the legislature in recent years and as early as possible. Printed Estimates I hand out the day they are ready.

1974 Estimates: DFS will handle the basic work. It is useful to have the figures finalised so that typing can begin in July. Mid September is the date for submission to UK. I advise reading three to four years Estimates Despatches before drafting. You'll see the form has changed.

We may need new heads in 1974 for Chairmen and Senior Advisors, Committee by Committee. If so, use vacant numbers, e.g. 230 for Social Services, but I think it unnecessary and the 1975 Estimates can show the complete re-structuring.

Annual Appropriation: The Annual Appropriation Bill takes the standard form. The AG has simplified it over the years. There must be provision for overdraft borrowing to meet the requirements of the Public Finance Law.

I have consulted Finance Committee about the content of budget speeches but not submitted a speech in draft. You will want to review the procedure if collective responsibility and cabinet government are introduced.

Supplementary Appropriation: I have been tolerant about virement and FII now lay down the rules. I try to resist supplementary provision for recurrent heads. I do not attempt to match up savings or increased revenue directly, which was the old special warrant procedure in a grant-aided territory. I make inspired guesses and, if necessary, reservations to match expenditure. These often have to be adjusted but as the year goes on the picture becomes clearer. I am constantly amazed at how little relationship estimates, especially on the capital side, bear to reality. I had hoped to avoid more than one supplementary bill each year, but have had to agree to three each year so far! This could be avoided by increasing the FS's powers with regard to contingencies but if this happened there is no doubt the civil service would presume that the FS really controls it all and the legislature is only a rubber stamp. Carelessness would increase. Each year, therefore, I have become more difficult about contingencies warrants and now take a very legalistic approach in an endeavour to improve financial responsibility. But it has never occurred to anyone that they might just have to wait until the next meeting of the legislature or even until next year! I have also never come across such weak basic control – money is not merely committed but frequently spent before an application for a supplementary is put forward. Control has, however, been greatly tightened in recent months and will improve still more with the introduction of super departments and ministries and much larger heads and subheads. To be fair much of the trouble has stemmed from the fragmentation of a small budget so that supplementary provision of under $A10 has not been unusual!

Colonial Regulations: I have not so far mentioned Colregs. To me they are simply the basis upon which the Public Finance Law and FII have been built. The FCO and, occasionally, Audit still mutter about them but they have remained unchanged for years and are often quite inappropriate if one is trying (a) to modernise financial management and (b) to progress in an orderly fashion along the road to self-government. However, if you have not looked at them in years it would be advisable to do so.

Accounts: Monthly summaries are available about the 7th of the next but one month. The Treasury is concerned with balancing its books. I am interested in actual revenue and expenditure. I think we could get the print out much sooner if the Treasury were not so fussed about advances and deposits. There is need here to have the priorities re-assessed and put right. One matters so much more overall than the other. I also suspect that we do not get the best out of our NCR machines. I personally analyse the revenue and expenditure figures each month and keep up the graphs in my office. I ring up heads of departments and comment where necessary, which at least makes them look at what is happening. It is unwise, however, to comment upon heavy under expenditure – better to keep that up one's sleeve until the estimates! The Treasury is always very pessimistic. In practice I find that my projections are far more accurate and I much regret having been pushed into seeking a supplementary grant-in-aid in 1972 which proved all but unnecessary, even though I asked for half of what the Treasury considered necessary.

Gross waste of expenditure occurs in the last couple of months of the financial year, but can be stopped completely as we found out in 1972. The argument has always been, 'why reduce grant-in-aid already agreed?' With a block system we will be allowed to retain surpluses, or part of them, for transfer to the capital account.

The annual accounts will be changing form for the 1972 accounts. There is no need for a written report and I have asked for straight accounts and no more.

Audit Report: I have given Audit all the support I can and made much of the annual report which, in turn, the Director has reduced in size and made easier to handle. There needs to be a PAC exercise on the 1972 accounts and thereafter. Govco showed keen interest in the last Audit Report.

Write-offs: SEO(F) handles these. Procedure needs tidying up. Now that legal powers have been increased you might delegate to DFS. When the amount exceeds local powers I put to Governing Council and then to the Secretary of State.

Financial Policy: read through recent papers in RF 456/2/1. The basic aim is to keep within revenue which can be raise locally. Grant-in aid is now likely to be fixed in advance. The toughest job, as usual, is to keep expenditure within reasonable bounds. The educational budget is the largest and needs careful watching, agriculture is growing and can be very wasteful and the police budget is also growing ahead of a reasonable percentage rise.

The FCO and ODA economists are rather naïve about projections. I have been disinclined to waste much time over bogus figures. I watch out-turns very closely, however, and in my experience the combination of all factors put together produces very specific trends which can be forecast for the budget as a whole. Attempting to split things up in so small an overall and so economically vulnerable a budget is of little value. For example, in 1973 we have much over-estimated the return from the new fishing industry. The budget was produced before final negotiations and in the event it is taking longer than expected to build up to the catches upon which estimates were based. At the same time we assumed a low figure for copra export duty because of poor prices and low production. As things are we will get very much more. I prefer, therefore, to work on an overall 5% increase in local revenue, which I would expect to increase to 10% quite soon and certainly earlier than my projections submitted to the FCO suggest.

Apart from the aim of eliminating grant-in-aid, and thereby much petty interference from the FCO, there is need to hold administrative expenditure and increase development sector expenditure. Social services expenditure also needs watching but has been held fairly well in health (although inflation seems to have hit drugs etc exceptionally hard) and in education executive capacity to spend is poor. The room for manoeuvre is limited and one can only achieve a good balance by gently nudging things in the right direction over the years. Heads of departments fight hard for increases and are often backed up by the FCO Advisors, who pay little attention to overall issues, concentrating on the status and survival of their professional interests.

The bigger departments habitually over-estimate executive capacity and this offers some slack each year, which is, however, hard to realise without stimulating monumental rows. For example, in 1972 the educational budget was $A250,000 under-spent, largely owing to slow recruitment and the inability of the voluntary agency schools to meet grant requirements, but the Director protested with bitterness when we knocked him back $A50,000 in his 1973 estimates and I am still not forgiven.

TAXATION POLICY

Income Tax: Direct taxation is over the hump and likely to take off. There is a flow of company tax at last, newly established firms of accountants are helping returns, wage levels are getting into the tax area etc. The Ordinance was amended in December 1972. I would not attempt to touch it again for a while. There were no changes proposed in rates but I failed to push through a reduction in personal allowances. But generally things were tidied up in a satisfactory manner. Tax holidays are largely unnecessary and I have taken a hard line but there is legal provision. I recommend holding company tax at 25% for at least another five years and preferably for longer in order to offer some inducement to processing industries and small manufacturing. A low rate of tax, access to the common market at preferential duty rates and low cost labour could entice both Australian and Japanese manufacturers into the area.

When negotiating an agreement lasting for more than ten years I have offered a guaranteed rate of company tax at 33% for the life of the agreement as an alternative to the prevailing rate. This seems a reasonable device although perhaps a bit unfair as I don't think any reasonable government would want to beyond a rate of 33%.

Customs and Excise: The tariff has been amended steadily and is now in a shape which permits reasonable growth without too much tampering. Searching for new growth areas is not easy. I have twice failed to raise the duty on flour. Petrol could possibly stand a bit more but 50 cents a gallon is a useful selling price which brings little complaint. Outboards are affected as well as road transport. Tobacco would also stand an increase (last done in 1971) and would be easy to get through but be cautious about twist tobacco, one of the few consumer incentives in the villages. I feel the same about beer and there is a strong temperance lobby that is concerned with morals not revenue!

The protective tariff on rice has had to be withdrawn because of crop failure. I would be disinclined to re-impose it. Fresh meat now qualifies for a greater measure of protection that I was hesitant to seek while GPL had a virtual monopoly. This should have been broken wide open by the end of 1973. I also think that there is a case for duties on fresh fruit and vegetables now that the local market can supply so much more, including a good variety of European vegetables. There will be a minor expatriate uproar but constant stimulation to the market is needed.

I have quietly reduced duties in development areas and this process should be continued. I am committed by precedent to the abolition of duty on chassis and engines for trucks, trailers and buses. The object is to develop a body building industry and provide some new work for the shipwrights whose timber hulls are tending to be displaced by concrete. The Malaita Development Company has been given remission on bus bodies recently. Duty on diesel has gone which helps the logging and copra industries as well as shipping. Four wheeled vehicles might also be exempt. None of these things would lose much revenue but would be worthwhile gestures.

As you will see from the file I am opposed to the preferential tariff which does us no good. I have agreed with the Comptroller that we should aim for a metric single line tariff to be introduced in 1974. He is working on this now.

As far as new industries and joint ventures are concerned I favour the Sukarno approach of a direct revenue which flows at once and can help to meet the increased costs of government services which new activity generates. I have, therefore, gone firmly for mining royalties and export duties on fish and even on palm oil. The fish duty is partly an incentive to canning and I also justify it as fishing is partly extractive. The fish is there without any local effort but I would oppose any duty on canned fish. The oil palm duty, as agreed, is on a sliding scale. This will need to be introduced into the tariff in due course. But I am in principle opposed to export duties on primary produce and they must be kept under constant review.

Copra Export Duty: Traditionally, copra export duty has been an important source of local revenue. It has to my mind also inhibited the development of the copra industry and as I have said above, needs to be kept constantly under review. In the 1971 budget we removed the $A7 per ton specific duty, which gave some relief to the industry at a time of steeply falling prices. You should read what I then said. Now that the price is rising again and is currently back to at 1970 levels, I would be in favour of making further concessions. We have been thinking of a sliding scale for some time and there are several proposals in the file. The Economist has suggested a very sound scheme which would give us a good flow of revenue at times of high prices but would automatically pull revenue down at times of low prices. There is still plenty of room for discussion about the actual set-off point, which the Economist puts at $A110 f.o.b. but which I feel ought to be $A90 or even $A80, and about the percentage rate. Ideally, we should have introduced a sliding scale before prices began to rise. At a time of high prices, however, the industry would have to pay more which it would resent and it might in practice be simpler to make a concession by reducing the 10% *ad valorem* duty to 7½% or even 5%. You will need to make a careful study of this prior to preparation of the 1974 budget. At the time of writing production has been very low but I understand that it is now picking up and if the price remains good we should be back to a reasonable tonnage by the end of the year.

CURRENCY

There are proposals for the introduction of a local currency in 1976. There is much to be done but until the election is over it is difficult to get on with it. I consider we have enough information available to go on with regard to denominations etc. I would press for the retention of dollar and cent nomenclature and argue for high quality printing and designs incorporating traditional money. There is a timetable in the file.

Exchange Control: The law is a mess as it was intended to protect sterling and since June 1972 there has been no obligation to do so. The Bank of England suggests abandoning control altogether but I am in favour of a simple law and have suggested amendments.

BANKING

A draft Banking Bill is ready for presentation. The Registrar could be the Registrar of Companies or, possibly, the DFS. The government banks with both the ANZ and the CTB. The decision as to where government should bank rests with the FS who must consult the Finance Committee as required by the Public Finance Ordinance. The ANZ is more competent at handling international business. Both managers fear that they do not get their fair share and come to complain from time to time. I try to keep in touch with them and both Waddell (ANZ) and Matthews (CTB) are pleasant and helpful people.

Generally, however, Australian banks are conservative and I have little respect for the operations of either of them. They seem to be greatly overstaffed for the size of their turnover and heavily expatriate staffed at that. Their lending policies are, however, becoming more liberal and Waddell has done a lot to bring bank credit within the reach of Solomon Islanders. I have, however, not discouraged the possibility of another bank and hoped that Barclays International, which has shown interest, might come in. The Hong Kong and Shanghai Banking Corporation has, however, beaten them to it and will be setting up shop later this year. It will be interesting to see how things progress as I doubt if there is really adequate business for three banks. We are under no obligation to give the Hong Kong and Shanghai any business but may find its terms attractive. ANZ and CTB are protesting about the possibility of the Hong Kong and Shanghai getting involved in savings bank business.

ECONOMIC POLICY

Perhaps the best way to see how things have gone in the economy is to read the budget speeches of the last three years. I have endeavoured to persuade people that some development is essential but not to make a fetish of growth. I have been cool towards tourism, keen on agricultural diversification, in favour of fishing for a quick revenue and employment catch and anxious to see one or two major developments well managed and properly off the ground for their demonstration effect. I have also advocated maximum utilisation of what we have and so have favoured home grown foodstuffs and better use of the coconut, 75% of which we currently throw away. If Jamaica, with a smaller annual production, can manufacture margarine, soap, coir and charcoal, I feel we ought to do better. Of course, we lack a good domestic market base but we are on the fringe of markets with high labour costs etc, which should give us an advantage.

Currently cattle seem a great hope. Agriculture is not too keen. It is well worth visiting Yandina to see what Lever's have achieved not only in copra and cattle development but in localisation as well.

For a while at least we must rely on copra for the biggest spread of income with timber and fish as supporters. I don't think we should be too easily frightened by threats that logging and fishing are taking manpower from agriculture. There is a mass of spare capacity all round, but the prophets of doom always adopt negative rather than positive approaches.

Better national accounts would help but we should soon be in a position to do more about this and I would recommend getting UNDAT assistance.

SIXTH DEVELOPMENT PLAN

The Sixth Development Plan is now in its third year. The Plan remains the base document. It is reviewed annually. The reviews to date have done little more than update plan projects and report implementation progress. As time goes on, assuming some spare capacity, it should be possible to include some specific appraisals and certainly there should be cross referencing to any work currently being undertaken, which could be of direct or indirect significance. For example, Watt in Forestry, produces bits and pieces of value which you may not even see.

I have made something of a fetish about implementation procedures and I don't think that I have carried everyone with me. I believe in a proper historical record for the sake of posterity as well as strict plan discipline. It is hard enough to keep a civil service to a plan, let alone a dynamic political government (which we currently lack). This doesn't mean inflexibility. The plan can be extremely flexible but it does mean recognised authorities for variation that forces some re-appraisal not only of objectives but priorities. The discipline of choice is also fundamental to the economic and political education of both legislature and civil service, namely 'Yes, you may have X but will you have it instead of A, B or C?'

ODA economists sneer at our elaborate project lists, which they castigate as shopping lists but, of course, they haven't usually looked at them very carefully. Some international agencies have, on the other hand, been very flattering and I believe that a sound project list, kept up to date and linked annually with the capital budget, is an essential control document. There are anomalies and by no means all concerned really understand some aspects of plan procedures. There is, for example, a failure to appreciate that there can be plan provision which will not be provided by the UK. Project 15201 for Rennell Mine land acquisition and infrastructure comprises a $A300,000 development aid project to meet our commitment under terms of the agreement with Mitsui and $A200,000, which will be paid by the mining company after the final agreement is signed. The total due from the company is $A700,000 but the project as it stands should be sufficient within this Plan period. After costs totalling $A1,000,000 have been met ($A300,000 by us and $700,000 by the company) any additional costs will be our responsibility again, presumably from a local transfer to the capital budget of sums earned from recurrent mining revenue.

Both local staff and FCO tend to assume, however, that any figure in the Plan must be tied into UK aid and get agitated about the size of provision etc. Again, if the ADB comes up trumps with loan finance for SIPL it will have nothing to do with UK aid project 192, which was a grant for equity in SIPL.

There has also been confusion over the Plan provision for carry over projects. All expenditure within the Plan period is intended to appear in the project list; it may or may not be 'new' money.

ODA also objects to unallocated balances in plans but I have told FCO and ODA quite firmly that it is none of their business. The object of unallocated balances is to provide flexibility where estimating has been inexact at an early stage in project identification and during a period of rising prices. At the same time it preserves sectoral balance and enforces plan discipline. The trouble is that the ODA men have little if any experience of administering a plan in a political environment.

SAS(D) is the key man for plan implementation. He reports to DFS. I have tried, once the Plan was approved, to keep away from detail except where variations involve either FS or Finance Committee and to approve the annual review. Personnel changes in the SAS(D) schedule can lead to misunderstanding and lack of continuity and I think in retrospect that I ought to have taken a closer interest in the submission of aid applications for actual projects, some of which have got very much out of hand.

Development aid project applications are usually drafted in the department concerned, a practice which I do not like but which is firmly entrenched. I think it is much better if the department sends the material and leaves the Planning Unit to draft around it a project in standard language and format. It would help if all projects could be discussed within F to ensure that everyone has all the relevant background. It is advisable to keep details as simple as possible to avoid subsequent audit queries and even disallowance. The Treasury has to submit an annual statement on each project and we receive quarterly advances based on a submission in the middle of each quarter. The quarterly returns and the annual statements are produced in £Stg because of the fluctuating rate of exchange. I have asked the FCO that we should in future produce them in $A. This is an outstanding issue and one of considerable concern as you will see from the papers. There are a few projects in dispute between FCO and us at present. SAS(D) can brief you on these. I also expect the FCO to be difficult about the Choiseul Bay sub-station project which has many unattractive features, notably that there is no population at Choiseul bay!

North Malaita Road: ODA has arranged for a cost benefit evaluation of the North Malaita Road. This first attempt at evaluation is being undertaken by a Brunel University student, called Carpenter. He has just started work. He seems fairly self-assured and most probably will get on with the job without too much bother. He is not, however, an economist and you may find that this causes extra work for Patrick Spread, who is doubtful of Carpenter's ability to handle the economic side of things.

SEVENTH DEVELOPMENT PLAN

The Seventh Development Plan covers the period 1975 to 1979. I have been opposed to shorter period plans and to rolling plans on the grounds that we do not have the executive capacity to do more than get a plan moving and keep it under annual review. Equally, I am opposed to inputs of ODA labour to help us plan. Experts not under firm control are a nuisance; ODA experts who make out that their opinion is all that matters, a damn nuisance. In fact Garth Armstrong, who was here before DP6, has far more influence on the FCO/ODA than I have. We spent about 2½ years preparing for the present plan, which was intended to have a three year life, and even before it had been born it was clear that we would need to extend it for a fourth year. A preliminary draft of plan objectives has been agreed by the Finance Committee and has been distributed. Patrick Spread, the economist, who writes well, has the task of guiding things along and producing the final draft. He will need a lot of assistance and guidance, particularly on the political side but I am sure he is capable of a workmanlike job. The final draft should go to Governing Council in August 1974 if you are going to have the plan ready and in print and some projects agreed and funded to start in January 1975. There will a certain number of carry-over projects from the Sixth Development Plan which ought to be incorporated in the new plan.

It has been agreed that the format of the Seventh Development Plan should follow that of the Sixth which has proved acceptable and is now generally understood. I have insisted on detailed project lists as far as public sector expenditures are concerned because in my experience this is the only effective way of controlling the Plan. Plan project numbers are also used as the capital subhead numbers in the annual Estimates. The numbering system is flexible and it should be possible to retain sector, sub-sector, programmes and sub-programme numbering from plan to plan.

Usually we have been completely orientated towards UK development aid and, certainly, a vast mass of our projects has been funded this way in the past. As a member of ADB, however, and with increased activity by Australia and New Zealand in the Pacific, there is no reason why we should not shop around much more for resources to implement the Seventh Plan. It will be a major exercise to convince the civil service here and the FCO that this can and should be done. I am strongly opposed to the practice of seeking bids from departments for aid offers from the new sources. If we cannot tie aid firmly into the plan we should reject it. I have tried to steer Australia into livestock support and New Zealand might be interested in forestry.

The FCO will want to see the plan in draft and will almost certainly comment upon some projects as being undesirable. If, however, they are wanted they should be retained. And we should look for funds from elsewhere if we think there will be UK objections. It will become even more essential now to convince the Treasury and the departments that the Development Plan project list, as annually amended, and the Capital Estimates are the controlling documents for the plan and not just development aid project memoranda. These are certainly important in regard to the projects with which they are concerned but as we progress into other areas of financing, the Treasury will have to make the adjustment and be more interested in the Plan and Capital Estimates than has been the case in the past. There has, however, been a great improvement in 1972 and 1973.

In general, I suggest that you reckon on expenditure of about $A5M a year excepting any expenditure such as equity contributions or loan finance for a joint venture, say a plan total of £A30M. You will need a ceiling to keep people's feet on the ground. I very much doubt if the country has the overall capacity to spend more. We have tended to have rather a lot of small projects in the present plan and it would be better to go for a few larger projects but this must be balanced against the length of time that a larger project takes to prepare and, therefore, the resulting delay in implementation as well as the fact that smaller projects seeking UK aid can be approved at a lower level than larger ones and so get through the pipe line much quicker.

The general emphasis is likely to be very similar to the present plan. I personally am in favour of putting as much as possible into communications infrastructure with roads and shipping services as the highest priorities. Social service spending will be needed and in the areas which result in greatly increased recurrent expenditure which, of course, needs to be avoided. Both economically and politically if grants can be obtained, money spent on public buildings of popular appeal, such as a sports stadium, would be well spent in the next period during which there will an increasing attempt to establish national identity.

AID, TECHNICAL ASSISTANCE AND VOLUNTEERS

F Branch is responsible for all aid and technical assistance, including volunteers. We do not get involved, if we can help it, in domestic problems of staff after arrival, which is the business of the host department. There is also need for close liaison with Establishments Branch. The main source of grant aid is ODA and we rely on ODA for TA as well, but increasingly look to UNDP. The UNDP regional representative, Bill Hussey, is in Apia. He is a forceful chap who rather rushes one along but he gets things moving and can be a great ally. In Suva there is UNDAT, which has economists, statisticians, public administration experts etc. and can get a chap here at the drop of a hat at absolutely no cost and with the minimum of palaver. If you have a specific assignment these are good men to use.

There is a swarm of ESCAFE experts on permanent offer. They need to be treated with caution. ESCAFE is the worst example of the proliferation of the aid industry that I have come across and membership is a waste of money. It was, however, a necessary passport to the ASDB and Govco chairmen get some benefit from its annual sessions.

ADB looks as though it may be useful. The approach is very legalistic and you must study the membership file carefully because you will undoubtedly have a lot more work to do in clearing up detail. The Reconnaissance Mission seems favourably disposed. Dr Ettlinger, the leader, is an old hand at the aid game, however, and can be difficult with respect to his personal whims and fancies. We are soon going to be swamped with ADB papers and filing needs to be sorted out.

WHO, ILO, UNESCO etc are all here under UNDP auspices. The battle is to prevent heads of departments from accepting every offer as a free gift. Each appointment costs us quite a lot and tends to lead to the creation of services we cannot afford.

Australian aid, SPAP, is likely to be stepped up and New Zealand is offering aid for the first time. The Commonwealth Secretariat has proved a speedy and efficient aid donor although funds and opportunities are very limited.

There have been far too many volunteers kicking around, often under-supervised and without a real job to do. It is now under control and F Committee examines volunteer programmes annually. Personally, I believe the day has passed for any but the most skilled and dedicated volunteers and if in doubt I have individuals sent home. Currently we have Peace Corps, UNA, CUSO and VSA. The VSO group has gone and will not be replaced.

The crucial thing is to incorporate all aid into the plan policy and reject what we don't really need.

MAJOR NEGOTIATIONS

The FS has supervised and usually chaired personally all major negotiations with overseas companies in recent years. With the establishment of the Commerce and Industry Committee of Governing Council I have tried to pass as much as possible on the smaller deals over to the SAS(C&I). Bigger deals, however, which involve other chairmen, e.g, Natural Resources, are best co-ordinated in F Branch which is responsible for the overall economy, although it is important to make it clear that the FS is not personally responsible for such matters as land acquisition, which must be handled by the department responsible. Negotiations with Mitsui, Taiyo, CDC and CEA have been a major part of my job.

I have had to learn a great deal as I have gone along, particularly with regard to technical aspects. I have found, however, this to be one of the most interesting and satisfying parts of my job in the Solomons.

Each major negotiation has a file in the restricted file series and I keep the reports concerning them close at hand. We have established certain precedents, which are not recorded in any one place, so I will list them here:

(1) Governing Council must be kept as fully in the picture as possible and it is entirely a matter for your judgement when and how this is done. A flow of information papers, as brief and as simple as possible, is perhaps one of the best ways. You will not want to be too tied by decisions when actually negotiating.

(2) Any final agreement must be ratified by Governing Council in public. The Taiyo Joint Venture Agreement provides a full precedent for the procedure. I have, however, opposed the idea that preliminary agreements or agreements in principle should be subject to ratification in public. According to their importance, they can be approved by Governing Council in private meeting or by the appropriate committee.

(3) Negotiations leading to final agreements being signed must be on home ground. Earlier technical and preliminary meetings can be away but preferably on your ground, thus we used the British Embassy in Tokyo.

(4) Always retain the initiative by chairing all negotiations yourself. Governments have this advantage over the private sector and it must not be lost. I have always determined the agenda and guided its direction. Although, of course, such matters have to be agreed mutually, there is much to be said for discussion revolving around your own draft.

(5) We usually accept responsibility for drafting the final documents. We did not do this in the case of CDC and I regret it. There are now sufficient precedents around for one to make a pretty good stab at it. The problem is usually one of time. Our law officers are not very experienced in commercial drafting and have not yet played much of a role. They need to be brought more into things even though we have a UN lawyer available as in the mining deals.

(6) We have used consultants, hired by ODA and at no cost to ourselves. Consultants Allan, Charlesworth & Co., city accountants, are so valuable that I have persuaded the FCO to retain them for any major negotiations. The background knowledge they now have of the Solomons is extremely valuable and the continuity factor will be particularly useful to you. John Laurence is my contact. I correspond with him freely and directly and, on the whole, once agreement for the services to be used has been reached, do not concern the FCO. Mackay & Schnellmann PTY. Ltd are our mining consultants who we should continue to use because of the knowledge built up. Dr Fitch is a former Director of Geological Surveys in Sarawak. His relations with our own Director are not particularly good, but he is certainly a useful man to have and Alan Hansel, the mining engineer, has a great deal of knowledge and experience which one cannot do without. Finally, we have made use of the United Nations to bring to the negotiating table an independent third party. Chuck Lipton on mineral legislation is in a unique position because he has attended so many similar negotiations all around the world. He can be difficult to handle, as can all the consultants, but I have found him an enormous asset. UN consultancies arranged through the regional representative of UNDP.

SOLOMON ISLANDS PLANTATIONS LTD.

The government has a Joint Venture Agreement with CDC to establish an oil palm plantation on the Guadalcanal plains. Our equity is 26%. The project is going well and is very effectively managed by Joe Mulholland. You will find, however, that he is protocol conscious and extremely reluctant to deal with anyone in government other than the FS. While I always get along well with him personally, he infuriates junior members of my staff whom he enjoys tying up in knots.

There are three current problems, one of which I fear, will recur throughout your stay. This is the question of land. It is not, of course, primarily a finance matter but I have found it essential to keep myself fully briefed and occasionally to seek compromise if things look as if they are breaking down. Brian Twomey understands the position intimately and you will do well to get a personal briefing. The second problem concerns the supply of seed. This has been obtained from Malaysia but the Malaysian Government has imposed a ban on export and things have got rather behindhand as a result. However, this month they have allowed us to take 50,000 germinated seeds and alternative sources of supply will be available from Papua New Guinea in another year or two. The third problem is one with which you must become immediately concerned. Our equity in SIPL is provided by a UK development aid grant. The UK is not, however, prepared to give us a grant or loan to provide the matching loan capital for which we are responsible. This amounts to about £A1 million, namely 26% of the total required. It seems likely that ADB will give favourable consideration to a loan at concessionary rates for the off-shore costs of establishing the mill and storage tanks. The amount involved is about $US 4 million which, of course, is more than we ourselves have to provide. ADB, however, understandably does not want to get involved in the arrangements between CDC and the government and thinks it will be much easier to offer loans to government for on-lending on a back-to-back basis to SIPL. ADB procurement procedures will have to be used and this could prove an obstacle in persuading the CDC. The matter has been taken up with the FCO and I will pursue it personally while in the UK.

Oil Palm Outgrowers Scheme

It is hoped to back up the SIPL project with an outgrower scheme. The initial target is 3,000 acres but it could grow to a much larger acreage in future years. The people on the plains are, however, extremely difficult to handle and we stumble from disaster to disaster. It really needs somebody of much higher calibre than we have available to coordinate the project. In general, my inclination is to leave well alone until pressure builds up as a result of a policy of deliberate neglect. This may, however, not be practicable and you will need to get the feel of the new Governing Council before making up your mind. The initiative ought to come from Agriculture and Natural Resources Committee but, in practice, everyone will wait upon you.

GPL RICE

Also on the Gualalcanal plains is a rice project. The company, GPL, is being taken over by an American corporation but full details are not yet known. There should be a substantial injection of capital but what the company really needs is management. The rice crop has failed once more owing to pest destruction which could have been avoided had management decisions been taken at the right time. The only person who knows anything about rice is Frank Corres who is currently on holiday in the Philippines. I have negotiated with the Philippine Government to ensure that he returns. He is liked by the Solomon Islander staff who respect him, but is at loggerheads with the Australians. He ought to be given a free hand and things will improve. The 2 cents protective duty has been removed.

The Agriculture Department is less than lukewarm about rice. I argue, however, that whether we like it or not, Solomon Islanders have taken to rice and moved away from locally produced roots. In time, as some wage earners have already begun to do, they will move from rice to wheat. Meanwhile we can produce rice here and by doing so can help to control imported inflation now (rice comes from affluent Australia not poverty line Asia) and the balance of payments in the future.

There is always a possibility of our having to invest to keep the industry alive. A good report was made last year by Dr Jordon and you should read this before coming to any conclusions.

TAIYO FISHERY COMPANY LIMITED

Government has a Joint Venture Agreement with the Taiyo Fishery Company of Japan in a commercial fishing venture in the Solomons under the auspices of a local company, called Solomon Taiyo. You should study the Allen, Charlesworth report on the Joint Venture Agreement which usefully consolidates all the key documents. This has been an area of major activity during my term of office and it would be as well if you could familiarise yourself with the files and debates in Governing Council. The company is still in its infancy and we are, of course, going through the difficulties of seeing that the agreement is kept. Mr Pepys-Cockerell is on special duties, fisheries and the maintenance of the agreement is his primary task but he is far from a fit man and you cannot rely upon him to gauge priorities and keep to timetables. Currently, charter agreements and marketing agreements to be made between Solomon Taiyo and the parent company are subject to approval. There are serious objections to both as you can see from the file. You will find Patrick Spread knowledgeable and helpful in this area and if needs be you should not hesitate to call upon the services of our consultants. It is my guess that Taiyo will try to promote long lining either by themselves or the local company or, possibly, by both. I don't think we should oppose this. A great deal of long-lining is going on in our waters and we may as well get in on the act. We have proved that Solomon Islanders can take to long lining and provide the major component of a ship's crew. Any agreement should insist on these employment opportunities, which are not only helpful to the economy (although the Director of Agriculture would dispute this) but lessen the social problems which foreign fishing crews produce. You may find that in reaching agreement on a long-lining operation you will have to accept a different basis for obtaining direct revenue. Much of the fish is caught in waters over which the Solomons has no jurisdiction. The larger tuna are likely to be wanted for canning locally and would not be transferred to a freezer ship, which can result in some deterioration in quality. Variation in price for larger tuna is enormous and it would be very hard to negotiate a fair f.o.b. value. I would suggest alteration of the law to increase the licence fee for long- liner ships and obtain revenue this way.

So long as Taiyo keep a front man here with whom you can communicate things go quite well. Morio Mito is easy to get along with and I believe is completely sincere. This, however, makes his masters rather suspicious of him and they may use my departure as an opportunity to pull in somebody else. I have refused to deal with a man called Kanna who was here for a while and utterly disastrous. Capt. Honda, the Managing Director and operations expert is a pleasant person who obviously enjoys the Solomons and wants the company to be a success. His English is getting better but it is still difficult to communicate effectively.

Mitsui – Bauxite mining on Rennell

The government has an agreement in principle to enter into a joint venture with the Mitsui Mining and Smelting Company of Japan to mine bauxite on Rennell Island. The best way to master the background would be to read the two volumes of the Allan, Charlesworth report which contain all the basic documents. For a variety of reasons Mitsui now seems rather unwilling to come to the wedding and we renegotiated a year's additional time at the end of 1972. We obtained from Mitsui payment of $A1,000,000 advance of mining revenue which is non-returnable in the event if things go wrong, but interest bearing should the mine go ahead. $A590,000, the second instalment, is due to be paid in June this year. It will inflate Geological Survey revenue two years running so be cautious! Mitsui has promised to deliver a final feasibility study in mid May and I have arranged a meeting in London on 8 June with our consultants to discuss it. I will report back thereafter. My guess is that Mitsui will attempt to renegotiate terms on the grounds that mining costs are much higher than were first expected. In all probability, the best solution may be to refuse to continue and hope that CRA, which seems prepared to go ahead on Vaghena, will pick up Rennell as well in due course.

I personally will be sorry to see this happen because I have grown to respect Mitsui and in many ways I think a Japanese managed enterprise is less likely to cause undue disruption in a place like Rennell. You will learn that there is a conservationist lobby, including the Duke of Edinburgh, which condemns our proposal to mine on Rennell at all. Internationally, the lobby is led by two Danish anthropologists, who spent a lot of time on Rennell and Bellona, and have mustered academic support far and wide. If mining does go ahead, it will be advisable for the government to seek the services of an economic anthropologist to help and advise the Rennellese people. To an old colonial hand like myself it seems unthinkable that this cannot be done more effectively by the district administration but there is little continuity or experience these days and specialists are probably needed to combat overseas criticism.

The danger would be to leave matters open and have the international lobby hire a lawyer to fight on behalf of the Rennellese.

The Rennellese have in fact never had it so good. The great tragedy is that they demand everything for themselves as individuals and we have not been able to establish trusts that could build up community projects of some value to future generations. The lessons we have learned from compensation difficulties on Rennell need to be well digested and passed on.

VAGHENA BAUXITE – CRA EXPLORATION PTY LTD.

There is a proposal by CRA to mine bauxite on Vaghena in the Western Solomons. Matters will come to a head by the middle of this year when CRA are likely to put up a detailed proposal. There is already some in formation available. CRA's proposal is to mine and sell at a substantial price which is in our interest. They accept the principle of a royalty payment and company taxation, but I am not sure it will be easy to negotiate any equity and it would certainly be much harder to obtain a free ride than it has been from the Japanese. I get on well with John Innes who negotiates on behalf of CRA and have found that a frank approach has been mutually appreciated and beneficial. This is likely to be the first major negotiation in which you will get involved.

CEMENT CLINKER

CRA and Blue Circle cement are talking with us in a desultory way about manufacturing cement clinker for export to Sydney where it would be ground and bagged. It is an interesting series of factors which makes this unlikely proposal worth further investigation.

AIR PACIFIC

The Solomons has an equity share in Air Pacific and the DFS is our director. The airline is not particularly well managed and there is a conflict between the interests of the major airlines and the small countries in the partnership. It is likely that the airline will break up if Fiji grows too ambitious for Quantas and BOAC. Our primary objective is to retain a good regional service and we should not be afraid of some competition.

SOLOMON ISLANDS TOBACCO CO LTD.

There has been a proposal to manufacture cigarettes in the Solomons where twist tobacco is already manufactured. You will see from the papers in the file that the project was only marginally attractive from the revenue point of view and for social reasons the government decided to refuse any special concessions. This has put some useful pressure on the company which may still well decide to manufacture. You will then have to negotiate an excise duty.

HOLIDAY INN

There is a currently active proposal; for a Holiday Inn hotel in Honiara in which government would take an equity share as a premium for land. SAS(C&I) is handling.

UNIVERSITY OF THE SOUTH PACIFIC (USP)

The financing of USP will provide a major headache as the years go by. We are in a very weak position. My view has been that if a regional status is to be preserved we must expect to pay for it but try to keep academic fancies within reason. I have had a personal interest in this but because of time have been unable to do much about it. I believe we should prepare for sixth form work here, possibly offering places to GEIC and NH, and opt out of Suva preliminary courses. Fiji will not need them much longer and neither will the University when the age range creeps down as it is bound to do and they find themselves with the care of sixteen year old girls. There is also the danger that one cannot easily pull back a student who has started a preliminary university course unless he fails abysmally. You are obliged to give him a scholarship for a degree course for which he may be unsuited.

EUROPEAN ECONOMIC COMMUNITY

We will soon have to make up our minds about the EEC. Activity will increase towards the end of 1974. My current thinking is that association will pay off if there is a chance of more processing industries and fish processing alone might justify it.

INVESTMENT AGENCY

You will find in the file my ideas for the proposed investment agency, which have not got off the ground because of the difficulty of justifying aid for starter funds. I have now advanced in my thinking. It seems to me that if we can get the existing statutory bodies together under one umbrella then there would be scope for higher calibre top management, redistribution and better utilisation of middle management, with rationalisation of accountancy services in particular, as well as an immediate cash flow. The bodies concerned are the Ports, Electricity and Housing Authorities and the Agricultural and Industrial Loans Board. The Copra Board could not easily be brought in because of its sacred cow position in the eyes of the planters. Its function is also essentially one of marketing and while it could usefully be within a larger organisation it may be better to wait until such an organisation has proved its effectiveness. The Tourist Authority is different again and best left alone unless the government at a latter date decides to promote rather than control tourism. These parts of a development corporation could be broadly classified into three divisions: Investment, Utilities and Property.

Within the Investment Division I would expect several departments to merge, ranging from the original concept of an investment agency managing the government portfolio and entering into partnerships with foreign investors to the Small Business Credit Scheme. One would hope that, with increased competition, the commercial banks would provide all the middle level credit facilities. I would see government handing over its investments as assets to help establish the umbrella organisation and seeking soft loans from the ADB, membership of which is another reason for the proposed new tactics. The ADB likes to have a local institution to undertake on-lending and the AILB would in any case need to be restructured to cope with much more business. It must have field staff – a point of disagreement between the present chairman and myself. He is only interested in agro based lending and believes his departmental staff is all that is required. He wants, of course, to increase his departmental staff!

Existing government investments are in SIPL, Solomon Taiyo and Air Pacific. Investments have been negotiated in Mitsui (BSIP) and Pacific Holiday Investments.

On the utilities side, apart from those now provided by statutory bodies, water supply in Honiara and main centres might be linked with electricity. There could be savings in meter reading, accounting, management etc. The present supply is viable. Two other possibilities, worthy of examination, are the marine workshops and slipway at Tulagi, which cry out for commercial utilisation and are the best such facility in the Solomons, and parts of the marine fleet. I would be opposed to any lock, stock and barrel transfer. The government has got to provide shipping between islands in exactly the same way as other governments provide roads on the mainland. For a long time services will be uneconomic and it might be as well to accept this and carry the burden directly rather than subsidise another organisation. There is also need for the police to have direct control of vessels in an emergency.

The Property Division might usefully move into all types of building and manage the property of the entire group – something which can make for economy and which is often forgotten – as well as providing good quality housing for purchase and rental by low level income groups.

I suggest that this is one of the areas where you will have most scope for innovation in the next year or so.

J.H. Smith

Financial Secretary

16 May 1973

Appendix B

First Impressions Despatch dated 13 November 1973

The Right Honourable Sir Alec Douglas-Home, KT MP,
Secretary of State for Foreign and Commonwealth Affairs,
The Foreign and Commonwealth office,
London SW1.

Sir,

Sir Arthur Grimble has written so ably and popularly about these remote and unusual islands that it is as impossible for a newcomer not to feel intimidated about offering first impressions as it is to arrive without preconceptions. But the islands and their peoples are no longer quite the same as those with whom Grimble first came into contact half a century ago and first impressions are of value because the absolute sameness of atoll ecology and equatorial climate quickly blunt the edge of perceptions, while the background of sun, surf and sand can encourage the unwary to fall into the relaxed mood of island life.

I have arrived in a pause before substantial constitutional advance. The present 'member' system has outworn its usefulness as the elected members of the Executive Council have grown in stature and become resentful of expatriate public service members. There is also a constitutional pause before a decision on the future of the Ellice Islands is implemented. Economically the Colony is in the twilight of mineral prosperity. Ocean Island phosphate will be worked out in 1978. It contributes the major part of external earnings, more than half the government revenue and five hundred jobs. Socially the effects of aid supported health and educational policies with which the general economy has not kept pace are beginning to be felt. An island environment fosters introversion and xenophobia and there is less appreciation of what is about to happen than is healthy.

The constitution to be introduced next year will confirm an elected majority in the legislature, establish it in the executive, introduce the principle of collective responsibility and put ministers firmly into a position to exercise general direction and control of departments of government. If transitional colonial constitutions are to lead smoothly from the one into the next the spirit in which they are operated must be in advance of the letter, and, when the new government is formed after a general election in April 1974, the colony will be not far short of internal self-government. The election itself is likely to bring not just change in members but in the educational and social background from which membership of the legislature is drawn. In particular the articulate urban wage earning class is likely to be represented for the first time and some younger, well educated civil servants, impatient of the pace of localisation and scornful of the older members who dominate the legislature, will turn to politics.

Constitutional change will also follow the decision on the future of the Ellice Islands. Gilbertese desire to be rid of the need to share their limited heritage with the Ellice is no less real because it has been muted in an endeavour to preserve an image of statesmanlike impartiality and to ensure that any opprobrium should fall on the Ellice Islanders who have actively sought separation. The Gilbertese position is now the most important element in the politics of separation and there would be a quick response to any withdrawal of Ellice pressure. The mechanics of separation will revolve around jobs: the Ellice unable to absorb all the trained manpower available and the Gilbertese determined to replace every Ellice Islander in employment.

That jobs will play a major role in the political scene, that labour is showing a new potential for organisation and leadership, and that the educated and political elite are restless are factors indicative of the economic and social change which has taken place in recent years. 25% of the population now live in South Tarawa, crowded into the three settlements of Betio, Bairiki and Bikenibeu, and 85% of the children of school age enjoy a nine year primary course.

His expectations aroused by Grimble, the expatriate will find the overcrowding, lack of sewage, inadequate water supply and confusion of litter that characterise urban Tarawa unattractive, and he may well be disappointed in its diffident and occasionally ungracious gum-clicking population. But urban Tarawa offers post primary education, electric power, shops, cinemas, dancehalls, bars, freedom from parental restraint and above all the chance to jingle money in one's pocket not once or twice a year but every week. It also provides the demonstration of expatriate ways of life even though it provokes the jealousies which relative affluence and occupation of choice beach sites are bound to arouse. In contrast the most obvious evidence of a century of British rule on the outer islands is the enormously tall flagpoles which thrust the Union Flag above the palm fronds to compete with the spires of the many and lavish churches. Remoteness and size of population have limited what could be done and the churches, whose policies have been conservative and law and order inclined, as are those of the island councils, have done little to hold the enterprising. The growth of urban Tarawa is the inevitable consequence of contact with an external economy just as the social changes taking place are the consequence of the exposure of an overwhelming proportion of the population to Western forms of education. It is neither desirable nor possible to put the clock back or halt the pace of change. But is essential to consider how the economy can withstand the shock.

For years it was assumed that it would be possible to graft on to the traditional economy and culture only the barest trimmings of the Western world. Over centuries the islanders had evolved a pattern of life which made their chosen atoll homes tolerable at a level of existence that would seem affluent to the poorest peoples of South East Asia. The more debilitating tropical diseases, including malaria, are unknown. The Gilberts (though not the Ellice) are outside the cyclone belt. There is an abundance of fish, coconuts, pandanus and taro that provides a balanced diet, shelter, and the accoutrements of culture. Born in a world in which the land is but a stroke of green between an immensity of sea and sky the Gilbertese have achieved their highest expression of art in the construction of canoes. Capable of great turns of speed the sailing canoe has reduced the loneliness of atoll existence, kept the people together and enabled a homogenous culture to survive.

But it was impossible to contain the intrusion of the Western world with its whalers, traders, missionaries and finally colonial administrators. Exposure to an external economy has introduced exchange where it had hardly been needed, encouraged specialization which previously had been tolerated only as demonstration of exceptional skill in canoe building or dance, and brought incentives to a society by custom suspicious of the individual who stepped out of line.

For a century copra and the one mineral resource, Ocean Island phosphate, have been adequate to permit the import of metal fish-hooks, kerosene lamps, cloth, tobacco and the other items a limited atoll economy might be expected to need and be unable to produce for itself. But convenience has dictated a diet of Queensland rice and bully beef for phosphate workers. Income appeared sufficient to indulge the taste and rice and canned meat have become staple foodstuffs. The common stocking and pricing policies of the co-operative trading has allowed the spread of imported food through out the islands. The pattern of trade has remained tied to Australia, now one of the more expensive markets in the world in which to buy and through which even cheaper British goods are channelled, with a consequent mark-up, because manufacturers sweep the entire Pacific into the ambit of their Sydney agents. The economy is feeling the strain of imported inflation and in 1972 the value of staple imports was more than double the value of copra exports.

It is not just imported food for which a taste has been acquired but also the social services which are enjoyed elsewhere. The demand has quickly grown and has been largely met by aid from the churches, from Britain, from the international agencies and most recently from Australia and New Zealand as well. Aid has produced its own distortions. The more aid there is, the greater the encouragement of local assumptions that it an obligation to redress exploitation, real or supposed, of earlier times. Aid is then demanded as a right rather than because it is needed in any particular circumstance. The attempt to achieve economies of scale has encouraged centralisation which, in its turn, has prompted urban growth. An enlarged and concentrated expatriate population needs an increasing amount of servicing. Lack of development on outer islands leads to guilt feelings. For example, it is believed that senior primary school fees of $A1 a year for a maximum of two children a family are excessive but charity raffle tickets are readily sold for 50 cents apiece.

The day of economic reckoning is near. The increasing population and the high price of imports will place new demands upon coconuts as food and reduce the amount of copra available for export. More important, Ocean Island phosphate will have been worked out by 1978. Efforts are, therefore, being made to improve the coconut crop which has in the past been left untended and 73% of which has been wasted because only copra has been marketed. There is little scope for other agriculture and the results of coconut development projects lie in the future. Reliance upon a single vegetable oil export is, moreover, in itself unsatisfactory. Immediate relief is being provided by a new source of income, worth nearly half a million dollars a year, from remittances sent home by foreign going seamen.

The establishment of the Merchant Marine Training School is perhaps the most exciting and useful achievement of British administration since the war and certainly has done more than anything else to bring the colony into the twentieth century. Deckhands, engine room greasers and stewards are trained and find employment in foreign shipping lines, mainly in a German consortium which supports the training. The doubts of the International Transport Workers' Federation have unfortunately placed the scheme in jeopardy and could put an end to it but by local standards the seamen are well paid. An 18 year old steward can earn as much as the captain of a colony ship or his former primary school headmaster and little less than a graduate district officer. There are just under a thousand men in employment. If this number is to be expanded skilled negotiation with international labour organisations and a dynamic approach in seeking new employers will be required. We also need to set our sights higher to keep pace with rising educational standards and look for something better than the bottom rung of the nautical ladder for the school's graduates.

As well as putting to economic use the natural seamanship of the Gilbertese and Ellice Islanders an effort is being made to exploit the sea itself by the development of commercial fishing. To date the approach has been costly, aid oriented, bureaucratic and timid of foreign investment. The lesson has now been learned that there will have to be an overseas partner who can bring operational and marketing skills as well as capital to match the local contribution of labour and fish. The Development Authority, established in 1972, will be able to provide the necessary commercial experience to permit effective negotiation.

While seafaring and commercial fishing can provide additional employment and income the natural limitation of total resources sets not only a level on the standard of living but a time scale as well. The population, despite a widely understood and accepted control programme, is growing apace and an ever increasing proportion can be expected to seek regular wage employment and urban amenities.

Although in the short term improved communications combined with effective decentralisation could assist the growth of other centres and Tarwa itself could contain more, the economy, already overstretched, will not for long be able to sustain the technology required to make a tolerable existence possible. It is time to seek opportunities not only for external employment but for settlement as well. The total population is not large. It could be absorbed in a single year's immigration quota into Australia and still leave room for as many again. The earlier evacuation of whole communities from drought plagued atolls to the Solomon Islands should not and need not be repeated. Whole island communities are hefty dumplings for a racial stew pot, but the young Gilbertese or Ellice Islander who has seen something of the outside world, wants to go back and, if given the chance, opt to settle. Redundant phosphate workers from Ocean Island in 1978, from Nauru in the 1990s, seamen looking for a land job after a decade or so at sea and unemployed secondary school leavers, whose numbers will undoubtedly increase despite rigid manpower policies, all need an outlet. The Gilbertese and Ellice Islander suffer from the limitations of their environment, but potential migrants would be English speaking, accustomed to the rule of law and Western democratic institutions, cash motivated and of proven assimilability. A group already happily settled in Melbourne through marriage may be pioneers of a new pattern of migration which could leave some of the atolls uninhabited fifty years hence. The alternative is for the rest of the world to pay for the technology necessary to keep islanders at home.

It is an alternative which could quickly degrade and reduce a decent and deserving people into decadence. The first development decade by-passed the Pacific, but so did the intense nationalism which accompanied it. The international pressure for de-colonisation is off and local leadership can easily be seduced by the apparent advantages of dependence politics. Aid concentrated on essential short-term infrastructure, insistence on properly safe-guarded commercial partnerships for viable projects, and the rapid promotion of localisation must all accompany forthcoming constitutional advance if the people are to be saved from themselves. There is also room for the development of regional institutions which could reduce the burden on a small island economy of the expensive services without which it is difficult to retain contact with the outside world and the confidence of the people. Civil aviation, marine navigation and specialist medical services are areas in which a dynamic common services organisation could provide what is needed at higher standards and lower costs than could otherwise be obtained.

I am hopeful that the election to be held next year will produce a Government ready and able to face the formidable but exciting challenge.

I have the honour etc.

John Smith

Appendix C

INDEPENDENCE

Questions to be answered before an independence constitution can be drafted.

A constitution is a set of rules for governing a country. Independence removes external influence and the people of the Gilbert Islands will have an opportunity to decide for themselves the rules by which they want to be governed. To help discussion of a set of rules for independence, a list of some questions which have to be answered is given below. The questions take into account the following:

> **(a)** Gilbertese custom, remembering that custom does not stand still but survives in everyday use by change and adaptation:
>
> **(b)** The experience of recent years as a nation taking part in regional affairs and dealing with international organisations; and
>
> **(c)** The present system of government to which people have become accustomed.

Name
1. Should the name of the country remain the Gilbert Islands or should it be changed?
2. If the name is to be changed how should a new name be found?
3. Have you a name you would prefer?

Place in the world
4. Should the Gilbert Islands remain in the Commonwealth?
5. Should the Gilbert Islands join the United Nations or only continue membership of the various UN agencies such as WHO?
6. Should the present fundamental human rights provisions be retained in the constitution?

7. If so, are there any changes which should be made?
8. Who should qualify to be a citizen of the Gilbert Islands?
9. Should there be any means by which those without constitutional qualification as citizens can become citizens?
10. If so, on whose authority?

Law-making
11. Should an elected assembly continue to make laws for the Gilbert Islands?
12. Should the name of the elected assembly remain House of Assembly?
13. Should the numbers of elected members remain as at present or should the House be enlarged?
14. If it should be enlarged how should it be enlarged – by extra constituencies in large islands or by some other means?
15. Do the qualifications for election need to be changed?
16. If so what should they be?
17. Is the present electoral system adequate or should it be changed?
18. Who should have the power to dissolve the House?
19. Should constituencies have the right of 'recall', that is to be able to decide that they don't want their member any more before the House is dissolved?
20. Should members be paid?
21. Who should decide what members should be paid?
22. Should the House continue to be presided over by an elected member or should someone who is not a member be elected by the members to preside?
23. Should the business of the House be so arranged that the proposals for laws (that is bills) must normally be made at one meeting (first reading) and then deferred until a subsequent meeting (committee stage and second reading) so that members can discuss them with their constituents?
24. Should proposals raised by individual members also be deferred so that a careful and considered reply can be given by the Government?
25. Is there any formal institutional way in which island *maneabas* could be associated with law-making?
26. Is there a need for a second or Upper House?

27. If so, how would it be chosen and what would be the qualifications for membership?

The Government

28. Should the House of Assembly continue to elect the chief executive (the Chief Minister) from among its members or should the chief executive be elected in some other way?
29. If the chief executive should be elected in some other way should it be by national election?
30. If not, how?
31. Once elected should the Chief Executive chose his own team of ministers to form a Government or should they be chosen in some other way?
32. If they should be chosen by some other way, by what way?
33. Should the members of the Government be drawn from the House or would it be acceptable for them to be draw from elsewhere (e.g. as in the USA)?
34. If ministers were chosen from elsewhere (for example a renowned fisherman to be Minister of Fisheries) should they still be responsible to the House and be *ex-officio* members?
35. Does a rigid distinction between minister and secretary (political and civil heads of a ministry) have validity in Gilbertese custom and an economy as small as that of the Gilbert Islands?

Head of State

36. Should the Gilbert Islands retain the British monarchy as the Head of State, the Queen being represented by a governor-general?
37. If yes, on whose advice should the Queen appoint the governor-general?
38. If no, should the chief executive also be the head of state, that is an executive president, or should there be a president who is head of state but not the chief executive?
39. If there is to be a president who is not the chief executive, how would he be chosen?
40. What powers, if any, should he have? (The powers of a governor-general are established by precedent in the United Kingdom and are not subject to discussion.)

The Judiciary
41. Should there be courts independent of the government?
42. Should all courts be subject to the control of a chief justice?
43. How should the chief justice be chosen?

The Public Service
44. Should the public service be independent of political control or not?
45. If yes, should it be controlled by an independent commission?
46. How should that commission be appointed?

The Police
47. Should the police force continue to have a special status guaranteed by the law?
48. How should the commissioner of police be appointed?

Finance and Audit
49. Should there continue to be a Public Accounts Committee?
50. If so, how should that committee be chosen?
51. Should the basic provisions of the Public Finance (Control and Audit) Ordinance be included in the constitution?

Variation of the Constitution
52. If a change is to be made in the constitution on whose authority should it be made?

Appendix D

Valedictory Despatch dated 3 May 1978

The Right Honourable Dr David Owen MP
Secretary of State for Foreign and Commonwealth Affairs
Foreign and Commonwealth Office
London SW1

Sir,

Farewells are seldom easy and a governor's farewell is the harder because, unlike an ambassador or a high commissioner, he has been not only an observer of the scene but an essential part of it. His valedictory may comment and forecast but it will also be a report on his own administration. In the twilight of empire, with responsibility for the remote and scattered remnants a minor and usually unexciting part of the broader field of affairs and with the need to fit them into the larger Foreign Office machine as overseas posts, we need to be reminded that our primary role in dependencies remains that of seeing that they are well administered. It is all too easy to become forgetful of our stewardship and of the spirit of British colonial policy in this century that the interests of the people we serve should be paramount.

Fortunately for these people, they usually have quite as much influence upon those who administer them as the reverse. One of the advantages of British colonialism has been that, until very recently, it has been mean, making territories pay for all services from local budgets and thus keeping the number of British down. The whip of popular imagination has in reality been a feather duster. Our particular brand of arrogance, moreover, convinces us that nobody can ever be exactly like ourselves. So, unlike the French, we have never tried to produce colonial copies. Because those of us on the ground have been few, and remote from the normal influences of our own society, we have the more easily absorbed local attitudes and, of course, prejudices. One has only to read Grimble, or to compare the life style of expatriates in the Gilbert Islands with that of expatriates in other Pacific dependencies to see the effect that these islands can have on those who live and work here.

I am thus aware that my departure will cause little more of a ripple across the lagoon than did my arrival. Indeed, until a few months ago I would have had to report that no other job or period of five years in my career had provided so little satisfaction in terms of achievement. I would have had to confess that in the atolls I had met my match. But, perhaps because the knowledge of imminent departure has clarified my thinking, in recent weeks the missing pieces to the jigsaw have quickly fitted in.

I can now happily accept that it is logical and sensible that everything takes longer to achieve in the Gilbert Islands than it does elsewhere. The Gilbertese have adapted with remarkable ability to their unusual and restricted atoll environment. Part of that adaptation has involved a slowing down of activity. To be born full of twentieth century go-go-go would mean the exhaustion of all life's possibilities within hours of adolescence. Island enthusiasms have been carefully channelled into *la passion du jeu*, to use the perceptive Father Sabatier's phrase, and it is in self made entertainment that the Gilbertese comes fully into his own. *'Il s'y jette avec frénesie; il enoublie le boire et le manger; il y passé des jours et des nuits.'*

Adaptation to environment has also provided a strong sense of community. The relations of each individual with the community are more important than relationships with other individuals. The community moves forward as a whole. The person who steps out of line is pulled back. So progress is not so obvious as it is in societies where the individual makes his own impact. It creeps up on one unawares. Everyone walks or rides a pushbike until suddenly it seems that everyone has access to a motorbike. Houses in a village are all traditional until it seems that everyone has started to build in permanent materials. Nobody seems interested in politics and then, as in the recent general election, there is a massive turn-out and every indication of an understanding and discriminating electorate. It is the entire community that is literate, not just an educated elite.

At the end of my commission, I must look not for personal achievement but examine how the community as a whole has advanced. And advance it has. Few dependencies will have entered the prelude to independence better equipped to work out a settlement which is essentially their own. There is high quality and a wide representation of interests in the legislature. The Government is able, determined and modest. It has overwhelming support and in return is committed to the close community consultation essential to the achievement of consensus. If the independence constitution proves unsuitable it will be our fault for failing to pay sufficient attention to Gilbertese views, which have been slow in formation and will, perhaps, be expressed only once because it is not in the nature of a society which places a premium on diffidence to argue forcefully. Anxious to secure citizenship and Banaban provisions to our liking, we are in danger of being impatient with matters of no direct British concern but fundamental to the future stability of the Gilbert Islands.

Not the least of the challenges which independence brings will be economic. With phosphate income ending in 1979 it would be easy to forecast doom, but to do so would ignore the degree of selectivity the Gilbertese displays with respect to imports and his ability when the need arises to return to the affluent subsistence the islands offer. Community preferences are respected. Motorbikes and buses are acceptable but there is little demand for cars. Mats are preferred to furniture. Everyone goes happily barefoot and there is little concern with fashion. Every boy, even in urban Tarawa, prides himself on his ability to cut toddy. The girls still learn how to provide an elaborate and tasty diet from coconuts, fish and pandanus. From the earliest age everyone acquires fishing skills. The palm and the pandanus can still provide every form of shelter and domestic utensil.

In my first impressions despatch I argued the need for emigration as an alternative to the rest of the world paying for the technology necessary to keep the islanders at home. I was mistaken. Emigration would still be a useful outlet, and in particular a safety valve, for those whose educational advantages have sown the seeds of western individualism and made them conscious of rights rather than duties and less ready to serve than to command, but there remains an enormous untapped potential within the limited resources of the atolls.

Only now is the achievement of the past few years in coconut replanting, in poultry and pig improvement, in inter-island communications and in marketing beginning to take effect. Much land remains under-utilised and the potential for reclamation is yet to be explored. There is opportunity for settlement in the Phoenix and Line Islands. The vast ocean setting of the islands is exploited by others who, since the establishment of a 200 mile fisheries zone last month, will no longer be able to ignore the legitimate rights of the Gilbertese. The infrastructure required to take advantage of unused or under-used assets is under way. The supply of educated and skilled manpower is growing. The basic buildings and tools needed for administration are under construction or planned. Much, of course, remains to be done and as the community moves forward it will stumble from time to time and its rate of progress will, perhaps, seem unnecessarily slow.

I also have regrets. In particular, I regret that the Banaban problem has so often come between the Gilbert Islands and orderly, peaceful progress. It has made excessive, if inevitable, demands on the time of departmental staff in the Foreign Office and has dominated discussion between us. It has diverted attention from the anachronistic early colonial arrangements under which phosphate has been mined and taxed. The experience and skill of the British Phosphate Commissioners are not in doubt, but their unique position in the Gilbert Islands would not have been tolerated elsewhere for so long. The Commissioners have enjoyed the advantages of unusual immunity from government control, wealth, isolation and continuity of management. The relationship has been unequal. While there has been improvement in recent years in response to political advance, and the shortage of time makes further changes nugatory, there is now no hope of avoiding the accusation that Britain's only interest in the Gilbert Islands has been phosphate, an interest to be abandoned when the last shovelful has been shipped.

But if I leave with regrets, I also leave with complete confidence in the ability of the people of the Gilbert Islands to manage their own affairs in a manner perfectly satisfactory to themselves and causing no undue difficulties to others. I shall take away the happiest of memories of an enriching experience, for I have learned much of value to me as a man, and my sadness at leaving will be tempered by contentment that I have been allowed to spend a small part of my life among so attractive a people who have provided me with warm friendship and so much fun.

Aware of my inadequacies, I have sometimes reflected upon the qualities with which I ought to have been endowed. Apart from the more obvious, there are those necessary to meet the exacting standards of Gilbertese hospitality and to command esteem in the *maneaba*. You need to be a good sailor in the smallest of ships and the roughest of seas; not merely unconcerned but demonstrably amused when capsized crossing the reef; and eager to bounce up the beach with smiling face, respond to all three verses of the national anthem in both languages and shake the hand of everyone on the island. Your stomach should be ready to digest a feast at every halt, no matter how many or how frequent or at what time; for fish, raw and fried, lobster, chicken and puddings may accompany the cakes even when the programme decrees but afternoon tea. The alternative to a working day spent in the double-lotus position is to sing or dance, for which an apprenticeship in both opera and ballet would have been a better preparation than anthropology and economics. Fortunately shyness is admired and nowhere could people be more tolerant of human weakness, making it the easier to become part of the community and settle into island ways.

It is hard that I may never again enjoy the exhilaration of racing a canoe across the lagoon or thrill to the emotion of the dance or watch the full moon rise through the palm trees. Because I leave not only the Gilbert Islands but the Pacific. It has come a long way since I first arrived in 1970. In January of that year, when the then assistant under secretary proposed 'an island in the autumn', not only did he have to send for a subordinate to list the possibilities but he was confident that the Pacific dependencies would remain so for another twenty-five years.

I will also be bidding farewell to twenty-seven years spent in de-colonisation. Like many of my colleagues I entered the colonial service not only conscious but because of its changing role. It has been an absorbing and worthwhile career which I would not have wanted in any way to change. It is sad but inevitable that it be misinterpreted both in the new nations that were formerly dependencies and in Britain herself. Our reward is in the satisfaction we have derived from our service.

I have the honour to be,
Sir, Your obedient servant,

John Smith

SELECT BIBLIOGRAPHY

Listed below are a few of the pertinent historical studies and accounts by participants and observers of the Islands and events about which I write prior to, during and after my departure.

At Kew, in the National Archives, the relevant files can be found in the CO and FCO series.

General

Deryck Scarr, *Fragments of Empire, a History of the Western Pacific High Commission 1877-1914*, Canberra 1967.

H.E Maude, *Of Islands & Men, Studies in Pacific History*, Melbourne 1968.

R.G. Crocombe, *The New South Pacific*, Suva 1973.

Ron Crocombe and Ahmed Ali (ed), *Foreign Forces in Pacific Politics*, Suva 1983.

Austin Coates, *Western Pacific Islands*, London 1970.

Robert Turnbull, *Tin Roofs and Palm Trees, a report on the New South Seas*, Canberra 1977.

The Solomon Islands

Glynn Cochrane, *Big Men and Cargo Cults*, Oxford 1970.

Francis Saemala, *Solomon Islands, Uniting the diversity*, in Ron Crocombe and Ahmed Ali (ed), *Politics in Melanesia*, Suva 1982.

Janet Kent, *The Solomon Islands*, Newton Abbot 1972.

Tom Russell, *I Have The Honour To Be*, Spennymoor 2003.

James L.O. Tedder, *Solomon Island Years*, Stuarts Point NSW 2008.

Peter Kenilorea, *Tell It As It Is*, Taipei 2008.

The Gilbert and Ellice Islands

Arthur Francis Grimble, *A Pattern of Islands*, London 1952.

Arthur Francis Grimble, *Return to the Islands*, London 1957.

Arthur Francis Grimble, *Tungaru Traditions, Writings on the Atoll Culture of the Gilbert Islands* (ed by H E Maude), Melbourne 1989.

Rosemary Grimble, *Migrations, Myth and Magic from the Gilbert Islands: Early Writings of Sir Arthur Grimble*, London 1972.

Ernest Sabatier, *Astride the Equator*, Melbourne 1977.

Barrie Macdonald, *Cinderellas of the Empire, Towards a History of Kiribati and Tuvalu*, Canberra 1982.

Martin G. Silverman, *Disconcerting Issue*, Chicago 1971.

Maslyn Williams, Barrie Macdonald, *The Phosphateers*, Melbourne 1983.

H.E Maude, *The Gilbertese Maneaba*, Suva 1980.

David .J Murray, *Constitutional Instruments in Kiribati and Tuvalu, A Case Study of Impact and Influence* in Hermann J Hiery. and John M. Mackenzie, (ed), *European Impact and Pacific Influence*, London 1997.

Eric Bailey, *The Christmas Island Story*, London 1977.

Tony Whincup, *Nareau's Nation, A Portrait of the Gilbert* Islands, London 1979.

Kiribati Extension Centre, University of the South Pacific, *Kiribati, Aspects of History*, Suva 1979.

Howard Van Trease (ed), *Atoll Politics, The Republic of* Kiribati, Suva 1993.

Kiribati Extension Centre, University of the South Pacific, *Politics in Kiribati*, Suva 1980.

INDEX

Page numbers 19-90 relate solely to the Solomon Island, pages 91-207 to the Gilbert and Ellice Islands. **n** refers to a footnote.

women's clubs *See* ladies' clubs
working hours 25
WWI 129, 131, 195, 196
WWII 195–196

Y

Yandina 77, 231
Yaxley, John 71, 211